Whit Lane Methodist church is to close. The Minister, the Rev Norman Skinner, will hold the last morning service on Sunday and in the evening he will be joined by the Superintendent Minister of the circuit, the Rev E Lincoln Minshull. The Mission will continue to use the building, which is being converted into a Youth Centre to meet the needs of young people in the Whit Lane area. (29.4.66)

One of Salford's oldest landmarks, the Windsor building on Cross Lane, is to be pulled down. The house, which dates from the 1790s, and the warehouse added later are owned by by Hall's Hygiene Co, Salford's oldest herbalist's. The firm, originally founded in America by Dr A Wilford Hall, started a branch in South Wales and moved from there to number 6 Broad Street before the Windsor building was acquired. It is now being run by Mr Wilford Hall's great-grandson, Basil John Hall. Mrs O M Hall and Miss Joy Hall are also active in the business, which will be moving to premises on Langworthy Road. (29.4.66)

The new Maternity Unit at Hope Hospital opens on Sunday, marking the first stage in its redevelopment as a District General Hospital. Building has taken 40 months and the total cost is £650,000. (29.4.66)

May 1966

Festivities to mark the twinning of Salford with Clermont-Ferrand will begin on Monday and last for three days. The key ceremony will be the signing of the twinning document in the Council Chamber on Monday morning. (13.5.66)

The new Salem Methodist Church and School were formally opened in Broughton on Saturday. The old church was demolished in February 1965 and building of the new began two months later. (20.5.66)

The small, self-contained Wallness housing estate adjoining Salford Technical College is being demolished. Among the buildings to go will be the Prince of Wales Feathers pub, which closed recently. (20.5.66)

Building costs of the new £1,750,000 Technical College were increased by unexpected problems underground. During the digging an unusual form of brick construction was discovered, thought to be the foundations of a cinema started before the war and never finished. (20.5.66)

At the start of the bowling season Seedley Park won their match against Victoria Park, who had been unbeaten at home since 1928. (20.5.66)

June 1966

Demolition work has begun on

Westwood Methodist Church, on the Height boundary. (10.6.66)

At the Salford Carnival on Saturday, the new Carnival Queen, Susan Pimblett, was crowned by actor Bernard Youens, best known for his rôle as Stan Ogden in "Coronation Street". (17.6.66)

The new social club was opened at Salford Rugby League Club's Willows ground on Thursday 16 June. (17.6.66)

Roy Mason, MP and Minister of State at the Board of Trade, will open the new Stella Maris hostel for seamen in Oldfield Road today. It replaces the old, non-residential hostel in Howard Street. (24.6.66)

July 1966

On Wednesday six new £18,000 Rolls Royce Sentinel diesel shunting engines arrived at Salford Docks and it was farewell to three faithful old steam locomotives. This is the end of the steam era on the Docks railway system. The port is now completely served by diesel locomotives, thirty-five of them valued at over £500,000. (8.7.66)

A local firm of exporters, Messrs Hogg & Toole, have bought the entire contents of the Grapes public house in Cross Lane, now in the course of demolition. They say the whole lot has been sold to a Chicago group who will probably build a new Grapes on a site in that city, though the new building will not look anything like the old one. (15.7.66)

The British Home Stores on Regent Road closes this weekend, after thirty-three years. This is a company decision

anc
in t

August 1966

Demolition of the last of the original houses on the Cholmondeley estate in Pendleton is now under way. (12.8.66)

The Centro Italiana Club opened recently at premises in Singleton Road, Broughton. It is the only club in Salford formed solely for the benefit of Italian immigrants. (19.8.66)

The new Mount Chapel, built to replace the Lightbown Hall which was condemned in the Ellor Street demolition scheme last year, opens tomorrow at the junction of Langworthy Road and Eccles Old Road. (19.8.66)

Salford City Swimming Club has won the Manchester & District Water Polo knock-out competition for the ninth successive season. (19.8.66)

September 1966

Salford's new Weights & Measures offices opened this week at the corner of Liverpool Street and Oldfield Road. (23.9.66)

A car park has been built over the old graveyard of Christ Church, Acton Square. There are other long-disused burial grounds in Salford which have become eyesores and while they cannot be used for building, they could be turned into gardens of rest, car parks or play areas. This is the first such conversion to be allowed in the city. (23.9.66)

Sir James Farmer Norton & Co, the Adelphi engineers, will close their foundry at the end of the month; 50 jobs will be lost. (23.9.66)

Hall's Hygiene Company, photographed in 1962

Salford's first ever purpose-built day centre for elderly people was officially opened on Wednesday 21 September. Located in Devonshire Street, Broughton, it was featured in an eight-minute slot on BBC television. (23.9.66)

Three large concrete totem poles have been erected in the forecourt of the new Technical College in Leaf Square, Pendleton. Built by a London sculptor, William Mitchell, the poles are around fifteen feet high and weigh between four and five tons each. (30.9.66)

Adelphi Lads' Club, founded in 1888, is to have extensions costing £9,000. There are seven clubs in Salford affiliated to the Manchester & District Federation of Boys' Clubs: Adelphi, Albert Schweitzer Boys' Club, Blackfriars Boys' Club, Brindleheath Lads' Club, North Salford Youth Club, St John's Cathedral Youth Club and Salford Lads' Club. (30.9.66)

The Woolpack Hotel, Pendleton, closed down on Wednesday night to make way for road improvements. More than a century old, it stands at the junction of two old toll roads - Eccles Old Road and Bolton Road - and its once famous bowling green was the birthplace of the Crown Green Bowling Association. (30.9.66)

October 1966

Plans to turn the Essoldo cinemas on Ford Lane and Ordsall Lane into bingo halls have been turned down by the City Council on the grounds of inadequate parking space. (14.10.66)

Salford's newest discothèque, the Disc-o-Jockey, has opened in the Racecourse Hotel, Littleton Road. (21.10.66)

Mr James Critchley, the clogger who has worked in Whit Lane for nearly forty years, is leaving. He took over the shop from Thomas Shoreman (also known as Thomas Shoreman Cleworth), who set up there as a clogger in the early 1890s. Ten years ago Mr Critchley helped to set up the clogger's shop in the Lark Hill Place street scene in Salford Museum; now the rest of the contents of his shop will be used there. (28.10.66)

November 1966

George Glass & Co, founded in Regent Road in 1932, has been taken over this week by the Combined English Stores group for £833,000. The business of George Glass & Co will retain its autonomy and identity, with the family still in charge as directors. (4.11.66)

Among the buildings affected by a Compulsory Purchase Order for six acres of land in the Windsor redevelopment area are the Unitarian Church, Cross Lane, the New Windsor Church School, the defunct Windsor Institute (founded a century ago as a ragged school) and the Albert Schweitzer Boys' Club. The world famous missionary and scientist visited the club named after him when it opened in 1933. At one period there was a membership of about a hundred boys of all denominations and Salford actor Albert Finney played for its rugby team for a time. The club closed about six months ago and has since been used as a recreation centre. (4.11.66)

The new Brentnall Primary School, Higher Broughton, which has cost

James Critchley at work in his clogger's shop

£128,000 to build and furnish, opened on Monday 7 November. The new school stands on the site of the former Broughton High School for Girls, part of which was Bella Vista, a handsome mansion with a glistening cupola on its roof which once served as the Greek consulate. (11.11.66)

December 1966

Colin Stewart, a former pupil of Tootal Road Secondary School, has recently been appointed Managing Director of the Coconut Growers' Association in Trinidad. Mr Stewart lived in Lune Street, Weaste, and went to Jamaica in 1953 to join a sugar manufacturing company, moving to Trinidad later in his career. A professional engineer with two degrees, he is a specialist in fats technology. Although he is now West Indian by adoption, he frequently visits his mother at her greengrocer's shop on the corner of Tatton Street and West Worsley Street. (2.12.66)

The new shopping centre on Regent Road, The Piazza, is open for business and soon to be completed, at a cost of £126,000. (9.12.66)

1967

January 1967

Park Place Lodging House, off Cross Lane, is in the final stages of demolition. (20.1.67)

Once in danger of being closed down as redundant, Salford's Liverpool Street Gas Works has taken on a new lease of life as a major storage depot for

Rag Week well established after a year: Bill Oddie presents the winner's cheque to the Rag Queen of 1968

liquid naphtha, from which low toxicity gas is produced. There will be twelve million gallons of storage capacity when the latest new tank is complete. (20.1.67)

Mr W H Strauss and his brother Mr S G Strauss, joint managing directors of Mandleberg's, the historic rainwear and rubber firm, have retired, breaking the link of purely local control which has existed since 1856, when the firm was founded. Both were born in Broughton and have been in the clothing trade all their lives.
(27.1.67)

February 1967

Aldine House, a six-storey office block built on the banks of the River Irwell at New Bailey Street, will be officially opened today. (3.2.67)

The Nuclear Block at Salford's university-designate is now "in business" but not yet fully equipped.
(3.2.67)

"Rag" came to Salford for the first time this week and will last until the grand procession around the city on Tuesday. It is the first time Salford Royal College of Advanced Technology (soon to be Salford University) has joined with Manchester University to promote a Rag Week for both cities. (3.2.67)

Mike Leigh (24), one of the bright theatrical stars nurtured by Salford Grammar School, has joined the Royal Shakespeare Company for its Stratford-on-Avon season as an assistant director. After producing and acting in several school plays, Mike won a scholarship to RADA and has appeared on television a number of times. (10.2.67)

The Royal College of Advanced Technology has been notified by the Clerk of the Privy Council that the Queen has approved the grant of a charter constituting and founding a university under the name and style of "The University of Salford". (17.2.67)

After forty-eight years Manchester Rugby Union Club is to leave Salford. Approval has been given for its amalgamation with Cheadle Hulme Cricket Club in a £100,000 sporting venture. (17.2.67)

March 1967

The "Manchester Progress", the latest in the Manchester Liners fleet, is due to leave Salford Docks today on her maiden voyage to Canada. (10.3.67)

The new £20,000 footbridge over the Irwell at Springfield Lane was opened to the public on Wednesday. It spans part of the thousand-foot-long excavation which is to become a new channel for the river following the cutting out of the Anaconda bend.
(17.3.67)

April 1967

On Monday the governing body of Salford Technical College held its first meeting in the new premises on the site of what was once Leaf Square. The buildings, which cost £1,750,000, will be officially opened by Prince Philip in June. (7.4.67)

After months of negotiations, Castle Irwell Racecourse has been bought by the University of Salford. The plan is to build residential accommodation for students and still leave space for public access. (7.4.67)

One of the oldest Toc H residences in the country, Mark XIV, is empty and

will shortly disappear to make way for the Broad Street (Woolpack) underpass. In the yard is the unusual tower building which for many years was the headquarters of Rover Scouts in the city. (14.4.67)

Due to open on Sunday 30 April is the new Georgian Theatre Club in Devonshire Street, owned by the Moss family, who came originally from Salford. Topping the bill on opening night is Lonnie Donegan. (28.4.67)

May 1967

The Julius Glass Heart Care Unit at Hope Hospital will be opened on Tuesday 9 May by his widow, Mrs Doris Glass Clive. (5.5.67)

The long-established building and shopfitting department of the CWS in Vere Street, Weaste, is to close. Three hundred men will be made redundant.
(19.5.67)

At the Salford works of David Brown Gear Industries Ltd, the world's largest gear-cutting machine is now in operation. Assembly of the 250-ton machine began in February. Capable of cutting gears up to forty feet in diameter, it is already working twenty-four hours a day, and can be operated by one man at a simple control panel.
(26.5.67)

June 1967

Salford Rugby Club has signed two international players, Chris Hesketh and Charlie Bott. (9.6.67)

Prince Philip, Duke of Edinburgh, came to Salford today to open the new Technical College and to be installed as the first Chancellor of Salford University. (16.6.67)

The new Salford Carnival Queen for 1967-68, Pam Armstrong, was crowned by disc jockey Jimmy Savile. Pam (19) of Albert Park Road, Broughton, was elected in May. (16.6.67)

July 1967

Described as the biggest development at Salford Docks for forty years, the new £400,000, "TV-controlled" transit shed will be officially opened on Tuesday. It is expected that the "Clan Graham", (9,308 tons) will be discharging at the berth. (7.7.67)

The new Booth's Charities estate of flats for senior citizens adjoining Holy Angels Church, the Height, was officially opened on Tuesday by the Mayor, Alderman A E Clark, JP.
(7.7.67)

At last week's Council meeting, a petition with eighty signatures was handed in, protesting against the curtailment of operating hours at Hodge Lane Wash House. (7.7.67)

Agreement over the new Pendleton Shopping Centre has finally been reached with the developers, Ravenseft

Building work between Pendleton Church and Salford Precinct

Properties. This brings to an end five years of frustrating delay, disagreement and whittling down of a development which it was once hoped would be among Europe's biggest and finest. Work will go ahead in March and linked with it will be a canopied market, built by Salford Corporation, to replace Cross Lane Market. (14.7.67)

St Matthias Church, Broughton, which has stood empty for the past five years, is to be demolished in August. The church was built in 1842 and the last service was held on 14 January 1962. (14.7.67)

Work is just starting on two 23-storey blocks of flats on the Ellor Street estate, the highest in Salford. These will almost certainly be the last, as well as the first, of their kind. A widespread dislike of "high living" is becoming increasingly apparent and any blocks in the Cheetham redevelopment plan will be at a four-storey limit. (14.7.67)

Salford and Manchester Police Forces are to merge on 1 April next year. The Manchester & Salford Police Act of 1792 provided for a single body of Police Commissioners for the two towns, but they operated separately and the merger brings to an end 175 years of independent policing. In modern times Salford Police Force has been much praised for its efficiency and enterprise. Police boxes ("mini police stations"), play streets, fog flares and distinctive white coats for officers on point duty are among Salford's innovations. (21.7.67)

Four street lighting columns 100 feet high are being erected this week at the Woolpack traffic junction. This type of lighting - white in colour - is a comparatively new idea and is appearing for the first time in this part of the North. (21.7.67)

August 1967

Brindle Heath Primary School closed for good at the end of the summer term on 28 July. (4.8.67)

At Esso's Mode Wheel oil terminal an operation believed to be the first of its type in Britain has been carried out. A tank fifty feet in diameter, thirty feet high and weighing seventy tons was moved 350 yards by first floating it on a cushion of air, then towing it along by tractor. A second tank is to be moved shortly. The principle is similar to that used in hovercraft. (4.8.67)

One of Salford's oldest firms, artesian well borers Thomas Matthews Ltd, has had to close down its plant after 97 years. (4.8.67)

The Manchester Liner "Manchester Exporter" (7,503 tons) is back in her home port of Salford after suffering a fire in one of her holds on the run to the Canadian Great Lakes. Now she awaits an examination to decide her future. (11.8.67)

The Rex Cinema on Chapel Street has been given a new lease of life as the city's latest bingo hall. Now part of the G B Snape circuit, it was opened last night, 10 August, by Miss Violet Carson (Ena Sharples of "Coronation Street"). (11.8.67)

September 1967

A massive fire at the Turner Wilberforce candle-making, starch and soap works in Watson Street, Lower Broughton, destroyed a store room containing nearly 100 tons of paraffin wax on Tuesday. Fifty firemen fought the blaze and a sea of molten wax caused many problems. (1.9.67)

John Shaw & Sons (Salford) Ltd of St Stephen Street have manufactured a 12,000-ton upstroking press, believed to be the largest of its kind ever built in Great Britain. (8.9.67)

At a meeting on Tuesday, the Companionship Circle's Carnival Committee voted unanimously to discontinue the Carnival and concentrate on a much-extended programme of events in the Homestead grounds. (15.9.67)

Ward & Goldstone, Salford's largest industrial employer, with seven factories and a labour force of several thousand, are celebrating the 75th anniversary of the company. (15.9.67)

New extensions to the Adelphi Lads' Club will be officially opened today. (29.9.67)

October 1967

Salford Corporation has bought the Cross Lane Drill Hall from the Ministry of Defence. Built in 1870, the Drill Hall was a mobilisation centre for local men answering the call to arms in the Boer War, the 1914-18 war and the Second World War. It was originally used by the 17th Rifle Fusiliers and two companies were raised there for the South African Campaign, in 1908 the 7th and 8th Lancashire Fusiliers took over and in 1914 2,000 men mustered there for action in the Middle East, France and Belgium. (13.10.67)

Just over a year after it opened, Salford Rugby Club's social club is booming. Colour television was installed in July and at the same time work began on an extension, which was opened on Wednesday, 11 October. (13.10.67)

The foundation stone of the new parish church of St Luke, the Height, was laid on Sunday by the Auxiliary Bishop of Salford, the Right Reverend G Burke. (20.10.67)

Salford Central Mission celebrates its 60th anniversary this month; it was opened on 19 October 1907. (27.10.67)

David Watkins, who signed for Salford on Thursday at a hotel in Tewkesbury, made his début against Oldham at the Willows on Friday night. He scored a try and two drop goals, and won Man of the Match. (27.10.67)

November 1967

Asda Queens Supermarket in Regent Road opened today. It is the eleventh in the country. (3.11.67)

The new Broughton Baths opens tomorrow, 11 November. This is the first addition to the city's swimming facilities for 57 years and could not be more timely, for Pendleton Baths (opened in 1885) has recently closed and Regent Road Baths (1892) is threatened with closure. (10.11.67)

Since winning the Commonwealth figure skating championship, Salford's ice skating star, Harold Williams (22),

Promise fulfilled: David Watkins receiving the Division 1 Championship Trophy for 1973/4. Also in the picture are Brian Snape and Graham Atkinson (left) and players Chris Hesketh, Colin Dixon and Paul Charlton

of Hodge Lane, has received the Gold Star, the highest award in the amateur ice skating world. He awaits a decision today as to whether he will be selected to skate for Britain in the next Olympic Games. (17.11.67)

One of the oldest businesses in the city, Briggs' National Tyre Service, has moved from Windsor Bridge to modern premises on the new Liverpool Street industrial estate. (17.11.67)

1968

January 1968

A massive redevelopment scheme is shortly to begin in Ordsall, involving 6,370 families housed in the 220-acre area. Salford's new policy of "rehousing on the spot" will be employed, ensuring that residents can have new homes in Ordsall and that the present close-knit community is preserved. (12.1.68)

Pendleton Town Hall is to be demolished at the end of its present lease. (12.1.68)

On Thursday, what is probably the largest single cargo ever to have been carried up the Ship Canal arrived at the private wharf of Brown & Polson in Trafford Park. It consisted of 13,710 tons of maize, carried by the merchant vessel "Carchester" on her maiden voyage from Japan. The "Carchester", 510 feet long and weighing 14,100 tons, was designed to bring the maximum amount of maize to the company and will be used exclusively for that purpose. (19.1.68)

British Rail is trying to sell the old railway tunnel that runs from Liverpool Street siding to Salford Docks. The tunnel is in three separate sections measuring a total of 936 yards. The first, from Liverpool Street to a point near Doddington Street, is 473 yards long, then there is a short open stretch between retaining walls before the second tunnel is reached. This runs between Martha Street and Robert Hall Street for another 291 yards. A third tunnel carries the line from West Park Street to Hulton Street for 172 yards, and from this point the line ascends to the level of the dock sidings at New Barns junction. (19.1.68)

The fate of all the shops on the south side of Bolton Road, Irlams o'th'Height - known as "the village"- has been sealed, with the confirmation by the Minister of Housing of the 1.94-acre Compulsory Purchase Order. The inspector says the buildings, except the pubs, are old, in poor condition and the area has a run-down appearance. (19.1.68)

February 1968

New premises for the Union Cold Storage Company are under construction on Ordsall Lane. (2.2.68)

Affected by work on the "Woolpack Underpass", the premises of A B Critchley, motor bodies, in Brindle Heath Road has had to be shored up. It was in this building, known locally as "The Smithy", that the Reporter Steam Printing Company was founded by the late Councillor Peter Hampson in 1879. Later the Reporter moved with its printing plant to bigger premises in Frederick Road, Pendleton. (9.2.68)

Plans for creating a new "heart" for Salford in the Ellor Street redevelopment have been refused. A new Civic Centre complex - Town Hall, Art Gallery and Museum, Central Baths and other Corporation structures - had been proposed, but the space is to be used for car parking for the shopping centre and the original £9 million plan has been reduced to £2 million. However, it is pleasing that the lovely old buildings of the existing Salford Museum and Art Gallery, and the Peel Building of the old Technical College - which might have been knocked down - will now be retained. (9.2.68)

The Flamingo Club, which opened in the former Co-op buildings on Broughton Road, Pendleton, at the end of September, closed on 27 January. It is to be refurbished and will reopen under new management on 28 February as the New Flamingo Club. (16.2.68)

The old John Street School in the heart of the Ellor Street redevelopment area is soon to be demolished. It has been empty for some time, sticking out like a sore thumb amid its new surroundings. (23.2.68)

The finishing touches are being made to the new Blackfriars Telephone Exchange adjoining Salford Town Hall. It is one of the biggest buildings of its kind in the country. (23.2.68)

Work has finished on the new chapel and school extension at De La Salle College in Weaste Lane. (23.2.68)

March 1968

Before the Second World War Salford had a flower show rivalling those of Southport and Shrewsbury. Now there are plans to reintroduce a Salford Horticultural Show which will put the city on this particular map again. (1.3.68)

Ordsall Redevelopment area in 1969: looking up Derby Street towards Regent Road

At midnight on Sunday, 176 years of Salford police history will come to an end as the force merges with that of Manchester in a combined service of more than two thousand men and women under the command of Mr W J Richards, at present Chief Constable of the Manchester force. It was in August 1792, at a meeting of Police Commissioners at the Kings Head, Chapel Street, that the Salford force was established as a separate entity from Manchester, which it now rejoins.
(29.3.68)

The Manchester Jewish Benevolent Society is to extend its "Gan Eden" block of flats for the elderly in Stanley Road, Higher Broughton. (29.3.68)

The second phase of the new St Paul's Primary School at Little Hulton is to be completed in the next week or so.
(29.3.68)

Salford Fire Service has just taken delivery of its new £18,000 Snorkel fire engine. The hydraulically operated platform can take six people up to a height of 65 feet. (29.3.68)

April 1968

Salford's Civil Defence Corps and Auxiliary Fire Service were formally disbanded on Monday, as part of a national decision. (5.4.68)

Having in turn lost control of its hospitals, gas, electricity and water undertakings, and on Sunday its police force, Salford now faces the near-certainty of having to surrender its bus services this year, probably around December. (5.4.68)

Salford still has more than twenty schools built before 1900, with the oldest dating back to the middle of the nineteenth century. (12.4.68)

History was made at the Willows on Monday 5 February when Salford became the first club team to play a Great Britain side. Unfortunately, deplorable conditions caused the game to be abandoned just before half-time, with the Reds trailing 12-0. The match was rearranged for Friday 5 April, and this time Great Britain won 20-5.
(12.4.68)

The Windsor Bingo & Social Club opened today in the old Essoldo Cinema (formerly the Dominion) on Ordsall Lane. (26.4.68)

This year marks the centenary of the world-renowned company of W T Glover & Co, cable manufacturers. Although its headquarters are now in Trafford Park, the company was started in Salford in 1868 by Walter T Glover. (26.4.68)

280 years of regimental history came to an end this week when the Lancashire Fusiliers, with which Salford has always been closely associated, amalgamated with other regiments to form the new Royal Regiment of Fusiliers. (26.4.68)

May 1968

Shelmerdine Gardens, the recently-completed Booth's Charities estate for the elderly in Cholmondeley Road, Pendleton, will be formally opened on Tuesday, 7 May. (3.5.68)

Further extensions to Salford Rugby Club's social club at the Willows began this week. They are to include a restaurant and concert room. (3.5.68)

Salford lad Albert McPherson has been with FA Cup winners West Bromwich Albion for two years, and his work as a trainer has helped to take the team from near-relegation to this week's

success. Albert was born in West Union Street, off Oldfield Road, and was a member of Salford and Adelphi Lads' Clubs. (24.5.68)

June 1968

Langworthy Rugby League Club is to move to the former Manchester Rugby Union FC ground at Moor Lane, Kersal, on a three-year lease. The ground now belongs to the Education Committee. (21.6.68)

July 1968

A new milestone in the history of Civic Welfare in Salford will be reached today with the official opening of two units for the elderly in the Broad Street/Ellor Street redevelopment area. They are the Lime Court Day Centre for the Elderly and the Goldstone Residential Home. (5.7.68)

The Plane Court block of flats on the Ellor Street development was officially opened this week. (5.7.68)

The Co-op Workers' Social Club on Bolton Road, Pendleton, which closed a year ago, reopened on Thursday 27 June as the Cumberland Club. The first night was by invitation only. (5.7.68)

A proposed £8 million development on the old railway goods yard in New Bailey Street is dead. The plan would have brought the "Guardian" and "Evening News" into Salford, creating a "Golden Gateway" entrance to the city from Manchester. Now negotiations are under way which will allow them to move into the northern headquarters of the "Daily Mail" group on Deansgate instead. (12.7.68)

Gravel Lane Methodist Church is to be demolished by the end of the year.
(12.7.68)

Building of the first new public house on the Ellor Street estate is to start shortly. The site is in Magnolia Court and work should be completed within twelve months. (12.7.68)

Among the victims of the Broad Street/Eccles Old Road development plan is one of the oldest established florist's in the area, run by Mr George Bryden. The business was established in the 1870s by his great-great-uncle, a Mr Pearson, in the days when the remains of the toll bars could still be seen on either side of the Woolpack Hotel. The mirrors framed in corkwork which lined the shop will be remembered by many. (12.7.68)

The Salem Independent Methodist Church on Ellor Street, Pendleton, will hold its last service on Sunday. After more than a hundred years in Ellor Street, the move will be made to a new church in Unwin Street, due to be opened officially on 28 September.
(19.7.68)

The Home Improvement Company announced their Grand Opening in the

The railway tunnel to the docks from Liverpool Street, photographed in 1964

former Lande's Stores building in Regent Road recently. (19.7.68)

The city's overspill estate at Cutnook Lane, Irlam, was completed yesterday with the opening of the final house. (26.7.68)

August 1968

Bank Lane Mission Hall is to be sold to the Evergreen Over Sixties' Club. (9.8.68)

September 1968

Salford's new-style "Carnival Gala" was held at the old Castle Irwell Racecourse on Saturday, 31 August. There was no procession this year and no Carnival Queen as previously. Instead, Miss Marcelle Hendricks became the first Salford Carnival Gala's "Miss Personality". (6.9.68)

The latest concept in cargo handling, "containerisation", has arrived in Salford. Large, steel-framed, aluminium, plywood-lined, 20-foot-long containers are being delivered to the Vere Street Docks gate. The makers of the containers, Metropolitan Cammell, who also build Salford bus bodies, have installed a £150,000 production line to handle an initial order for 400 containers a month. (13.9.68)

Mount Carmel Pipe Band have just returned to Salford with yet another trophy to add to this season's massive collection. After winning the grand slam of major events in 1968 in last week's European Championship (Grade 3), they became the first band outside Scotland to win the coveted Supreme Champions Award. Already this year the Salford lads, led by Pipe Major Walter McMinn, have won the World Championship for their grade and taken the British, All England and Scottish Championships. Mount Carmel have now amassed twenty-eight trophies in all, ten of them coming this season. (13.9.68)

Salford's new City Librarian has proposed some drastic new measures, including the closure of four branches and the use of mobile libraries. (13.9.68)

The official opening of Langworthy Rugby Club's new ground at Moor Lane, Kersal, is on 14 September, when Langworthy entertain Salford "A" team. (13.9.68)

Salford's first Horticultural Society's Show was a huge success. More than 1,200 people visited Chaseley Fields and there was plenty to see. A wonderful display of roses was just one of over 600 exhibits which varied from flower arrangements to budgerigars and the Mayor, Alderman Sidney Hamburger, was there to present the prizes. (13.9.68)

The former Regent Road Health Offices have been converted into fifteen maisonettes, which will soon be available for lease. (20.9.68)

After some months of enquiries and negotiations, Salford Corporation has bought a 1964 Rolls Royce Silver Cloud for Mayoral duties, to replace the present outworn Daimler. Salford's previous Mayoral Rolls did many years' service and is understood to be still working in America. (20.9.68)

A fire completely destroyed the renovated Kings Cinema on Regent Road in the early hours of Tuesday morning. The cinema, owned by British Railways and one of the city's finest, was closed some years ago, but had been undergoing an extensive facelift which had been put back repeatedly by outbreaks of vandalism. (20.9.68)

The new Gravel Lane Methodist Church will be opened on 21 September, when members of the community will walk in procession from their old place of worship to the "temporary" church in Lowcock Street, Broughton. The pre-cast building took only a week to erect. (20.9.68)

The Right Reverend Geoffrey Burke, Auxiliary Bishop of Salford, opened the new Monton House Preparatory School for the Adelphi House Grammar School this week. (20.9.68)

The buildings of the 65-year-old Tootal Road School, closed this year as being surplus to the needs of the education service, are to be brought into multi-purpose use. There will be a centre for school music on the top floor, a centre for selected youth activities on the second floor and a furniture and equipment store in the rest of the space. (20.9.68)

The Flamingo Club, Pendleton, which closed in July, has had its licence revoked. (20.9.68)

For the first time, Salford has gone in for advertising on its buses. The contractors will be a London firm, Associated Publicity Holdings. They will pay £10,575 in the first year and £17,473.10s in the second and subsequent years. (20.9.68)

Mike Coulman, the British Lions Rugby Union forward, signed for Salford on Thursday 16 September. (27.9.68)

October 1968

The death knell of "skyscraper housing" was sounded this week with recommendations for the Ordsall No.1 redevelopment area. There will be no more than two seventeen-storey blocks and the development will otherwise rely entirely on two and three-storey homes. Although efficient in terms of cost, it is realised that high living is anti-social and productive of much unhappiness. (4.10.68)

A Hammond organ valued at £5,500 has been installed at the Salford SOGAT Club in Great George Street. Brought over from Chicago specially for the club, it is the latest design in de luxe electric organs and the first to be installed in the North of England, and possibly in the country. (11.10.68)

Part of the area originally designated for the new Civic Centre is to be freed for building 70 or 80 flats or maisonettes around Nursery Street. When the Civic Centre scheme was dropped in February, it was thought that the whole space would be used for car parking. (18.10.68)

The new Willows Restaurant opens next Thursday, 24 October, at the Salford Rugby Club ground. (18.10.68)

Practice makes perfect! Mount Carmel Pipe Band photographed leading a Whit Walk in the 1950s. The shop on the left is Durkin's outfitter's

November 1968

Britain's first deep-water container ship, the SS "Manchester Challenge", is due to sail for Canada on Sunday from Salford Docks. This is the first stage of a £10m plan on which the future prosperity - and possible existence - of the Docks depends. The "Challenge" - 530 feet long, with a beam of 63 feet 6 inches and a gross tonnage of 12,000 tons - is the first of three such ships. The second, the "Manchester Courage", is already launched and the third, the "Manchester Concorde", will be launched later this year. The vessels will carry up to five hundred twenty-foot containers, all under deck, a feature which no other container ship in the world can guarantee. (1.11.68)

A large black bell, standing about 20 inches high and complete with the original rope, was discovered two weeks ago in the cellar of the Flying Angel Mission to Seamen, Gladys Street, Trafford Road. The manageress, Mrs Frances Bradley, cleaned it up and discovered it was made of brass and inscribed "MS Europa".

Her enquiries have now revealed that a German liner called "Europa" was built in 1927 and received the Blue Riband for her maiden voyage across the Atlantic. The 51,839-ton ship was handed to the French after the war, rebuilt and renamed the "Liberté". She did twelve years service before being broken up. However, the bell seems to have come to Salford before the rebuilding, for the resident Minister at the Mission in 1940 has told Mrs Bradley that it was there then. (1.11.68)

December 1968

The Minister of Transport has agreed to a proposal by British Railways to close Exchange Station and divert all services from there into Victoria Station. Ironically, Exchange Station makes a handsome profit each year. (6.12.68)

This week Salford and other local councils received from Whitehall regulations relating to illuminated "lollipops" for use at school crossings in darkness or fog. It was stated that these had been drawn up after experiments in five London boroughs, but illuminated lollipops were in fact pioneered by Salford with much success, and were only dropped after Home Office objections. (20.12.68)

Salford's first underpass, part of the Broad Street improvement scheme, was completed last week. (27.12.68)

Salford Rugby Club signed two more players this week. They are Colin Dixon from Halifax and Bill Burgess from Barrow, both internationals. (27.12.68)

1969

January 1969

The new Manchester Liners building at Salford Docks had its topping out ceremony last week. The design is curved to represent the bridge of the company's ship "Manchester Miller". (17.1.69)

Salford Education Committee has started an introductory course on the local history of Salford. The first speakers were: Mr E Gray, speaking on "Transport in Salford from 1824"; Mr V I Tomlinson on "The Growth of Salford", Miss E Vigeon on "Queen Victoria at Peel Park" and Mr J Smith, "The Architecture of Salford and Manchester". (24.1.69)

From 6 July Salford's sludge-removal ship, the "Salford City" is to link up with Manchester's "Percy Dawson" and "Mancunian". The move is expected to save on costs, not least by insuring the ships as a single fleet rather than separately. The ships take sewage sludge from the local treatment plant down the canal and out into Liverpool Bay, where it is dumped. (31.1.69)

February 1969

The former Mission of the Good Shepherd in Liverpool Street, which now stands in the middle of the industrial estate, is to be pulled down by Messrs T A Anders and replaced by a two-storey warehouse for their adjoining glass processing premises. (14.2.69)

The building which was once Broughton Drill Hall is to be taken over by Great Clowes Street Warehouse, who have premises across the road. (14.2.69)

The new St Luke's Church will be opened in Swinton Park Road on Thursday, adjoining the present building. St Luke's parish was formed from parts of the parishes of St James, Pendleton and St Mary's, Swinton, in 1922, and for two years Masses were held in the Height Parish Hall and in a house in Moorfield Road, until the present church was opened on 14 December 1924. (21.2.69)

Members of the Education Committee have unanimously approved a plan to merge Salford Grammar School and Salford Technical High School in September. (21.2.69)

March 1969

The Baths Committee, which had recommended closing Holland Street Wash House in preference to Regent Road Baths, withdrew their recommendation at the Council meeting on Wednesday. Their decision had angered housewives from the Charlestown area and a protest group gathered outside the wash house in the last week of February. (7.3.69)

Salford have reached the semi-final of the Rugby League Challenge Cup, following a 20-7 victory over Widnes before a crowd of 20,000 at the Willows on Sunday. (7.3.69)

Over the next two years the tenants of eleven blocks of flats - ten of them in the Ellor Street and High Street areas, and Oakhill Court in Mandley Park -

Tootal Road School when it was new

will have to move out while structural strengthening and replacing of the gas supply is carried out. This follows the Ronan Point disaster in London last year, when a block of flats partially collapsed after a gas explosion.

(14.3.69)

On Sunday night one of the new container ships, the "Manchester Courage", crashed into the lock gates at Irlam, blocking the lock and trapping a further fifteen ships at Salford Docks. Small vessels such as the Guinness boats will be able to pass through the small adjoining lock. A similar situation was experienced in 1961, when a sand barge sank at Stockton Heath and closed the port for 27 days. (14.3.69)

Salford Rugby Club has qualified for the final of the Rugby League Challenge Cup to be played at Wembley. The team beat Warrington in the semi-final at Wigan by 15 points to 8. It is thirty years since Salford played at Wembley and the lads are assured of a civic reception when they return - win or lose. (22.3.69)

April 1969

The 150th anniversary of the birth of Sir Charles Hallé, the founder of the Hallé orchestra, was marked by a tribute to his memory at his graveside at Weaste Cemetery on Friday 11 April. (18.4.69)

May 1969

On Tuesday the foundation stone was laid for a three-bed ward extension to the Julius Glass Intensive Heart Care Unit at Hope Hospital. (2.5.69)

Another Booth's Charities scheme will be officially opened on 6 May. It is Mainprice Close, built at the junction

of Eccles Old Road and Broad Street on the site of the former Toc H Mark XIV hostel. As well as the living accommodation there is the new Midwood Hall, capable of holding 250 people. (2.5.69)

The City of Salford's first sauna bath will be open at Broughton Baths from 6 May. (2.5.69)

At the new Pendleton shopping precinct the foundations are laid and some of the steelwork has been erected. (9.5.69)

It was not Salford's day in the Challenge Cup Final at Wembley. They were beaten 11-6 by Castleford. All could have been different, though, if the referee had allowed a try by Chris Hesketh which most Salford supporters claim he definitely scored. (17.5.69)

Frank Willis, the British Real Tennis champion, was beaten in the World Championship, the first leg of which was held in New York, and the second in Salford. (23.5.69)

Mount Carmel Pipe Band, competing in the "Festival of Scotland" at Richmond on Saturday, came away victors in the open pipe band contest, with the major awards of the day for band and the drum section also winning their trophy. This is the fourth successive year in which the band has triumphed. (23.5.69)

The new £50,000 geriatric unit was opened at Ladywell Hospital on Friday. (30.5.69)

Due to be opened on Tuesday is the new £1,750,000 Civil Engineering building, part of the University overlooking the Meadows at the Crescent. (30.5.69)

June 1969

The Margaret Whitehead school for mentally handicapped children was opened on Saturday. Alderman Miss Margaret Whitehead, after whom the school was named, unveiled a commemorative plaque in the entrance hall. (6.6.69)

The Queens Arms on Chapel Street has been renamed the Tallow Tub, the nickname by which it has been known for many years. Legend has it that there used to be a candle works near the pub and that the lads, when going for a drink, used to say that they were going down to the Tallow Tub. (6.6.69)

The Mayoress, Mrs E Handley, crowned Miss Gail Chapman Salford's "Miss Personality 1969" at the Salford Carnival Gala held at the Homestead on Saturday. (20.6.69)

July 1969

The Pendleton branch of the British Legion, whose premises in Seedley Road are affected by the Broad Street Compulsory Purchase Order, is to lease the former Seedley Junior Training Centre, Langworthy Road, from Salford Corporation. (11.7.69)

The foundation stone of the Canon Green Youth Centre was laid on Tuesday 15 July. (18.7.69)

The former Lower Broughton Synagogue in Cambridge Street has been taken over by a firm of builders' merchants. It was known locally as the "Tin Synagogue" because of the corrugated iron in its construction. (18.7.69)

For the first time in many years, the floral display which decorates the Irwell embankment at the Crescent is missing. It usually takes the form of a crest bearing Salford's coat of arms, and on occasion has represented outstanding events taking place in the city. The Parks Director says that it was sacrificed as a cost-cutting measure. 25.7.69)

Claiming to be the oldest amateur Rugby League club in the business, Seedley Rangers, founded over sixty years ago, is re-emerging this season as an active playing side. After the first fifty years, there came a period of inactivity on the field, although the Old Boys' Association lived on. The Rangers' new home will be behind the Cumberland Club, Bolton Road. (25.7.69)

August 1969

An application by Sir A McAlpine & Son for permission to extract sandstone at Mount Vernon sand quarry, off Eccles New Road, Weaste, has been granted. The permit lasts until 30 December 1970. (8.8.69)

Salford Rugby Club opened their season with a visit to Huyton, in a

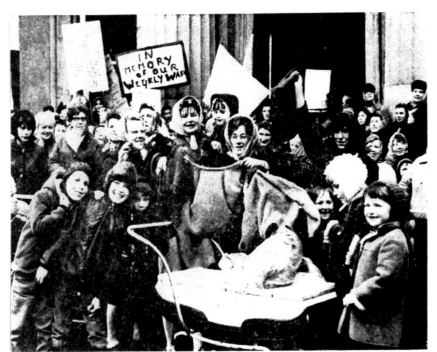

February 1969: a group protesting against the closure of Holland Street Wash House

game which marked the official opening of the new Alt Park ground. Salford won the match 60-5. (15.8.69)

Ivy Court, the purpose-built home for elderly and handicapped persons in George Street, Broughton, was officially opened on Thursday.
(22.8.69)

The old West Liverpool Street School has just been demolished. Pupils said goodbye to the old building before the Easter holidays, when they helped to carry the furniture to the waiting vans.
(22.8.69)

September 1969

St John's Cathedral is currently cocooned in scaffolding, ready for workmen to start the battle against dry rot. (5.9.69)

Higher Broughton Synagogue in Duncan Street officially closed its doors on Saturday after more than sixty years. (5.9.69)

As a result of containerisation, transit time between Salford Docks and Montreal has been cut to six and a half days. (5.9.69)

The new Parish Hall for St John's, the Height, was opened on Saturday.
(19.9.69)

Just a fortnight after the news that the Oakwood Hotel on Lancaster Road is to lose its bowling green for a car park, it appears that the same is to happen at the Griffin Hotel, Lower Broughton. Both pubs are owned by Whitbread.
(19.9.69)

St John's Methodist Church Hall, Seedley, has been demolished.
(26.9.69)

Police recruiting for the "Specials" at Salford Carnival Gala

So successful were the local history lectures given in January this year as part of Salford Education Committee's new venture that a programme for the winter session has been arranged. The Salford Local History Group will meet once again at Hope Hall Further Education Centre, Eccles New Road, and the first lecture will be on 7 October. (26.9.69)

October 1969

Included in the recent amalgamation of the Salford and Manchester Police Forces was the Mounted Section. The Manchester stables at Moss Lane East can accommodate twenty horses, all of which are named after Dickensian characters, such as "Little Nell" and "David Copperfield". Copperfield (known by his "surname" for short) is claimed to be the tallest horse in the whole country, standing at eighteen hands. In the Salford section, stabled at Oakwood Park, there are four horses whose names have associations with the city: "Pendleton," "Kersal," "Byrom" and "Miss Bexley". (17.10.69)

Maurice Richards, Salford's latest big signing, made his début at the Willows against a Leigh side who had won their thirteen previous games. The match, played on Wednesday evening, was won by Salford 15-5. (17.10.69)

St Anne's Church, Brindleheath, closes on Sunday, after which the parish will be divided into three and the areas added to the parishes of St Thomas, Pendleton; Holy Angels, the Height and St John's, the Height. The first St Anne's Church was consecrated in 1863. (24.10.69)

Barney Hudson, one of Salford's - and Rugby League's - greatest wingmen, is leaving the city to retire to his native County Durham. (24.10.69)

Two "new signings" for Salford Rugby Club made their début against St Helens on Wednesday. Paul Charlton and Ken Roberts helped their new team to win by 16 points to 12.
(31.10.69)

November 1969

Mr Alfred Jermy, a member of the Salford Grand Division of the Sons of Temperance, has been appointed the National President of the movement -

The Mounted Section of Salford Police on Chapel Street

the first Salford member to hold the position for sixty years. (7.11.69)

After forty-five years in the Transport Department of Salford Corporation, Mr Clifford Jones of Pendleton retired on Friday, the last man to do so before the Department's merger with the Passenger Transport Authority. (7.11.69)

Salford's bus services have become part of SELNEC, the South East Lancashire, North East Cheshire section of the new Passenger Transport Authority. Statistics for Salford up to the merger are as follows: staff employed - 1,400; mileage operated 1968-69 - 8,839,828; passengers carried - 67,500,175; total revenue - £2,039,058; financial result - a surplus of £76,783. The bus fleet strength is 271, of which 223 have been purchased since 1962. The latest batch of twenty were put into service in August 1969, twenty more are on order and by 1972 there will be no buses over the age of ten years. Two and a half million pounds worth of assets were handed over to the SELNEC PTA on 1 November and not one penny will be received in compensation. (7.11.69)

At a meeting held at Salford Town Hall this week, a Lions Club for Salford was established. The International Association of Lions Clubs (the full name of the organisation) was formed in America in 1917, to give service to the community without regard to politics, religion, race, or in any way furthering the personal interests of its members. (7.11.69)

Planning permission has been given this week for the conversion of the former Groves & Whitnall pub, the Springfield Tavern on Springfield Lane, for office storage and light industrial purposes. (21.11.69)

St George's Methodist Church, Kenyon Way, Little Hulton, is to close down. Built only seven years ago following the demolition of Hankinson Street Methodist Church, Pendleton, it has suffered continual problems with vandalism. (21.11.69)

Salford's oldest Free Church, the Chapel Street Congregational Church, celebrates its 150th anniversary this weekend. In 1817 a building known as the old Cloth Hall in the Greengate area was opened for worship and two years later the preacher, Mr John Coombs, opened the new church in Chapel Street; it became known to the locals as "Coombs' Church". (28.11.69)

December 1969

Vaughan's Club on the Ladywell Estate - the former Salford Corporation Employees' Social Club - has been refused a drinks licence because it did not give sufficient notice of its application. It will now be February before an application can be heard. (5.12.69)

The ten-storey Manchester Liners House was opened today by Mr Charles Ritchie, High Commissioner for Canada. The 32-foot-high Canadian Indian totem pole adjacent to the main entrance is a permanent visual testimony to the trade links maintained by Manchester Liners between Canada and Salford Docks. The pole was specially carved for the firm by the Kwakiutl tribe of Indians in British Columbia. The pole has four symbolic representations: the eagle, the killer whale, the raven and a chief

holding engraved ceremonial coppers in his hands; the metal signifies his wealth and power. (12.12.69)

At the Punch Bowl pub on Chapel Street last week, decorators stripping off multiple layers of paint uncovered a whole row of murals. Among the paintings, believed to have been done in oils, is one of the old Flat Iron Market which used to adjoin Sacred Trinity Church opposite the pub. There is also a large seascape and a punch bowl. Another link with the past may be in the bar shelves, for the carvings on them suggest that they could at one time have been part of a choir stall. (12.12.69)

On Saturday 20 December there is wrestling at the Scala Cinema, Ford Lane, featuring Count Bartelli versus Rough-house Alf Cadman (Salford's "iron man"). (12.12.69)

Work has started on the New Windsor School on Unwin Street. (12.12.69)

The police section houses in Hankinson Street, Pendleton, and the various police boxes scattered about the city which are no longer in use, are to be demolished. (12.12.69)

Prince Philip, Duke of Edinburgh, was in Salford on Friday afternoon to confer degrees on students at Salford University. Among them was the first girl to gain a BSc in Mechanical Engineering at the University. She is Miss Angela McKay, aged 24. (19.12.69)

Tootal Road School is now open as a music centre. (19.12.69)

Threlfall's Royal Hotel, Church Street, Pendleton, next to the proposed Civic Market, has had its interior completely refurbished. The main theme of the decoration is the history of markets in Salford and various old flat irons are on show in glass cases and on shelves to go with the new name - the "Flat Iron". (19.12.69)

A tender of £4,200 has been accepted for the demolition of the now vacant Pendleton Town Hall. (26.12.69)

Further information on the Punch Bowl murals has come to light. Mr J Doyle of Swinton, who was the tenant of the pub when the seascape was painted in 1960, has sent a description of it to the local paper. It consisted of three sailing ships, with cherubs representing the East and West Winds, and also the points of the compass, and took one of the workmen of the decorating firm, James Goodall, over a week to paint. The other paintings - the punch and punch bowl on a chimney breast and Trinity Church and the Flat Iron Market on the wall of the News and Views Room - were done about 1950 by a previous tenant, Mr Harry Comish. Another contributor, Mr Scattergood, confirms Mr Doyle's recollections. (26.12.69)

A Salford Corporation bus repainted in SELNEC livery leaving Frederick Road Depot

1970

January 1970

Last orders were called at the Queens Arms, Ordsall Lane, on Thursday night. In a short time the building, in the heart of the demolition area, will be pulled down. Other Ordsall pubs which have recently gone the same way are the Clough Inn, the Egerton Inn, the Leamington and the Northumberland House. (16.1.70)

The Georgian Group, a national body dedicated to preserving good examples of Georgian architecture, has lodged an objection to the proposed demolition of 35-36 Crescent and the adjacent house, 6 Hulme Place, which are listed buildings. (23.1.70)

The foundation stone of the new £90,000 Windsor Church and Youth Club, Pendleton, will be laid on 24 January. (23.1.70)

For the first time in Salford, the market traders have joined together to form the Salford Open Market Traders' Association. A meeting of over twenty traders was held in the Bridge Inn, Lower Broughton Road. (30.1.70)

February 1970

The first new public house on the Ellor Street estate, the Pied Piper, is open, another is well on the way, a third was recently started and a fourth is under construction in the shopping precinct. This week provisional licences for two more have been granted.

The Woodman will be on site No.2, immediately behind the Reporter offices and the Rose & Crown premises on Broad Street. When these are demolished, the new pub will face on to the main road. In return for the new licence Wilsons Brewery will surrender the licences of the Grapes (Cross Lane), the Prince of Wales Feathers and the Grove Inn (Church Street).

On site No.7, the Woolpack will replace the Wheatsheaf Hotel. The Wheatsheaf and one other licence will be surrendered.

Elsewhere in Salford, a licence has been granted to another new pub, the Lima in Peru Street. The Regency Club on Regent Road has decided not to seek a gaming licence and proposes to drop its identity as a "club" and change the emphasis to dancing and meals. Vaughan's Club, Eccles New Road, was refused a licence but advised to try again when its objectives were more clearly defined. (6.2.70)

The Canon Peter Green Centre held an informal "open night" on Tuesday to mark its official opening. (6.2.70)

The Housing Committee has rejected a plan for deck access housing on the six-acre Brindleheath site because it included blocks of up to eleven storeys high. (6.2.70)

Salford's coronary ambulance (Whiskey One), based at Hope Hospital, went into full twenty-four hour operation on 17 February. The mobile unit is the third of its kind in the British Isles. (20.2.70)

In front of a crowd of almost 2,000 on Sunday 22 February, Langworthy Rugby Club defeated the French team Celtic de Paris by 17 points to 3. This gave the Salford team an aggregate win of 28 points to 16 in the final of the Dubonnet Trophy Competition. (27.2.70)

After renovations, the old lecture hall at Brunswick Methodist Church, Pendleton, will be officially reopened tomorrow, 28 February. The hall, which in the past has been used as a five-a-side football pitch and a general "dumping ground" for the church youth club, has been transformed into a second church and meeting room. (27.2.70)

March 1970

Salford's latest pub opened its doors on Thursday 19 March. The Lima Arms in Peru Street is a "theme pub", with various murals and paintings giving an insight into Inca life and traditions. The rooms have been named the Andes Room and the Inca Room. (20.3.70)

This week saw the 150th anniversary celebrations at Regent Hall Methodist Church, Ordsall. (20.3.70)

Work on Cherry Tree Court, the first of the five blocks of flats that have to be vacated and strengthened to new Ministry standards, will start soon. The first tenants to leave will be moved next week to Albion Towers on the High Street estate. (20.3.70)

April 1970

Within the next three weeks, work is to start on a new three-storey office block on the site of the old Cromwell Cinema. (10.4.70)

The Priory Hotel in Broughton, overlooking the cricket club, has been modernised. The whole of the interior has been torn out, the old flag floors and little cosy niches have gone, replaced by carpets and two large rooms. (10.4.70)

Work has begun on the demolition of Pendleton Town Hall. (17.4.70)

After seven years of planning and preparation, the 220-acre Ordsall redevelopment was officially launched by the Mayor, Alderman V Hemingway, JP, on Friday. He operated a giant piledriver to start the foundation work for the first block of flats. (24.4.70)

May 1970

Forty yards below one of Salford's busiest streets, work is going on round the clock to pump 1,000 gallons of water a minute away from the latest addition to the city's subterranean labyrinth. A tunnel is being built to take additional telephone cables which will link with the new trunk equipment in Dial House. The new tunnel will connect with the existing tunnel which runs from Ardwick to Islington Street, Salford. (1.5.70)

The Amalgamated Inn in Gloucester Street, Ordsall, seen by television viewers as the Rovers Return in

Prince Philip on one of his visits to Salford University in the late 1960s

"Coronation Street", will soon be no more. The landlord, Mr Cyril Plant, and his wife Betty move out today to make way for the demolition men.

The pub was chosen years ago by Granada as an ideal setting for exterior scenes at the "Rovers". Since then they have made several visits, notably to film Annie Walker's arrival from Paris in a Rolls Royce. Though the Amalgamated may be dying, its memory will live on, as an exact replica has been built in the Granada studios for further episodes of the programme.   (1.5.70)

The demolition of "Tommy Bradford's" works at the Windsor roundabout, announced two years ago, has begun. The firm produced famous laundry machinery for over a century, and made one of the world's first automatic washing machines. Part of the site will be used for a car park for 255 vehicles.   (8.5.70)

Alderman G M Joplin, elected as Mayor of Salford on Wednesday, will at the age of 36 be the youngest ever of Salford's 93 mayors.   (22.5.70)

The last three "tipplers" have vanished from Salford. These old water closets worked by water being poured into them directly, or from a household liquid waste disposal pipe. When full, the tank would "tipple over" into the closet below and flush away the contents. The Salford Reporter stated

that the last "tipplers" had been replaced by the standard type of water closet, but did not say where they were.   (22.5.70)

Mr Cliff Evans, one of Salford's original Red Devils, has been appointed as the new coach in place of Griff Jenkins, whose departure was announced a fortnight ago.   (29.5.70)

June 1970

On Saturday, 13 June, there will be stock car racing at the Albion Stadium. The event is advertised as a "Sensational Opening Meeting", with "Hell Drivers and Hot Rods".   (5.6.70)

"Miss Salford Personality 1970" is Miss Jo Ann Casey, who will be presented with her sash at the annual Carnival Gala at the Homestead, Stott Lane, on 13 June.   (12.6.70)

On Sunday 13 June the last "Time, please" was called at the White Swan, Bolton Road, the Height. The building, first licensed in the 1860s, is due to be demolished.   (19.6.70)

July 1970

Salford Players' Theatre Club, the city's oldest surviving drama society, will move into the former Lyons ice cream works on Cross Lane, which they will use for two or three years until new premises are built. The final production at the old theatre in Nursery Street was shown in the first

week of June, before the building was closed for demolition.   (3.7.70)

Salford has been reprieved by the new Conservative government. The Maud Report plan for local government reform, as accepted by the Labour government, would have doomed it to extinction as an independent city.
                                    (3.7.70)

The death occurred last week of Mr Henry Cobden Turner, the engineering and organising genius who built up the great Salford Electrical Instruments business. Mr Turner, a Salfordian who started at the bottom of the ladder, was responsible for many inventions of the electronic age and it was at his Silk Street works that the famous "proximity fuse" was first devised and radar improved.   (17.7.70)

The New Regency Club on Regent Road has reopened for dancing, dining and drinking every night except Sundays.   (17.7.70)

In the opinion of the City Engineer's experts, St Paul's Church on Broadwalk, Ellor Street, Pendleton, is architecturally out of keeping with the estate and structurally not worth reconditioning. However, the Rector, the Rev David Wyatt, has said that to pull the church down, as suggested by Councillor Williams, would be an act of vandalism; £100,000 could not replace it.   (17.7.70)

The new aviary has opened in Buile Hill Park, inside the large glass conservatory.   (17.7.70)

Among the victims of redevelopment at the Height is the old turnstile manufacturing works of W T Ellison, on the corner of Bolton Road and Jackson's Buildings, which is already partly demolished.   (31.7.70)

August 1970

A recent article in the Sunday Times tells of the origins of the Renold's Chains company. In 1864 James Slater, owner of a small Salford engineering workshop, patented a new type of driving chain. His factory was later acquired by the Swiss engineer Hans Renold, who invented the bushes which turned Slater's chain into the bush roller chain on which the modern precision chain industry was built.
                                    (7.8.70)

James Prescott Joule, the famous Salford-born physicist who died in 1889, was honoured this week when a moon crater was named after him.
                                    (28.8.70)

September 1970

Salford has its own civic flag at last. It has been entitled to one for years, but no action has been taken to acquire one until recently. Properly constituted by the College of Arms, it was shown to members of the City Council on

The Amalgamated Inn, Gloucester Street, filmed as the Rovers Return in television's "Coronation Street"

Wednesday. The flag measures nine feet by six feet and carries, on a background of blue and yellow, the bees, sheaves, shuttle, mill-rinds and bale which can be seen on the Salford coat of arms. It will be flown on all those occasions when a Union Jack is not flown - at the Mayor making ceremony, for example, or when foreign dignitaries visit the city or a councillor dies. Salford also recently acquired a flag for the Mayoral car; this will be used only when the Mayor is a passenger and when he is wearing his chain of office.   (4.9.70)

Salford's latest pub opened yesterday on the Ellor Street estate. Tales of cloth workers who are said to have settled here in medieval times gave rise to the name, "Flemish Weaver" and to the interior décor. This is Threlfall's first new house in the area following the demolition of seven of their pubs in the last eight years: the Druids Rest, Red Lion, Horse Shoe, Royal Oak, Wellington, Priory and Coomassie.
          (4.9.70)

A proposal to include an eighteen-storey tower block in the second phase of the Ordsall redevelopment was turned down flat.   (11.9.70)

Mr V J P Scerri made local civic history this week when he was appointed as Salford's first ever Director of Social Services, to unify and administer all the civic welfare, children's and home health services.   (11.9.70)

October 1970

The new "Turret" trunk telephone exchange on St Stephen Street was officially opened on Tuesday by the Mayor of Salford, Alderman G M Joplin. It will handle a million calls a week, which will be carried by the underground cable network, or by the microwave radio network via the communications tower at Heaton Park. Part of the building came into operation in July to relieve the pressure on Dial House, Chapel Street, which had become overloaded. A casualty of the new service was the Duke of Lancaster public house, which had to be demolished during preparation work on the site.   (9.10.70)

Manchester Liners are to start a new container service between Salford and Eastern Mediterranean ports. A new £1 million container vessel, the "Manchester Merit", will begin operations early in 1971.   (9.10.70)

Two long-established Salford businesses are about to cede to the developers. Kenyon's pawn shop is to go for the widening of Broad Street, though tentative enquiries have been made about the chance of having a pawn shop in the new shopping precinct. Lamb's house furnishers, who began at Windsor between the wars and have been at the Cross Lane shop since the 1940s, will soon close under the city's clearance programme.
          (9.10.70)

On Monday 19 October Salford Market will move to its new site alongside the Pendleton shopping precinct. The current market at Cross Lane will close and its large clock tower and white-tiled offices - local landmarks - will be demolished for housing development.
          (16.10.70)

Advertised as England's first triple entertainments complex, the former Carlton Cinema will reopen on 15 October as Studios 1 and 2, with a bingo/social club under the same roof.
          (9.10.70)

£1 million a day of customs revenue, as well as control of all the betting offices in the country, will be handled in the new five-storey Custom House adjoining the Manchester Liners headquarters in Salford Docks. Hoards of confiscated cannabis and a large illicit still used for making white rum were among the exhibits on show to the many distinguished visitors to the building on opening day, Thursday 8 October.   (16.10.70)

Salford's first female bus drivers, Mrs Nan Collins of Seedley and Miss Jean Rogers of Peel Green, will soon be working out of Weaste bus depot. Both passed their Public Service Vehicle driving test this week, after a three-week course at Manchester's Hyde Road depot.   (23.10.70)

Salford will become the home of Britain's biggest School of Chiropody next year when the College of Technology and Manchester Foot Hospital schools are merged. About 240 students will be in training at any one time, a quarter of the national total.
          (23.10.70)

Actor Michael Williams, whose parents formerly lived in Salford, is to marry actress Judi Dench. Mr and Mrs Leonard Williams moved to West Derby, Liverpool, when Michael was only a baby thirty-five years ago.
          (23.10.70)

Demolition is under way at Pendleton Baths on Frederick Road; the building has stood empty for some time.
          (23.10.70)

November 1970

The Salford Local History Group, meeting at Hope Hall Secondary Modern School, have decided to form a Salford Local History Society.
          (13.11.70)

Wednesday of this week was a busy day for Salford. The new market and food hall was officially opened by the

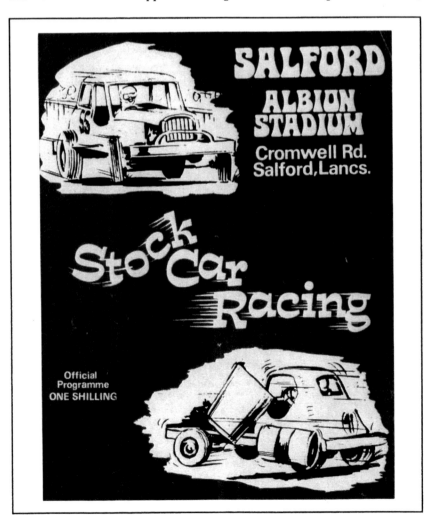

Programme for the first meeting of "Hell Drivers and Hot Rods" at the Albion Stadium, June 1970

Mayor, Alderman G M Joplin. Higher Broughton Conservative Club opened their new £3,000 extension. And Salford Rugby Club opened their new banqueting suite, to coincide with the visit of the New Zealand rugby team. (20.11.70)

December 1970

Memories of the dramatic days of World War Two were reawakened on Thursday when Salford railway station was invaded for the filming of an episode of the popular ITV series "A Family at War". (11.12.70)

A provisional licence has been granted for the Keystone, a Walker Cain public house now under construction in the new Salford shopping centre. The pub will have two unusual features: it will be octagonal in shape, giving the opportunity for what is claimed to be the most advanced pub layout in Britain, and it will be a lock-up house, the only one in the city. (11.12.70)

The Wheatsheaf Hotel, Broad Street, Pendleton, will close on Monday night and the following day the new Woolpack Hotel behind it will be opened. The new pub was built with factory-made segments and was assembled very quickly. (18.12.70)

1971

January 1971

The foundation stone of new flats for the elderly in Lancaster Road, Pendleton, was laid this week. (1.1.71)

The Salford Players' Theatre Club are hoping that they will soon have their own Playhouse again. After 21 years in their "little theatre" in Nursery Street, Pendleton, they had to leave because the land was required for development, and conversion work on the old Lyons ice cream factory on Cross Lane has proved more difficult than was at first thought. In the meantime, to keep faith with their patrons they have been presenting the comedy "All Things Bright and Beautiful" at the Salford College of Technology. (8.1.71)

In June last year it was announced that animals brought into this country for Belle Vue, Chester and other famous zoos were to spend a quarantine period in Salford, and a new storage building and offices were built in Liverpool Street Gas Works. Salford was chosen because it was thought to be a safe distance from any farms with beasts that might be affected by blue-fly disease, which could be brought in with the wild animals. The quarantine centre is now well established and is housing at present 66 unusual cloven-hoofed animals, including two rare black giraffes as well as ten other sorts; thirteen scimitar-horned onyx, two

gorals (a cross between a goat and an antelope), with other rare antelopes and a gnu or two. (8.1.71)

Another pub is due to close on 11 January, the Bay Horse on Broad Street. The last licensee, Mrs Cath Collier, has been there for 21 years. The pub has been nicknamed "The Monkey" since a former licensee, Bob McKinna, kept a pet monkey many years ago. Some of the customers also remember when there was a horse trough outside the building. (8.1.71)

All the upper floors of the former Health Offices on Regent Road have now been converted into large-family maisonettes. Homes with four to seven bedrooms have been created for fifteen families. The ground floor is still used for Health Department Clinics. (8.1.71)

Salford's twentieth Smoke Control Order was approved this week, bringing 92 per cent of the city area under clean air control. (15.1.71)

The Greyhound pub on Broad Street was closed on Wednesday, 13 January.

The last landlady was Mrs Janet Hinman. (15.1.71)

Salford is to lose yet another of its famous industrial firms. Churchill's of the Crescent were taken over by Unbrako Ltd of Coventry in August. They will move to new premises in Trafford Park. (22.1.71)

The Vine Inn on Broad Street is to close this week, and with it will go the line of pewter tankards built up over the years as a result of the tradition in the pub of giving a tankard to the young regulars when they reach the age of twenty-one. (22.1.71)

This week SELNEC began running one-man, double-decker buses in Salford. (22.1.71)

Because of the demolition of its offices for the Broad Street road widening, the Salford City Reporter has today moved to temporary accommodation in the former Civic Welfare Offices, Broughton Road, Pendleton. (29.1.71)

The Thatched House pub on Broad Street is to close on 1 March. It will be

The clock tower at Cross Lane Market

the last to go for the Broad Street widening scheme. (29.1.71)

February 1971

The newly-formed Salford Local History Society held its first meeting on Tuesday, 26 January, at Hope Hall School, Pendleton. The highlight of the meeting was a talk from Mr V I Tomlinson, JP, the headmaster of the school. (5.2.71)

The Salford Reformed Burial Society, formed in 1818 to enable people to pay the price of a decent funeral, is being wound up. Its assets of about £10,000 are to be shared out between its eligible members. (12.2.71)

The new offices for the Manchester district branch of the Amalgamated Society of Boilermakers, Shipwrights, Blacksmiths and Structural Workers, situated in Frederick Road, Pendleton, were officially opened last Wednesday. (12.2.71)

The first reaction of the Mayor, Alderman G M Joplin, to the local government reform plans announced on Tuesday was, "This is our D-Day, Deliverance Day from Manchester". His second was to announce that he is going all out to seek friendship with the neighbouring towns which will join in the new Greater Salford community. (19.2.71)

Salford Planning and Development Committee have refused applications to use a room at the Racecourse Hotel, Littleton Road and one at the Salisbury Hotel, Trafford Road, as licensed betting offices. In December they rejected a proposal to convert the off

sales department at the Lima Arms, Peru Street, into a fish and chip shop. (19.2.71)

The key to the 10,000th home built in the city since the war was handed over by the Mayor, Alderman G M Joplin, to Mr D Coates of Salford, in a ceremony to mark the occasion on Monday. The house is No.1 Barnfield Close in the Athole Street redevelopment area, Seedley. (26.2.71)

March 1971

Last orders were called at the Rovers Return public house in Tatton Street, Ordsall, on Saturday and the licensee, Mr Frank Hall, moved out on Monday. The pub, originally called the Park Inn until it was renamed some years ago, will soon be knocked down. (5.3.71)

The Secretary of State for Education and Science, Mrs Margaret Thatcher, came to Salford on Monday to open officially two new schools, St Boniface's Roman Catholic Primary School, Broughton and New Windsor Infants' School. In addition, she unveiled plaques at Albert Park County Primary School, Grecian Street and Broadwalk Primary School, Pendleton. (19.3.71)

At the age of fifty-five Joe Barlow of Kersal will make his début as a Hell Driver at the first meeting of the season at Salford's Albion Stadium tomorrow (Saturday). More than sixty drivers will compete for the March Hare trophy. (19.3.71)

This weekend Windsor Church and Youth Centre on Unwin Street, off Cross Lane, will be opened by Mr R W

Wyse, GM. The Chairman will be the Mayor, Alderman G M Joplin and the speaker will be the Rev Philip Hacking. (26.3.71)

April 1971

The first calf born at Salford's quarantine zoo is a fawn-coloured deer named Cleo. She is the first of her breed, the rare, scimitar-horned onyx, to be born in the country for over a hundred years. (16.4.71)

Manchester Liners Ltd have begun the first direct container service between Salford and the Great Lakes. The "Manchester Progress" sailed from Salford last Tuesday and is due to arrive in mid-April. A ten-day frequency is to be maintained, operated by four modern cargo ships; the other three are the "Manchester Port", the "Manchester Renown" and the "Manchester City". (16.4.71)

A stone fireplace thought to be several hundred years old has been discovered during restoration work in Kersal Cell. It was found behind one of the walls in an upstairs room and is now in the dining room downstairs. (23.4.71)

May 1971

Tesco, the first store to begin trading in the new Pendleton Shopping Centre, was opened on Tuesday 4 May by the comedian Dick Emery. Before the ceremony, a kilted piper played to the waiting crowd and a lady gave an impromptu knees-up to his accompaniment. (7.5.71)

The Wellington Inn, one of the handful of teams to start Sunday football before the Salford Sunday Football League was officially formed in 1948, celebrated the team's Silver Jubilee this year by winning the "double" of League Championship and Lowther Shield.

In their first games, teams turned up in bib-and-brace overalls, football socks and boots and used any old case ball, but by the time the League started, thanks to the support they received from the pubs and their supporters, they wore the full football attire. The "Lilywhites", as the Wellington were known then, played in white shirts and black shorts.

In an early Shield semi-final against the Grove, the Wellington played at Bute Street, watched by crowds that were six deep around the touchlines. Flat-top lorries had been backed on to the ground to form stands and the cemetery walls were filled to capacity. (14.5.71)

Lees Mission in Liverpool Street was officially opened on Saturday by Mr James Neil Lees and Mr Alan James Lees, the son and grandson of the founder of the original Hodge Lane Mission, Mr James Lees. (21.5.71)

Tilly Bramer behind the bar of the Rovers Return (formerly the Park Inn) on Tatton Street

Marks & Spencer opened their new store in the Pendleton Shopping Centre on Thursday 20 May. (21.5.71)

June 1971

Buile Hill Park Science Museum will close on 21 July and not reopen until late 1972, from when it will concentrate solely on the history of coal mining. This is as a result of the policy of specialisation by museums in the region. The fighting lions, stuffed elephant and the rhinoceros - half full-bellied and half skeleton - will go. (11.6.71)

St James' Roman Catholic Church, Pendleton, is to be demolished and replaced by a new building. The oldest Catholic church in Pendleton, it was opened in 1875 and consecrated on 8 September 1926. (25.6.71)

The death occurred on Friday of one of Salford's greatest and best loved players, Barney Hudson, who was one of the original Red Devils. He retired from Salford City Transport in October 1969 after thirty years' service with Salford Corporation and was one of the last two men to do so before the new Passenger Transport Authority took over. (25.6.71)

July 1971

The latest pub in Salford Shopping Centre, the Keystone, opened this week. The upper floor features a central circular bar and is to be used as a discothèque with multi-coloured lighting effects. The ground floor has a Keystone Cops theme, with silent films projected on to a screen, and "Roaring Twenties" memorabilia forms much of the décor. (16.7.71)

Salford Rugby Club's new North Stand is finished and ready for the new season. The building work has been going on since February. (16.7.71)

Stonemasons and other craftsmen are at work renovating St Paul with Christ Church, Ellor Street, Pendleton. A new floor has already been laid in the building. (23.7.71)

Prince Philip, Duke of Edinburgh, visited Salford on Thursday and Friday, when the 75th anniversary of the original Salford Technical Institute was celebrated. He toured the Ellor Street estate and new shopping centre, and opened the new Salford University library. (23.7.71)

John Virgo of Salford gained one of his biggest successes on Sunday, when he won a televised snooker competition by two frames to nil. John lived in West Ashton Street, went to Trafford Road Junior School and learnt his snooker at Stowell Youth Club. (23.7.71)

The new Jazz Palace will open in Regent Road tomorrow, Saturday 24 July, in the Gloucester Arms pub building. (23.7.71)

On Friday the Mayor of Salford, Alderman Ralph Evans, officially opened the new gramophone record library at the Salford Central Library, Peel Park. (30.7.71)

August 1971

The City Council has taken over the first two blocks of flats to be completed in the Ordsall Redevelopment Area. From 20 August, eighteen families will move into one of the three-storey blocks, Windmill Field

in West Park Street. The next block of flats to be let will be Garnet Wolseley. (20.8.71)

Work has started on the Salford University development at Castle Irwell Racecourse, initially by knocking down the old buildings at the Cromwell Road end. (20.8.71)

Bumpers, Salford's latest discothèque, opens in West Street, the Height, next Thursday. (27.8.71)

A fire engulfed the derelict John Street Board School on the Ellor Street estate on Tuesday. The school is the last of the older schools in the redevelopment area to be demolished. (27.8.71)

A new container crane with a capacity of 35 tons is in use at Salford Docks. They now have two in operation. (27.8.71)

September 1971

Higher Broughton Presbyterian Church is to close. The foundation stone was laid on 10 September 1873 and the final service will be held on 12 September. (10.9.71)

Manchester Liners have sold two ships, the "Manchester City" and the "Manchester Renown", both built in 1964, to the Korean Shipping Corporation. (10.9.71)

Langworthy Park Veterans' Centre overlooking the bowling green was opened today by the Mayor of Salford. (17.9.71)

October 1971

Salford Astronomical Society's new observatory at Chaseley Fields, Pendleton, will be officially opened on Tuesday 26 October by the Mayor, Alderman Ralph Evans. The £10,000 observatory was offered to the Society by Jodrell Bank in January, and the dome and large, eighteen-inch telescope were erected on their present site in the last week of August. (15.10.71)

The Norwest Co-operative Society Superstore in the new Salford Shopping Precinct will be opened on 21 October by Ken Dodd. (15.10.71)

Greenall Whitley have announced that on 10 March 1972 the Groves & Whitnall brewery in Salford will cease production and close. The brewery is over a hundred years old and was taken over by Greenalls in 1961. (22.10.71)

Salford Hundred Court of Record, which has its origins in Anglo-Saxon times, will come to an end on 31 December. The court takes its name from, and covers the district of, one of the six "hundreds" into which the area between the rivers Ribble and Mersey was divided in olden times. Its work will be taken over by Manchester County Court. (22.10.71)

John Street Board School on Ellor Street in its last days

The Salford City Reporter has moved to its new home at 496 Liverpool Street, Pendleton. (22.10.71)

Langworthy Rugby Club, which has been in temporary residence at the Moor Lane, Kersal, sports ground has been given notice to quit by 30 July next year. The site is required for the new Kersal Primary School. (22.10.71)

A house in Lower Seedley Road has been converted into a Hare Krishna temple. (22.10.71)

November 1971

The new Broadwalk County Primary School was officially opened on Friday 29 October by the Prime Minister, Mr Edward Heath. He was met by a group of demonstrators and there were chants of "Heath out!" and "Bring back free milk!" (5.11.71)

The Williams & Glyn's Bank, Pendleton, moved to new premises on Monday and is now in Mather Way in the new Salford Shopping Centre. The bank, earlier Williams Deacon's, first opened in Pendleton in 1888. (12.11.71)

Last week the country's first urban motorway was opened, the new Eccles bypass and interchange with the M62 and M63. (12.11.71)

The Salford Quarter Sessions opened on Monday for the last time, ending more than eighty years of independence in the administration of justice. Queen Victoria granted a separate Court of Quarter Sessions on 7 September 1889, in response to a series of petitions. All Salford cases in which the city magistrates have no direct jurisdiction will in future be sent on to the Crown Court in Manchester, which is the nearest. (26.11.71)

December 1971

People living near the Albion Greyhound Stadium, Cromwell Road, Pendleton, have triumphed in their campaign to end the "Hell Drivers" car racing which began in June last year and has continued with fortnightly meetings. (3.12.71)

The Hanging Gate public house in Ordsall is closed pending repairs to a back wall after an adjoining house partially collapsed. (10.12.71)

The Victoria Theatre, Broughton, is likely to close for good after the pantomime season which starts today, Friday. The "Save the Victoria" action group has disbanded because it failed to reach its cash target and the future of the building as a theatre is very much in doubt. (10.12.71)

Post Office contractors are tunnelling sixty feet deep under the Manchester Ship Canal, off Ordsall Lane and near Trafford Road Bridge. The tunnel into Manchester is forty-two inches in diameter and over three hundred yards long. (10.12.71)

Salford has enjoyed some good sporting publicity this month. Not only is Don Whillans included in the new Everest team, but steeplechase jockey Stan Mellor achieved his world record 1,000th win on Saturday 18 December. His first winner was "Straight Border" at Wolverhampton in 1954. (10.12.71)

At 11.30 next Friday morning the Mayor, Alderman Ralph Evans, will switch on Salford's first Pelican traffic crossing. It is sited at the junction of Hankinson Way and Broadwalk, next to the Shopping Precinct. (17.12.71)

Buile Hill Park bandstand is to be demolished because it is too costly to repair at £2,800. (24.12.71)

1972

January 1972

Mrs Elizabeth Tomlinson, known to hundreds in Salford as "Auntie Lily", has died at the age of seventy-five. She began as one of the famous dancing troupe of Tiller girls and went on to start her well-known juvenile troupes, "The Dinky Dots". Between 1925 and 1942 she trained local young girls who had never been on the stage before for panto and revue. Since 1945 she had lived in Middlesex. (7.1.72)

Berry Wiggins & Co closed their oil refinery in Eccles New Road on Saturday. Its work has been transferred to one of the firm's larger and more modern depots. (21.1.72)

Reliance Laundry (Lancashire) Ltd, which began sixty-four years ago in a small cottage in Park Place, Pendleton, is to close shortly, as the land and building have been acquired for extensions to Hope Hospital. The business was started by Frank and Lily Beard in 1907, using a hand cart to

Happier days: an advertisement for the Victoria Theatre from 1967

collect and distribute the clothes, and was then called Reliance Steam Laundry. The firm grew over the years and moved into larger, purpose-built premises nearby, but it has always tried to live up to the company slogan, "True to its Name". (28.1.72)

Salford Military Band, formed in 1903, is looking for a new home. For the past twelve years it has been using the New Ship Inn, Blackfriars Road, but this is soon to be demolished. The band was formed by theatre musicians from the Regent and Victoria Theatres in Salford and the Queens, Bridge Street, Manchester, who were soon joined by musicians from Salford Hippodrome when it opened the following year. Originally they rehearsed in the Buffaloes Club near Ordsall Park. (28.1.72)

February 1972

Charlestown Congregational Church closed last Sunday after 107 years, mainly because of the effects of vandalism. However, the church will still be occupied by the Lancashire Congregational Union, who are the trustees. (4.2.72)

Salford Corporation want to build houses on "Spike Island" - the Frederick Road recreation ground - but it will cost them £2,350 to get rid of restrictive covenants imposed in 1891, when the land was bought from the late Mr S W Clowes. The money will be payable to Major L A Clowes. "Spike Island" is one of the least-used recreation grounds in the city, but has for years been a popular area for fairs. (11.2.72)

Salfordian Jim Thorpe has been selected to referee the World Snooker Championships next week, at the Selly Park British Legion in Birmingham. (18.2.72)

March 1972

On Saturday 26 February the first Salford Boat Race was held, when a team from Salford University challenged one from Manchester University. The race started at Albert Bridge, from where the teams rowed the one and a half miles to Mark Addy Bridge and then back again. The winners - Manchester - were presented with the Greengate & Irwell Trophy. (3.3.72)

Pendleton's new main post office opens on Monday 13 March in the Salford City Shopping Precinct. It replaces the existing office in Broad Street, which will close on 11 March. (10.3.72)

The new £58,000 parish church of St Aidan, Lower Kersal, will be consecrated by the Bishop of Manchester, the Right Reverend P C Rodger, on Saturday 11 March. (10.3.72)

Salford-born Don Whillans, one of the world's leading mountaineers, set out for a new assault on Mount Everest on Saturday, only months after a previous expedition failed. This time the four-man British squad will team up with German climbers. (17.3.72)

The former police station on Regent Road is to be demolished, despite an application for tenancy of the ground floor. Mr Qureshi, a former bus

Stan Mellor

employee, had proposed opening the "Bus Wallah Club", but his application was refused as the Council committee felt it would be injurious to the reasonable quiet of the neighbourhood. (17.3.72)

"Harrold's", the long-established grocer's on Cross Lane, closed down for good at 6.30pm on Tuesday night. The business was started in the 1930s by Mr Weikert and his wife Hilda. (24.3.72)

April 1972

West Liverpool Street Primary School was officially opened on Thursday 13 April, although it has been occupied by pupils and staff since January. It replaces the old school, which occupied adjacent sites and had been in use since 1894. (14.4.72)

After many years of progressive restoration, held up at times through lack of finances and even calls to knock it down, Ordsall Hall will be officially opened on 27 April by the Mayor, Alderman Ralph Evans. It will be opened to the public as a museum on Saturday 29 April. (21.4.72)

The Unicorn on Liverpool Road, Peel Green, has just been reopened as a "theme" pub. Renamed the Jules Verne, it has five separate bars, all with décor and names which are said to derive from Jules Verne stories. The bars are called "Pukka Sahib Bar", "Mr Fix's Office", "Shanghai Waterfront Bar", "Last Chance Saloon" and "Davy Jones's Locker". (21.4.72)

The Victoria Theatre, Great Clowes Street, Broughton and the ABC Cinema (formerly the Rialto) in Bury New Road are to become bingo halls. Permission for change of use has been granted by the Planning and Development Committee. (21.4.72)

The Victoria Theatre, Great Clowes Street, in its days as a bingo hall

Two Salfordians have achieved international fame recently. Lieutenant Colonel Dick Crawshaw, born in Weaste and now Labour MP for Toxteth, Liverpool, walked non-stop for 76 hours, 21 minutes round the Aintree car racing circuit to set a new world record. He broke the British and European record of 201.77 miles after 123 laps in 56 hours, 12 minutes, and the world record of 230.8 miles in 67 hours, 5 minutes, before going on to set the new record of 255.84 miles.

Salford's Yvonne Blake was in New York last week to collect the Oscar that she won for costume design in the film, "Nicholas and Alexandra". (28.4.72)

May 1972

Charlestown Civic Youth Centre was officially opened on Tuesday 9 May by Alderman G F Pollard, Chairman of the Salford Education Committee's Youth Sub-committee. The new centre is located in London Street. (12.5.72)

Following Planning and Development Committee approval, the Salford licensing justices have refused an application for a gaming licence for bingo at the Rialto Cinema, Broughton. (26.5.72)

June 1972

Formed fifty years ago, the Pendleton & District Sunday School Orme Billiard League added "Snooker" to its title in 1956 and today the League remains the only organised billiards competition in Salford. (9.6.72)

The Cobden Hotel, Brindleheath, closed its doors for the last time on Sunday. It has been the only building

left standing in the area for some time, and is itself due to be demolished. (23.6.72)

In a change from recent years, Salford's Carnival Gala on Saturday 24 June was preceded by a procession of fifteen decorated lorries with tableaux, starting from the old market place in Cross Lane and finishing at the Homestead, Stott Lane. This year's "Miss Personality Girl", twenty-three-year-old Pauline Tarr, was crowned by the Mayor of Salford, Councillor Joe Hardman. (30.6.72)

July 1972

The Church of St Paul the Apostle (Paddington), Pendleton, was re-hallowed on Sunday by the Bishop of Manchester, the Right Reverend Patrick Rodger. The church, first consecrated in 1856, had fallen into a dilapidated state and there were calls for its demolition, but the Rector, the Rev David Wyatt, was determined to see the building restored.

Work commenced in May 1971, and many parts of the church have been replaced on a tight budget, often using furnishings and fittings from other churches in the area due for demolition. Some fittings and all the pews came from St Anne's, Brindleheath; from St Gabriel's, Hulme, came the altar and some beautiful ironwork; the marble and alabaster font is from St Alban's, Rochdale and the Church of St Saviour, Deane Road, Bolton provided more wrought ironwork and chandeliers. An 1852 period piece organ came from a Baptist chapel in Nottingham. (7.7.72)

Broomhouse Lane Primary School, Eccles Old Road, Pendleton, closed today, following a farewell open day on Saturday 15 July. (21.7.72)

During restoration work by the present owners of the 14th to 16th century Kersal Cell, Littleton Road, some discoveries have been made which could put it into the list of buildings of national importance. They include cruck frames to the end walls, plaster friezes of post-medieval date and wattle-and-daub plasterwork. (21.7.72)

Smiley's Disco has opened in Vaughan's Club, the former Direct Works Social Club on Eccles New Road. (28.7.72)

August 1972

After over a hundred years of trading in Bolton Road, the Height, Tinker's Chemist's, one of Salford's oldest pharmacies, ceased business on Saturday. The first shop was opened near Queen Street in the late 1860s by a Mr Holland, who earned a reputation for pulling teeth long before dentists became established! At the beginning of the century the business, by then on its present site on the corner of Bank Lane, was taken over by Mr Henry Tinker, who ran it single-handed until 1926. Mr Tinker was succeeded by Mr Walter Wilkinson and Mr Wilkinson was joined in 1955 by Mr John Tomlinson, the last proprietor. (4.8.72)

The Health Committee's final Smoke Control Orders of 10 December 1971 came into operation on 1 July, making Salford the first city in Europe to achieve smoke control covering the whole of its area. (18.8.72)

Mike Leigh's "Bleak Moments", which received rave reviews when recently premièred in London, has won the Grand Prix at the Locarno Film Festival. The film was written and directed by Mike Leigh, produced by Les Blair and financed by Albert Finney, all of whom are old boys of Salford Grammar School. (18.8.72)

A "pets' corner" or "animal farm", as it is being called, has just been opened in Buile Hill Park, Pendleton. (25.8.72)

September 1972

A new footbridge has been built over Blackfriars Road, next to the Broughton Tavern, in double quick time. The engineers arrived at 8.00am on Sunday and by the time they left at 5.00pm, the brand new bridge was in place with 16ft 8in clearance. The paving and some guard rails have still to be completed. (8.9.72)

Over 2,000 people took part in Sunday's Ellor Street Festival, which was so successful that it is to become an annual event. (8.9.72)

Salford Corporation is to pay £3,928 for the disused railway line which crosses

Young visitors to the pets' corner at Buile Hill Park

the Ordsall Redevelopment Area, mainly via a tunnel which was laid down by the Ship Canal Company many years ago. (15.9.72)

The Mount Carmel Pipe Band, which took part in the Inter-Continental Championships in Toronto recently, were placed sixteenth out of twenty-eight Grade One bands. They were the only English band of their class to take part in the contest, in which 76 bands from all over the world competed, and although Mount Carmel did not bring home any prizes, they proved that they can compete with the world's best. (15.9.72)

The Pendleton Branch of the Royal British Legion in Langworthy Road will be officially opened on Sunday 24 September by Major Harris. The Mayor and Mayoress, Councillor and Mrs J Hardman, will be among the dignitaries present. The club has, in fact, been open to members for the past twelve months and Sunday's ceremony will coincide with the first birthday of the premises. The standard will be dedicated at St Thomas's Church by the vicar, the Rev M V Deas, who is a past president of the Pendleton Legion.

Formed in 1945 at St Anne's School, Brindleheath, the Pendleton group met for some time in the Woolpack Hotel before moving to premises of their own at 52 Seedley Road in 1948. By this time there were about two hundred members and on 3 August 1950 the branch was granted club status by the Legion. When the site of their headquarters was acquired for

the building of Sutton House, they moved across the road to number 25, then to the Langworthy Road premises on 14 September 1971. (15.9.72)

The Lancashire Aero Club, based at Barton Airport since 1946, celebrated its 50th anniversary last weekend. It started with three men building a glider in 1922, and now there are more than 500 members and a fleet of modern aeroplanes. (22.9.72)

Sir Keith Joseph, the Secretary of State for Social Services, came to Salford on Monday to open officially three new public buildings. The Charles House Training Centre for mentally handicapped adults and children has been in operation next to the Ambulance Depot in Charles Street, Pendleton, since June. The other two are the Sahal Court home for the elderly and the Lower Broughton Health Centre, Salford's first. (29.9.72)

A new parish room, choir vestries and rectory are to be built adjoining the newly refurbished St Paul's with Christ Church, Broadwalk, Pendleton. On the ground floor of the two-storey building will be the city's only cloister, on which work is expected to start soon.

Stonework from demolished chapels in Weaste Cemetery and St Matthew's, Ardwick, will be used for the rectory flat and parish hall. Slates for the roof and walls, provided free of charge by demolition contractors Palmer, are to come from houses being demolished around the Woodbine Street area. (29.9.72)

October 1972

Composer Peter Maxwell Davies, whose opera "Taverner" is currently being performed at Covent Garden, was born in Salford in 1934, the son of a theodolite maker. His parents moved to Swinton when he was eight. He has recently scored two films for Ken Russell, "The Devils" and "The Boyfriend". (13.10.72)

Work on the "Anaconda Cut" to eliminate the bend in the River Irwell at Broughton has now been completed. (13.10.72)

Forty-one years after defeating Swinton to win the Lancashire Cup, Salford did it again on Saturday 21 October, beating them by 25 points to 11 in the final at Wilderspool, Warrington. (27.10.72)

November 1972

The new high altar in St John's Cathedral was consecrated on Saturday by the Bishop of Salford, the Right Reverend Thomas Holland, DSC. (3.11.72)

The new £12,000 club house for De La Salle Old Boys was opened on Sunday 12 November by the Mayor, Councillor J Hardman. The new building overlooks the college playing fields on Lancaster Road, a big improvement on their previous headquarters, which was a converted house in Radcliffe Park Road. (3.11.72)

Spillers Ltd closed down their factory on Ordsall Lane on Friday 3 November. (10.11.72)

The new extension to Salford Rugby Club's social club is now complete, and will in future be known as "The Willows Variety Centre". (17.11.72)

A petition to save the Fountain Head public house, which is on part of the new Blackfriars Park site, has been rejected by the Planning and Development Committee. (24.11.72)

A fire swept through several works in Ford Lane, Pendleton, on Sunday morning, 19 November, causing severe damage which could cost up to £1,000,000. The firms affected were Marsden & Co, Milford Astor Ltd, Textile Mercury Ltd and Kelvin Fenton Packaging Ltd. The Salford and Manchester Rifle Club was also badly damaged, but the Church Inn was almost untouched. (24.11.72)

December 1972

Following the fire in Ford Lane, the Salford and Manchester Rifle Club members are looking for a new home. They had occupied the top floor in a building next to the Church Inn for ten years and all their furniture, trophies and records have been lost. The club was founded at the beginning of the century, but its popularity grew when it moved to Pendleton and it is

Barton Airport, photographed on the 50th anniversary of the Lancashire Aero Club

recognised as one of the finest shooting clubs in the North West. The club has another indoor and outdoor practice area in Eccles New Road, but vandalism makes it impossible to use the premises as a main headquarters. (1.12.72)

The main stand at Salford Rugby Club was gutted by fire on Sunday 26 November. (1.12.72)

The new Ordsall Housing Scheme, built by Fram Gerrard of Swinton (part of the Leonard Fairclough Group) is finished. The contract, valued at £2,300,000, took two years and five months to complete. (8.12.72)

Salford's last gas lamp has been taken down from outside 187 Eccles Old Road, where it has been in continuous use for more than a century. Mr Jack Potter, the last gas fitter employed by the Corporation Street Lighting Department in Frederick Road, Pendleton, will be retiring next year.

The old green gas lamps will be missed, not only for the light they shed, but also by the children of Salford, as they served as swings and cricket stumps in the summer and as goal posts in the football season. They were also popular as a meeting place for courting couples all the year round. (8.12.72)

"Chalky's Place" in Gravel Lane, Salford's newest disco club, was opened on Thursday 14 December by the Mayor, Councillor J Hardman. (15.12.72)

Salford Parks Department's floral reproduction of the city's coat of arms is being planted again for the 1973 season. (15.12.72)

The former Tower Club in Broughton Lane has opened as the Wagon Wheels Club. (15.12.72)

The Sunday Cinemas charitable levy, which used to raise thousands of pounds a year in Salford at its peak, has now been officially ended. (22.12.72)

The new Friday market at Salford started on 1 December. (22.12.72)

1973

January 1973

The death occurred on Monday of Dr John Lancelot Burn, former Medical Officer of Health for Salford for twenty-eight years. Under his guidance, Salford became the first city in Britain to wipe out diphtheria, the first to register a nil figure for maternal mortality and the first to tackle tuberculosis by a mass X-ray of all the citizens. He also saw the first smokeless zones introduced to the city. (5.1.73)

With all its Victorian splendour restored, the Victoria Theatre, Broughton, reopened on Thursday 11 January as the Victoria Social Club. The entertainer Norman Vaughan performed the opening ceremony. (19.1.73)

The reigning Miss World (Belinda Green of Australia) delighted Salford shoppers when she called at the Norweb showroom in Pendleton Shopping Precinct on Thursday 25 January. (26.1.73)

February 1973

The exterior of St John's Cathedral is being cleaned. (2.2.73)

The ABC (Rialto) Cinema, Broughton, which opened in 1927, will close on 3 February. The last films to be shown are "From Russia with Love" and "You Only Live Twice". (2.2.73)

As from Monday, the home of Salford Hospital Management Committee will be the new Peel House office block on Monton Road, Eccles. (2.2.73)

On Friday 9 February the Right Honourable Geoffrey Rippon, Secretary of State for the Environment, announced that the new Metropolitan District 12E is to be named "Salford". This decision overrules the recommendation of the District Standing Conference, which on 18 January rejected "Salford" in favour of "Irwell" by eight votes to seven.

In the reorganised District, Salford will keep its magistrates' courts as a Petty Sessions Division of its own. (16.2.73)

One of the world's most famous railway engines, the "Flying Scotsman", passed through Salford recently, en route from Liverpool to York, where it will go into the Railway Museum. (23.2.73)

The RAOB held their last meeting at the Royal Archer Hotel in Lower Broughton Road on Sunday 18 February. The pub has been the home of the Royal Archer Lodge No.38 Grand Council since 1892; in future they will meet at the Royal Hotel, Weaste. (23.2.73)

March 1973

In 1851 Alderman Livingstone, Chairman of the Salford Union Board of Guardians, laid the foundation stone of a new Salford Workhouse in Eccles New Road, and was presented with a richly chased silver trowel as a memento of the occasion. On Tuesday that same trowel was handed over to the Mayor, Councillor J Hardman, to mark the opening of three new homes - Richmond Hill, Unwin Court and Cromwell Court - which provide up-to-date facilities for the elderly.

The workhouse, built under the historic Poor Law, was succeeded by the Homestead Old People's Home in Stott Lane, Pendleton, which was built in the late 1920s, when the National Assistance Board was being set up. More recently, under Welfare State legislation, the trend has been towards a series of smaller homes, accommodating around forty residents each, and the three just opened complete a crash programme to provide for the last of the Homestead's residents. In July 1970 the Regional Hospital Board was given permission to acquire the buildings and site of the Homestead, which has now closed. In due course the building will be demolished to make way for extensions to the adjoining Hope Hospital. (2.3.73)

Williams Garments' Social Club on Broughton Road, off Frederick Road, was opened on Saturday by the Mayor,

A photograph taken a week after the fire on Ford Lane in November 1972. The Church Inn stands intact amid the burnt-out property around it

Councillor J Hardman. Forty-nine per cent of the profits from the club will go to Salford Companionship Circle for the Elderly. (9.3.73)

Regent Hall Methodist Church, Regent Road, has closed only days before the 153rd anniversary of its foundation. The present building, which dates from 1870, will be demolished in the next few weeks. (16.3.73)

Murray's, the first newsagent's to open on the Height sixty-seven years ago, closes for good on 17 March because of road widening. (16.3.73)

Salford's churches are taking advantage of "Operation Eyesore" grants for the cleaning of public buildings and many are having a century of grime sandblasted away. Churches throughout the city are affected, among them St John's, the Height; St Luke's, Weaste; St John's Cathedral; St Thomas's, Pendleton and St Philip's with St Stephen. (23.3.73)

The Williams Garments' Social Club changed its name to the Condren Club this week. Mr Williams married the daughter of the late Fred Condren, who lived in Longfellow Street, "Poet's Corner". Mr Condren was a former member of the Companionship Circle for the Elderly and did great work in collecting money to help it, so Mr Williams has named the club in his memory. (30.3.73)

On Tuesday evening, 27 March, six citizens had the honorary Freedom of the City bestowed upon them, in the last such ceremony before Salford becomes part of the Metropolitan District. The six recipients were: Mrs Charis U Frankenburg, JP (the first woman to be so honoured), Mr Harry

Calderwood, Mr Sampson Goldstone, JP, Mr J H Lester, Mr D E P Norton and Mr J Roberts. (30.3.73)

The Georgian Theatre Club in Devonshire Street, Broughton, was completely gutted by fire on Sunday morning. (30.3.73)

For the first time in almost forty years a Clan Line vessel has loaded outwards from Salford Docks. Clan Line vessels call regularly with imports from South Africa and Asia, but the last to load outward was the "Clan Macbeth" on 28 August 1934. This week the "Clan Macintosh" loaded 4,900 tonnes of cargo at South 6 Dock. (30.3.73)

In the Players Number Six final against Leeds at Fartown, Huddersfield, on Saturday, Salford Rugby Club was beaten by twelve points to seven. (30.3.73)

April 1973

The Wellington team completed an undefeated season in the Salford Sunday Football League when they beat the Joiners Arms 2-0 and took the title for the third successive time. (6.4.73)

Salford's new £1 million incinerator at Wallness has passed its operating tests and has been taken over by the Corporation. (20.4.73)

May 1973

St Philip's School, Salford and St Luke's, Weaste, the city's latest, were opened officially today by the Bishop of Manchester, the Right Reverend Patrick Rodger. (11.5.73)

The first elections to the districts which

will comprise the new Salford Metropolitan District Council were held on 10 May, with Labour taking control of the Council with a majority of 50-16. (18.5.73)

On Wednesday, Councillor Harry Williams became the last Mayor of the old City of Salford before the new Metropolitan District is formed next year. (25.5.73)

The Salford University development now nearing completion on the old racecourse site at Castle Irwell has been officially renamed "University Village". (25.5.73)

June 1973

Another bit of Salford's industrial history is about to vanish. Remembered by most people for its "Thom's Castile Soap", David Thom's soap works on Indigo Street, Whit Lane, is in the course of demolition. (1.6.73)

The seven-acre site of the famous Richard Haworth's cotton mill in Ordsall Lane is to be developed as a new trading estate. Demolition work on the mill has already started. (22.6.73)

On Sunday the Mayor, Councillor Harry Williams, attended the last Mayor's Civic Service before the structure of local government is reorganised next April. Following the Manchester and Salford Police Band and the mace bearer, the Mayor and Mayoress, accompanied by the Chief Executive, Mr R C Rees, led the procession from the Town Hall to Sacred Trinity Church. (22.6.73)

A new world record of singing non-stop for 71 hours, 31 minutes was created this week at the Talk of the North Club, Eccles. Mr Eamonn McGirr beat his own record in an event which was sponsored by the Arnold Burlin Piles of Pennies Contests, in which many Salford pubs took part. (29.6.73)

The smallest parish in Salford, St Barnabas, Pendleton, is to merge with St George's, Charlestown, probably in the autumn. (29.6.73)

An Old Boys' Reunion was held on Saturday 23 June as a nostalgic farewell to the old Garnett Street School, now called the Marlborough Road Boys' School. Opened in 1880, it was one of the first Board Schools in Salford and is due to be demolished when new premises have been built. (29.6.73)

July 1973

The new Salvation Army hall in Edgehill Close was opened on Saturday 21 July. (27.7.73)

August 1973

After a campaign by local residents, it has been decided that the clock at St

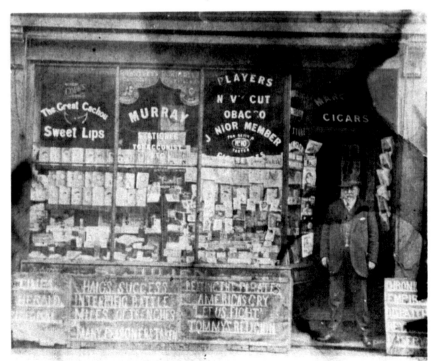

Murray's newsagent's on Bolton Road, the Height, photographed at the time of the First World War

George's Church of England Primary School, Charlestown, a famous landmark, will be saved. It will be transferred to the new school when that is built. (10.8.73)

Salford inventor Joe Dawson has completed work on a revolutionary new fire detector which is now available for hotels, homes and caravans. The detector alarm has three reference points: one, when all is normal; two, when there is smoke before a fire breaks out; and three, when there is fire. Salford Fire Brigade are evaluating the invention and a spokesman said, "The theory is good, and the cost is attractive." Joe also recently invented an in-car fog detector. (10.8.73)

Mrs Betty Knightly made electoral history this week when she was unanimously chosen as prospective Conservative Parliamentary candidate for Salford East, the first woman ever to be chosen to fight a Salford Parliamentary seat. (24.8.73)

Salford Carnival's "Personality Girl" this year was Miss Irene Conaghan of Higher Broughton, who was crowned by Granada TV's Brian Morris. There was no Carnival procession this year. (31.8.73)

September 1973

Salford's latest luxury night spot, the Water-Splash Club, opened on Tuesday 4 September in the refurbished Co-op Hall on Ford Lane, Pendleton. The previous club venture there was the Flamingo Club a few years ago. (7.9.73)

St Sebastian's Church, Charlestown, was officially opened by the Bishop of Salford, the Right Reverend Thomas Holland, DSC, on Tuesday 11 September. (14.9.73)

Workmen renovating the Duchy Inn, Brindleheath, have found a mural painted on plaster which shows the pub surrounded by buildings that are Elizabethan in style. The Duchy was a beerhouse dating from about 1860 and since it was almost entirely rebuilt in 1904 and altered again in 1909, the mural does not match the age of the pub. (14.9.73)

De La Salle Rugby Union Club's first team recorded their biggest-ever win on Saturday, when they beat Burmunians, the Bury team, by 82 points to 6. (14.9.73)

During the past three months ten Charlestown pubs have disappeared because of demolition. The Bird in Hand, Irwell Castle, Wellington, Clarence, Albert, Elephant & Castle, Jubilee Inn, Royal Oak, Britannia and Three Terriers have all served their last pints and more local landmarks will disappear in the course of redevelopment. So far, only one public house is being built to replace them. (28.9.73)

October 1973

The new Parish Hall and Community Centre of St Luke's, Weaste, was officially opened by Lord Clitheroe, the Lord Lieutenant of Lancashire, on Wednesday 10 October. The building has been in use since August and the first sod was cut on Sunday 16 July last year. (12.10.73)

The outfitters and furnishers H Bescoby & Co Ltd, who have served in Salford since 1895, have moved to new premises in Littleton Road, near the Racecourse Hotel. Bescoby's was founded in St Stephen Street and moved around the turn of the century to Cromwell Road, Pendleton, where they remained until recently. (19.10.73)

On Saturday 13 October Salford Rugby Club's team was at Wilderspool,

Warrington, in the Lancashire Cup Final, defending the trophy won last year. But this time Salford went down to Wigan by 19 points to 9. (19.10.73)

The last Masses at the ninety-eight-year-old St James's Church, Pendleton, will be held on Sunday. The building will then close for demolition, to make way for a new church. (26.10.73)

Just opened at Pomona Dock is the new "floating pub", the North Westward Ho, known locally as "The Boat". The 800-ton ship was built in 1938 and is a former ferry which assisted with the Dunkirk evacuation. It has been completely refurbished to provide dining facilities, a disco and a function room. The official opening is scheduled for Wednesday 6 February 1974. (26.10.73)

November 1973

There has been some disruption to shipping at Salford Docks this week, after the 3,600-ton container ship, "The Frontier", smashed into two lock gates at Mode Wheel last Thursday night. (23.11.73)

Another slice of Salford's history will vanish shortly when the Ship Inn at the corner of Cross Lane and Eccles New Road is demolished. Built in the late nineteenth century, the Ship was taken over by Walker & Homfrays in 1896, and subsequently by Wilsons, Watney Mann Breweries and finally by Grand Metropolitan. The licensee, Mr Robert Twamley, will be moving to the Wheatsheaf in Regent Road. (23.11.73)

Two well-known Salford churches closed on Sunday, St Barnabas in Frederick Road, Pendleton and Enys Street Methodist, off Whit Lane, Charlestown. (30.11.73)

Following complaints from Salford's Planning and Development Committee, the rebuilt Craven Heifer pub on Cross Lane, due to reopen by Christmas, will now be named the Golden Gate, and not the Barbary Coast, as originally planned by Whitbread's brewery. The Committee said the description "Barbary Coast" was bestowed on the Cross Lane/Trafford Road area many years ago, when it was notorious for prostitutes and drunks. (30.11.73)

December 1973

Pinky's Place, Salford's newest night spot, has opened in Hilton Street, opposite Broughton Baths. The club is named after the owner's black cat, "Pinky". (7.12.73)

The new Salford Metropolitan District, formed from the merger of Salford and four neighbouring towns, is to be granted a Borough Charter by the Queen on the advice of her Privy Council. This will enable the new authority to assume borough powers

The Borough Inn, Regent Road, with gasholder in the background. Gas-making in Salford ended in 1973

and appoint dignitaries, including a Mayor, Deputy Mayor and Freemen.

(28.12.73)

The Ghana Club has opened in Regent Road, over the premises of John Collier, tailors and outfitters. (28.12.73)

1974

January 1974

The first Mayor of the new Salford Metropolitan District, due to take office on 1 April, will be Councillor Harold Singleton, JP, a former Mayor of Swinton and Pendlebury. The first Deputy Mayor will be Councillor Mrs Nellie Openshaw, who was Mayoress of Salford in 1956/7 (when her father-in-law, the late Councillor James Openshaw, was Mayor) and again in 1966/7 with the late Alderman F Dewhurst as Mayor. (1.1.74)

Hyndman Hall, once the home of socialism in Salford and a landmark in Liverpool Street, is in the course of demolition. (11.1.74)

Work is going ahead to fill in the old railway tunnel of the derelict Ordsall branch railway. Over 17,000 cubic yards of rubble is being used to block the hole, most of it coming from a roadworks site in Whit Lane. The line once carried goods to the Docks from Pendleton and was said to be too narrow to convert to a road; financial approval for its demolition was given last November. (25.1.74)

February 1974

Following a boom in membership, CAMRA, the Campaign for Real Ale, is forming a North Manchester Branch which includes Salford. The National Organiser, Mr Graham Lees, was born in Salford and his parents live in Lower Kersal; the national Campaign headquarters is in Keats Court, Lower Kersal. (15.2.74)

Nearly four hundred pieces of pottery illustrated with a picture in pink of the old Pendleton Town Hall have been found during the clearance of cupboards in the Homestead Old People's Home, Stott Lane. After the city's historical interests have been safeguarded, they will be sold.

(22.2.74)

Work has started this week on the new Height Methodist Church on King Street, on the site of the old joinery works facing the library. The old Methodist Church in Bolton Road will be demolished soon for the A6 road widening scheme. (22.2.74)

March 1974

The ABC Cinema, Eccles, formerly the Broadway, closes officially on 9 March.

(8.3.74)

April 1974

Salford lost its one-boat navy on 1 April. The "Salford City" travels three times a week down the Ship Canal and out into Liverpool Bay to dump sludge from the Weaste Sewage Works. Now the works and the ship have been taken over by the new Regional Water Authority. (5.4.74)

On 1 April Salford was joined by the neighbouring townships of Eccles, Worsley, Swinton & Pendlebury and Irlam to form the new Salford Metropolitan District. (1.4.74)

The new district headquarters will be in the more modern building of Swinton Town Hall. Among the furnishings transferred from the Town Hall in Bexley Square was a grandfather clock which used to stand in the entrance hall. The clock was presented to Sir George Haworth on the jubilee in 1904 of Richard Haworth's mills in Ordsall Lane, at that time among the biggest in Europe. It was presented to Salford when the old mill was closed down. On the front of the clock is the legend, "I count the hours, doesn't thou?" (12.4.74)

The Horseshoe Inn in Cleggs Lane, Little Hulton, has been virtually rebuilt and tomorrow its brand new concert lounge will be opened.

(12.4.74)

The new Littleton Road Sports Centre was opened by Councillor Joseph Holt on Saturday 6 April. The new facility has changing rooms, toilets and showers, squash courts and a lounge and bar. (12.4.74)

The Campaign for Real Ale has moved from Keats Court, Lower Kersal, to a new full-time office in St Albans.

(19.4.74)

Salford are Rugby League champions for the first time since 1939. Their 24 points to 21 win at Leigh on Saturday clinched the title. They will be presented with the trophy at the Willows on Sunday, before the game against Bradford. (19.4.74)

May 1974

Wellington Street School, which was built as an infants' school in 1885, is to close later this year. (10.5.74)

After more than thirty-five years at Jesmond Dene in Eccles Old Road, Pendleton, the West Salford Conservative Association has moved to new headquarters in Weaste Lane. The first meeting in the new premises took place on 31 January and the official opening was on Saturday 11 May.

(17.5.74)

The Britannia Inn, Whit Lane, Charlestown, known locally as "Yeb's" after a previous landlord, has closed. The last landlady was Mrs Ellen Scott, whose family has been connected with the pub for nearly a hundred years.

(17.5.74)

The Hyndman Hall being demolished in 1974

Following the recent local government reorganisation, the new county names in England and Wales become part of postal addresses from July 1 - with only two exceptions. The rules are different for Hereford & Worcester and Greater Manchester, so Salford is one of the few areas in the country whose postal address will stay the same. Like Bolton and Oldham, Salford will not need a county in the address when the postcode is used. In fact, the Post Office has warned that people switching to "Greater Manchester" may find their mail delayed. The local paper, which had campaigned against changing the address and criticised Salford firms who used "Manchester" on vehicles and stationery, was delighted and announced firmly, "Salford should be addressed Salford".   (24.5.74)

June 1974

The new Salford, granted city status by the Queen on Monday 21 January, this week received an official inscribed and framed copy of its Royal Charter. This replaces the Salford Charter of April 1926, which became null and void when the old government area was reorganised on 1 April 1974.   (7.6.74)

The new footbridge across Broad Street, linking the College of Technology in Frederick Road with Belvedere Road, was put into place on Sunday 9 June.   (14.6.74)

Work started this week on clearing the "Spike Island" site adjoining the River Irwell on Frederick Road, for the building of 96 houses.   (21.6.74)

July 1974

The Wardley Hall skull, believed to be

that of local martyr St Ambrose Barlow, is to be taken from Wardley Hall to Salford Cathedral for special services. The first of three Holy Year services in honour of St Ambrose will be held on Sunday 14 July. The martyr was born at Barlow Hall, West Didsbury in 1585, worked as a priest in Lancashire for over twenty years and fell victim to the religious persecution of the period. In 1641 he was hanged, drawn and quartered at Lancaster. His head was saved and kept in Wardley Hall, which is now the residence of the Bishop of Salford. Pope Paul VI proclaimed the Blessed Ambrose Barlow a saint in 1970.   (12.7.74)

A meeting of former staff and pupils of St George's "clock" School will be held on Tuesday 14 July to mark the closing of the school in Charlestown. (12.7.74)

The Salford Carnival Gala was held at the Homestead on Saturday 13 July. There was a parade of vintage cars from Salford Precinct and the star guest was actor Peter Adamson (Len Fairclough of "Coronation Street"). For the first time there was no Personality Girl crowned.   (19.7.74)

Broughton Methodist Church on Alexandra Street, built to replace the chapel in Gravel Lane founded in 1791, and Cheetham Hill Methodist Society, started before 1820 and now in their third building, come to the end of an era on Sunday 28 July, when both churches close down.   (26.7.74)

August 1974

The Reverend Elizabeth Hodgkiss, born in Salford and a former member of Brunswick Methodist Church, Pendleton, was ordained at the Methodist Conference in Bristol

recently. She is Salford's first woman Methodist minister.   (2.8.74)

Miss Enid Mills, a former pupil of Langworthy Road Primary School and of Pendleton High School, has been made a Freeman of the City of London. The honour, which has been conferred on distinguished statesmen such as Winston Churchill, comes to Miss Mills as head of the English Department at the City of London School for Girls. Miss Mills lived in York Street, Pendleton, which was demolished at the time of the development around Churchill Way. Her mother lives in Burns House, Lower Kersal.   (2.8.74)

The last service at Broughton Methodist Church on Sunday was disturbed by an unexpected incident. As the Reverend George Artingstall led the final hymn, an eighteen-inch wooden spike came hurtling through the window above his head, ricocheted off his shoulder and clattered to the floor. However, the minister continued calmly with the next verse of a Charles Wesley hymn, apparently quite unperturbed.   (2.8.74)

Eamonn McGirr of Lower Broughton has reclaimed the record for non-stop singing which he set last year. His former record was soon beaten by an American, Jerry Cammarata, with 75 hours, but this time Eamonn set a more difficult target of 105 hours, which he reached last Saturday.   (16.8.74)

The M602 extension up to the Eccles (Ladywell) roundabout was opened on Thursday 22 August.   (23.8.74)

The Simo Club has opened over John Collier's tailor's in Regent Road, replacing the Ghana Club.   (23.8.74)

Brindleheath Lads' Club will be forty

Salford win the 1973/74 season

years old this year and the man who founded the organisation in 1935, Mr James Oakes, is still the chairman. (30.8.74)

September 1974

The former Fairfair Social Club in Ordsall Lane is reopening on Thursday 12 September as the Top Flight Club. (6.9.74)

The Old Curiosity Shop on Chapel Street, opposite Sacred Trinity Church, is closing down. The business has been a feature of local life since 1868, when the present owner's grandfather, Barnet Gilbert, started off in Marsden Square, Manchester. The shop moved to nine other premises over the years before coming to Chapel Street. (6.9.74)

Salford novelist and playwright Walter Greenwood was found dead in bed at his flat in Douglas, Isle of Man, on Friday. He was most famous for his book "Love on the Dole". (20.9.74)

Salford-born Alistair Cooke was the principal speaker on Wednesday at the United States House of Representatives to mark the 200th anniversary of the first meeting of the Continental Congress, the forerunner of the present-day governing body. Only three other Englishmen have addressed the United States Congress - Winston Churchill, Anthony Eden and Clement Attlee. (27.9.74)

October 1974

Due to open on Wednesday 9 October is the Harem Club at 376 Regent Road, just next door to the Simo Club over John Collier's tailor's at 374. (4.10.74)

The RAOB Club in Charles Street, Brindleheath, is now open. (18.10.74)

Swinton Rugby Club has announced ground developments costing £750,000 over the next five years. The plans include squash courts, a social club, a restaurant and a new stand. (25.10.74)

Washington House in New Bailey Street, the first phase of the Capital Centre development, was opened on Tuesday 22 October by Lord George-Brown, PC. The Capital Centre is on the site of the former New Bailey Prison, the scene of many public hangings between 1790 and 1868. It has since been a railway goods yard and latterly a car park. (25.10.74)

During research for a book he is preparing, the organist and choirmaster of Holy Angels Church, the Height, Peter McEvitt, discovered that the church organ built in 1927 for less than £2,000 is now worth £32,000. (25.10.74)

November 1974

The Regional Water Authority say that we could soon see fish in the River Irwell, as more and more anti-pollution laws take effect. The amount of effluent discharged into the river is being reduced all the time, and as the river gets cleaner, the wildlife should return. (1.11.74)

For the third year in succession Salford reached the final of the Lancashire Cup. They lost to Widnes at Central Park by 6 points to 2. (8.11.74)

The parade ground of the old Drill Hall on Cross Lane is in the process of being broken up. (15.11.74)

One of the world's greatest boxing coaches visited Salford this week. Angelo Dundee, trainer to Muhammad Ali, arrived at the Langworthy Hotel in Langworthy Road, Seedley, to visit his friends Johnny Lamb, the pub manager and Tom Burke, who runs the Cumberland Club in Bolton Road. (22.11.74)

The American girl singing group, "Thunderthighs", made a promotional visit to Salford Shopping Precinct this week. They inspected the record selection in Boots store and visited George Glass, Pecons men's wear shop and Marks & Spencer. (22.11.74)

The new £30,000 St Boniface's Youth Centre, Lower Broughton Road, was officially opened on Monday 25 November by the Auxiliary Bishop of Salford, the Right Reverend Geoffrey Burke. (29.11.74)

December 1974

In Salford Council's first-ever operation of this kind, it is deleting from its clearance programme houses in one of the few remaining areas of old Pendleton, the part behind the Broad Street Gardens, where wealthy cotton magnates and their ladies used to parade over a century ago. Some of the houses are so old that they have grazing rights included in their leases. Bounded by Broad Street, Frederick Road, the railway and Broughton Road, the area contains over two hundred houses in Eades Street, Upper Gloucester Street, Strawberry Road, Gerrard Street and Nicholls Street. (6.12.74)

Salford's latest pub, the Kettledrum, has just opened in Heywood Way, overlooking the market. (20.12.74)

1975

January 1975

Part of the first episode of the new Granada Television comedy series, "My Brother's Keeper", was shot in Salford. Two of the characters are seen talking in a police car in Gore Crescent, Weaste. Some months ago Buckland Road, Pendleton, provided a television setting, while the latest "Bootsie and Snudge" also uses Salford as a location. (3.1.75)

Cleveland House at the corner of Eccles Old Road and Lancaster Road, Pendleton, which is a day centre for twenty-five people classed as mentally ill, was featured in the Granada Television programme "Outside In". The showing of the programme was followed by many complaints about the bad language used. (10.1.75)

The Buck public house on Cross Lane closed on Thursday 16 January, signalling the end of an era for the family who have run it for half a

Gravel Lane Chapel, photographed in 1972 when it was occupied by a firm of fancy goods dealers

century. Mr James Hindle has been the manager for the past five years and his mother-in-law, Mrs Vina Lewis, remembers her father taking the pub over in the 1920s. Different members of Vina's family have held licences in Salford since the 1890s. (24.1.75)

On Tuesday 28 January the Mayor, Councillor H Singleton, JP, opened the Ordsall District Library and then went across the city to open a second new library, Broughton District Library on Bury New Road. (31.1.75)

Mrs Sophie Massey, who works out of Frederick Road bus depot, is thought to be the first lady bus inspector in the country. Her husband William is also an outside inspector based at Victoria. (31.1.75)

Langworthy Juniors are looking for a new home again. They have been told they must leave their Stott Lane ground by the end of the season. (31.1.75)

Salford won the BBC2 Floodlight Trophy on Tuesday 28 January when they beat Warrington at Wilderspool by 10 points to 5. The match was a replay of the nil-nil draw at the Willows on Tuesday 17 December - this was the first final in the ten-year history of the competition to end in a draw. (31.1.75)

February 1975

Planning permission has been given for redevelopment of the former Salford Corporation Gasworks site between Chapel Street and William Street. (7.2.75)

Sir James Farmer Norton & Co, the world-famous Salford engineering firm, have been granted outline planning permission to build a 40,000-foot single-storey extension to their premises. (7.2.75)

The trustees of Booth's Charities may apply to be allowed to extend the scope of their operations to include the whole of the new city. This would be only the second major change in more than three hundred years. The last one was when Pendleton and Broughton were incorporated into the Borough in 1853. (14.2.75)

The lake in Drinkwater Park was restocked on Saturday with the first consignment of £2,000 worth of fish. The lake was polluted by a broken sewer two years ago. (14.2.75)

Salford Local History Society has moved from Hope High School, where meetings have been held for the past four years. The new home of the society is at Midwood Hall, Mainprice Close, Eccles Old Road. (14.2.75)

The Talk of the North Club, Eccles, is due to reopen on Friday 21 March. (14.2.75)

Amid much controversy, Greater Manchester Transport is to make extensive changes to bus routes in Salford. Among them is a plan, announced in January, to scrap the Weaste to Mandley Park, Broughton, No.1 service, which has been running since the 1920s. (14.2.75)

A painting of staff and pupils of the first ever Salford Grammar School - "Dr Clayton's School" - is to be sold by auction at Christie's. The painting, currently housed in Manchester Grammar School, dates from 1738 and is by a well-known artist of the day, Arthur Devis. It depicts "Breaking Up Day" and identifiable in the picture are Edward Byrom, son of the poet and a boy reading one of Byrom's poems called "Three Black Crows". Salford Cultural Services Committee considered bidding for the painting but have decided the time is not right

to spend up to £30,000 on such a project. (23.2.75)

March 1975

A takeover bid has been made for Cussons, the Kersal Vale soap and toiletries firm, by Manchester-based merchants Paterson Zochonis. Cussons, the only independent soap firm in Britain, was founded eighty years ago by the late Alexander Cussons in a room above his father's chemist's shop in Swinton. It became a public company in the 1940s. (7.3.75)

The Salford Spiritualist Church, Lord Duncan Street, has been included in a Compulsory Purchase Order, with compensation to allow for reinstatement. The alternative site to be leased to the church authorities will front Liverpool Street and be bounded by Cross Lane and what was once Southport Street. (7.3.75)

The new City of Salford's second Job Centre was officially opened on Friday 28 February at the Swinton Shopping Precinct. (7.3.75)

Binnes' drapery shop, opened in Cromwell Road in 1926 by Mrs E Binnes, is to be demolished for a road widening scheme. (14.3.75)

The Duke and Duchess of Gloucester visited Salford last week and were taken on a tour of the city by the Mayor, Councillor H Singleton. Among the places they visited was the Manchester Liners building. (21.3.75)

Salford Boys were beaten in the semi-final of the English Schools' Trophy played at Old Trafford on the night of Wednesday 19 March. Their opponents, Barking Boys, won by one goal to nil. (21.3.75)

Park House home for the elderly, Ordsall, was opened on Wednesday 26 March by the Mayor of Salford, Councillor H Singleton. This is the last of the homes built in a crash programme because of the sale of the Homestead in Stott Lane; the others were Sahal Court, Richmond Hill, Unwin Court and Cromwell Court. (28.3.75)

A recent "This is Your Life" programme with Eamonn Andrews revealed that Nina Baden-Semper, the actress of "Love Thy Neighbour" fame, has links with Salford. She did her SRN training at Hope Hospital between 1954 and 1958, before going into acting. In addition, the producer of the programme, Ronnie Baxter, was brought up in Salford. (28.3.75)

April 1975

After standing empty for twelve months waiting for the bulldozers, the Church of St Bartholomew in Ordsall was swept by fire on Good Friday afternoon. The foundation stone for the church was laid in 1841 and work was completed the following year.

Members of Salford Local History Society: a meeting in the 1970s

Structural damage forced its closure at the beginning of 1974 and the last service was on Sunday 6 January.
(4.4.75)

A new disco club advertising this week is Sobers at Rialto Corner, Bury New Road. (11.4.75)

By beating Batley 40-3, Swinton Rugby Club's players have clinched a place in the First Division next season. (11.4.75)

Work has started on the building of the new Little Theatre for the Salford Players. It should be ready by next autumn. (18.4.75)

Salford Ladies' hockey team won the Manchester Women's League knockout competition on Saturday 12 April. They beat Withington 3-1 at the ICI ground in Lower Crumpsall.
(18.4.75)

The old Huddart Street canteen in Ordsall is being converted into a community centre. (25.4.75)

May 1975

Watched by a crowd of several thousands, the Royal Regiment of Fusiliers received the freedom of the City of Salford on Saturday 26 April. The Lancashire Fusiliers were granted the freedom of the old city nearly thirty years ago, and the latest ceremony extends the privilege to all the boroughs of the new Salford Metropolitan District. (2.5.75)

In the Salford Sunday League Lowther Shield final at Barton, Joiners Libs beat Wellington for the third year running to retain the trophy. (2.5.75)

The Peel Building, which is used by several departments of the University of Salford, has recently been listed as a building of special architectural and

historical interest, under the Town & Country Planning Act of 1971. Designed by Henry Lord and built in 1896 to house the Royal Technical Institute, it was considered remarkable at the time for being lit entirely by electricity and for having a combined central heating and air conditioning system. How strange that just fourteen years ago there were calls to pull it down to make way for a more modern building! (16.5.75)

Today the Duke of Edinburgh came to Salford, to hand to the retiring Mayor, Councillor H Singleton, JP, the Charter conferring the title of City on the new Metropolitan District. Prince Philip then watched as the new Mayor, Councillor Mrs Nellie Openshaw, was sworn in. (23.5.75)

Egerton Church of England Primary School, Ordsall, is to become Salford's first experimental Community School. It will act as a focal centre for the area's cultural and sports activities and will provide facilities for young and old, parents and pensioners. This is a new idea which is spreading rapidly in Britain and overseas. (30.5.75)

June 1975

Potters, the new snooker club at Rialto Corner, Great Cheetham Street, opened on Wednesday 4 June. Its first big attraction will be a 15-frame challenge match on Sunday 8 June, between John Spencer and Alex Higgins. (6.6.75)

Roberts' wholesale warehouse and wool retailer's of Lower Broughton Road will close shortly owing to compulsory purchase. Founded in 1883, the business has been run by three generations of the Roberts family and is claimed to be the oldest family

business in Salford. The present owners, Mr Edwin Roberts and his wife Vanessa, are planning to move to a new shop on Bolton Road, the Height. (13.6.75)

The first betting shop opened by the late Mr Fred Done in 1967 is closing down this week and the centre of their "World of Sport" is being transferred a short distance to their new premises in Cromwell Road, Charlestown.
(13.6.75)

Barr Hill Lads' Club has qualified to represent England in a "Mini World Cup" in Canada next year. The football tournament is for players of fifteen years or under at 1 January 1976, and the team picked to play have not been beaten for two years. They will compete against teams from Germany, Sweden, Bermuda, America, Trinidad, Mexico, Canada, and perhaps other countries. (13.6.75)

On Saturday 14 June the new Height Methodist Church was opened by the Superintendent of the Swinton Methodist Circuit, the Reverend John Hully. The Reverend Gordon Wakefield, Chairman of the Manchester & Stockport District, dedicated the church. The last service in the old church took place on Sunday 8 June. (20.6.75)

July 1975

The demolition of their homes has not subdued the people of Ordsall. Instead, friends and neighbours in Harry Street organised an old-fashioned street party as a send-off. The street was decked out in bunting and a large banner said "Goodbye, Harry Street". (4.7.75)

The new St Philip's Roman Catholic Church in Northallerton Road, Lower Kersal, was opened on the night of Thursday 3 July. The Right Reverend Geoffrey Burke, Auxiliary Bishop of Salford, blessed the building and then celebrated Mass together with fifteen other priests from surrounding parishes. (11.7.75)

World famous Salford artist L S Lowry was honoured by Salford University on Friday 11 July when he received an honorary D Litt degree from the Vice Chancellor, Dr J H Horlock. At the same ceremony Councillor Harold Singleton, last year's Mayor, received an honorary MA and Pendlebury-born Mrs Marie Patterson, President of the Trades Union Congress, was awarded a DSc. (18.7.75)

Princess Margaret, Countess of Snowdon, today officially opened the headquarters of the Salford Area Health Authority and its School of Nursing at Peel House, Eccles. (25.7.75)

The new Elim Pentecostal Church has been opened by the Reverend W Smyth. The old church was in Nursery Street, Pendleton and when it was demolished, the congregation moved

Salford Central Spiritualist Church, Lord Duncan Street, as it was in 1974

to a temporary home in the former clinic in Police Street. The opening of the new church coincides with the group's Silver Jubilee year. (25.7.75)

August 1975

The Condren Club, Broughton Road, has been extended to include an eight-table pool room and a darts centre with electronic scoreboard. It will reopen on Wednesday 13 August as the Condren Sporting Club. (8.8.75)

The Chequerboard, Ordsall's latest pub, opened on the night of Tuesday 5 August, when the first landlord, Mr Dennis Byrom, gave away 400 free pints. (8.8.75)

On Tuesday 19 August Gledhill Street, Ordsall, relived VE Day. Beer, bunting, butties, welcome-home banners, street music and dancing were all part of the scene recreated for a Granada Television documentary intended to show how ordinary people lived in 1945, when food rationing was still in force. Gledhill Street was chosen because it has changed so little since the war ended thirty years ago. (22.8.75)

September 1975

Salford actor Robert Powell, recently chosen to play Jesus in the forthcoming television series on the life of Christ, has been married to Babs Lord, a dancer with Pan's People. (5.9.75)

The long-established Co-operative store in Bolton Road, the Height, closed on Saturday 6 September. The shop, which dates from 1909, is to be demolished for road widening. (12.9.75)

Regent Road Baths, opened in 1892, has had to be demolished owing to vandalism and the dangerous state of the building. (12.9.75)

The Pack Horse Hotel, the Height, closed down on Sunday 14 September. Across the road, the Britannia Inn is already in the course of demolition. Both pubs will go to make way for the new Height roundabout. Work on the scheme is due to start on Wednesday 1 October, and will involve the lowering of the East Lancashire Road and about 1,300 yards of dual carriageway. (19.9.75)

The City Council has made a Compulsory Purchase Order for the Albion Greyhound Stadium, as they want the land for housing. (26.9.75)

St Philip's with St Stephen's Church celebrated the 150th anniversary of its consecration on Sunday 21 September. After the Battle of Waterloo £1 million was made available for building churches all over the country and they became known as the "Million Pounds" or "Waterloo" churches. St Philip's, designed by Sir Robert Smirke, was one of them. (26.9.75)

October 1975

The Bishop of Salford, the Right Reverend Thomas Henshaw, DSC, will open the new St James' Church, Pendleton, next to the Salford Shopping Precinct. Appropriately, this is the centenary year of the opening of the old church, which stood in Church Street. It was opened in April 1875, consecrated in 1926, closed in October 1973 and has since been demolished. (3.10.75)

Players from Salford Rugby Club took part in their fourth consecutive Lancashire Cup final on Saturday, but were beaten for the second time running by Widnes, 16-7. (10.10.75)

Mr Leslie Walsh, Salford's Stipendiary Magistrate for twenty-four years, retired on Friday 17 October. His replacement is Mr John Nimmo Coffey. (24.10.75)

The former library in Gardner Street, Pendleton, has been demolished because the building had become unsafe. Latterly it had been in commercial use, but for some years it was the venue for a Council club for handicapped people. (31.10.75)

November 1975

A lecture given last week at the monthly meeting of the Salford Local History Society must have brought back many memories of Wood Street Mission, Manchester. The Mission was founded in 1869 by Alfred Alsop, a stationer in his early twenties who saw the poverty, degradation and vice in the area and decided that something must be done to make life more bearable for the inhabitants. Its first home was in Lombard Street, but it later moved to Wood Street and by the time Alsop died in 1892 was a much respected institution. A home for fallen girls was added in 1893 and early this century its shelter for the homeless saved many lives. (7.11.75)

There was a fire on the night of Friday 31 October in the Cottage Club building in Gravel Lane. (7.11.75)

A meeting was called at the Willows variety centre last week by Mr David Berger, with the object of founding a trade union for beauty queens, to be called the BBQA (The British Beauty Queens' Association). (14.11.75)

A famous landmark on the East Lancashire Road will soon be no more. Burton's factory, which was designed to look like a giant sewing machine from the air, is almost demolished. The factory was closed down some time ago by Burton's, who have moved to a new tailor-made headquarters at Walkden. (21.11.75)

Beau, the resident organist at the Oakwood Hotel in Lancaster Road, broke the world record for continuous organ playing on Friday 21 November. By closing time, 11.00pm, he had beaten the previous record of 148 hours, 37 minutes by three and a half hours. Beau (44) decided to attempt the record to celebrate his ten years of working at the Oakwood. (28.11.75)

Farewell to Harry Street, Ordsall

December 1975

Once again, Salford has been filmed for the television series "My Brother's Keeper". The Town Hall in Bexley Square will appear as Leighley Town Hall in the series.   (12.12.75)

1976

January 1976

Swinton Rugby Club's new sports complex, which includes squash courts, gymnasium, sauna, and lounge and two bars, was opened on Wednesday 21 January.   (23.1.76)

February 1976

The Co-operative Funeral Services have moved into their new premises on the corner of Liverpool Street and Cross Lane. They left the old premises in Broad Street, Pendleton, on Tuesday 3 February. The new complex includes three staff houses.   (6.2.76)

Mr Appleyard, manager of the EMI Social Club, says he will be contacting the Guinness Book of Records to have a new world record entered - for bingo. This week at the club, a Salford woman called a full house in just 28 numbers, beating the previous world record by 5 numbers.   (13.2.76)

Angling in Salford seems to have a bright future. Salford Inter-Clubs anglers have taken over the running of the Clifton Marina and Clowes Park Lake from the City Council, and this extra seventeen acres of water will greatly improve facilities. In the past the only waters available to Salford anglers were the Bolton-Bury Canal (this stretch was filled in four years ago), the Greenall Whitley-owned facilities in Drinkwater Park, the Old River at Irlam, the Bridgewater Canal and Clowes Park, which was overrun by youngsters.   (13.2.76)

Tony Wilson, a former pupil of De La Salle College, is making a name for himself. He is to present the new Granada Television popular music show, "So It Goes", and is also a regular on the "Granada Reports" and "What's On" programmes.   (20.2.76)

The Cumberland Club, which closed on 10 January, is to be demolished for the Bolton Road A6 widening scheme.   (20.2.76)

Salford artist L S Lowry died on Monday 23 February at the age of 88. He had retired to Mottram-in-Longdendale, near Stalybridge and passed away in the local cottage hospital.   (27.2.76)

Tommy Brown, one of Salford's famous boxers, has died at the age of sixty-five. He started boxing at the age of fourteen with the Adelphi Lads' Club. In his prime, he beat Angelmann, later European champion and four times contender for the World Flyweight title. At his best, Brown was practically unbeatable in the UK.   (27.2.76)

March 1976

Now part of Greater Manchester Police, the dog section of the former Salford City Police force has moved to new County Headquarters on the other side of Manchester. The mounted section left some time ago.   (19.3.76)

The proposed closure of Seedley Baths has raised concern about the future of Salford Water Polo Club. There would be a lack of deep water facilities, which would mean that the team could not train adequately and might have to disband. Among their honours to date are the following: Bolton & District League and Knockout Champions 1958-74; Manchester & District League and Knockout Champions 1958-73; Lancashire Under-18 Knockout Champions 1971-72; Northern Counties Senior Knockout Champions 1965, Under-18 Champions 1970-71; English Under-18 Knockout semi-finalists 1970-71.   (19.3.76)

Folly Lane, one of Rugby League's most famous amateur teams, changed their name to Folly Borough during the summer.   (19.3.76)

Fifteen-year-old Gary Harford of the Salford Shotokan Club has become the youngest karate black belt in the country. He passed a Senior Dan Grade examination at Coventry, under the eye of Mr Enoeda, head of Shotokan Karate in Great Britain, to become a Black Belt, 1st Dan.   (26.3.76)

April 1976

Williams Garments, the Pendleton clothing firm, is to close, with a loss of two hundred jobs.   (2.4.76)

The Lance Burn Health Centre on Churchill Way, Pendleton, was opened on Wednesday by the Mayor, Mrs Nellie Openshaw, in the presence of the wife and children of the late Dr Lance Burn.   (2.4.76)

The members of the Height Congregational Church said a touching goodbye to the old building on the night of Sunday 4 April before the demolition men moved in on Monday. Many folk who had moved out of the area came back for the final service.   (9.4.76)

Salford Rugby Club won at Keighley on Sunday 25 April, by 18 points to 10, regaining the Championship of the First Division which was surrendered to St Helens last season. Sadly, neighbours Swinton finished bottom of the League and are relegated to the Second Division next season.   (30.4.76)

Brewers Greenall Whitley have been given permission to develop their block of premises in Lower Broughton Road comprising the Poets Corner and Beehive pubs and three shops in between. The whole property will be knocked through to make one large public house.   (30.4.76)

There was a fire on board "The Plainsman" at Salford Docks on Tuesday 27 April.   (30.4.76)

May 1976

Exactly fifty-five years to the day since the troop was founded, members of the 43rd Salford Scouts opened their new headquarters at Lancaster Road on Tuesday, 4 May. The ceremony was performed by the founder-scoutmaster, Mr Arthur Brown, OBE.   (14.5.76)

While some streets said goodbye, Gledhill Street remembered the past. This "V E Day Party" was recreated in 1975 for a television documentary

Where was "t'Hole in Wall?" One answer to this question, raised in the Salford City Reporter recently, is that "t'Hole in Wall" was a narrow thoroughfare running between Broad Street and Ellor Street, near the former Nelson Inn. Another reader thinks that it ran at the side of the Cross Keys pub on Broad Street, ending at Peel Street, where the street widened into Cross Street. (14.5.76)

Jane Evans of the Height has won an Emmy award for her costume design for the Thames Television series "Jenny". She is the daughter of the former Salford Rugby League coach and attended Adelphi House School. (21.5.76)

Langworthy Juniors Rugby Club is hoping to move into new premises at Oakwood Park, Pendleton. The old house and stables, recently vacated by the mounted police and police dog section, will make a good home for the club. (28.5.76)

Councillor Ken Edwards became the third Mayor of the new City of Salford on Wednesday 26 May, when he received the chain of office from his predecessor, Mrs Nellie Openshaw. (28.5.76)

A scheme to decorate the front of a brick-built cottage in the Claremont Road/Queen Street area of the Height has been vetoed by the Council. The row of cottages is part of the original Height village and is of particular architectural and historical interest. (28.5.76)

Salford Rugby Club was beaten 15-2 by St Helens in the final of the Premiership Trophy. The match took place at Swinton on Saturday 22 April in front of a crowd of 18,082. (28.5.76)

June 1976

Mr Gerard McDonald, chairman of John McDonald & Son, the city's well known Catholic funeral directors, has vowed to fight the bulldozers threatening to put him out of business. He is refusing to move out of his premises, which are in the way of the Bolton Road A6 widening scheme, despite a sheriff's order served on him to leave. (4.6.76)

M Brook, the tailors, will close on 12 June after eighty years of trading in Chapel Street. Mr Morris Brook started the business at 41 Chapel Street in 1896 and by 1901 had moved to the present premises (now number 114). The present proprietor, Mr Norman Brook, has been in the shop for nearly twenty years. (11.6.76)

A ship that has sailed the equivalent of twenty-four times round the world without ever being far away from Salford was "retired" on Tuesday 1 June. The "Salford City" is the smallest of five ships operated by the North West Water Authority to empty sewage sludge into the Irish Sea and has made over 7,500 trips in the past forty-nine years. Built in Glasgow, she had her engines converted from steam to diesel thirteen years ago. Now she will be broken up and parts used for spares for another of the Authority's ships, the "Mancunian". "Salford City's" twenty-foot lifeboat will go to the North West Sea Cadets Corps. (4.6.76)

Salford looks set to become the "snooker capital" of the country. Hurricane Higgins is already living in the city, top amateur John Virgo is ready to turn professional and Paul Medati is rapidly making a name for himself. (4.6.76)

The foundation stone of the new Salford Methodist Community Church near Salford Precinct was laid on Saturday 12 June. (18.6.76)

There has been a month of street parties, with the residents of Gledhill Street, Lord Napier Street, Hartington, Halliwell and West Park Streets all saying farewell with a "bit of a do". (18.6.76)

Brendan Foster, Britain's number one hope for a medal in the Montreal Olympic Games, is the nephew of Brother Lawrence, who was for many years deputy headmaster of De La Salle College, Pendleton. (25.6.76)

July 1976

L S Lowry has bequeathed four of his paintings to the Salford Art Gallery. (16.7.76)

On the Height, St John's Primary School in King Street is soon to be demolished. Its replacement, the new St John's School at present being built at Daisy Bank, should be complete by the end of the year. (23.7.76)

A new crossing over the Ship Canal, a dream of City Councillors for generations, is under consideration once again. The scheme was shelved in the 1960s and was also raised before the war. (30.7.76)

August 1976

It was announced on Saturday 31 July that the previous night's meeting at the Albion Greyhound Stadium had been the last. There was no forewarning and bookmakers and punters alike were shocked by the news. The Albion track opened in April 1928. (6.8.76)

Salford City Council is to build houses on the ten-acre Albion Stadium site; the scheme will include the first section of the city's long-planned Riverside Walk. (13.8.76)

A price of £27,000 has been agreed by the Council for the purchase of Smiley's club in Eccles New Road. The club was purpose-built to replace the old Direct Works Social Club on Cross Lane, but after lack of success it was taken over and became Vaughan's

The Tallow Tub on Chapel Street, with Brook's tailor's shop next door in the course of demolition. Threlfall's Brewery is in the background

Club, then Smiley's disco club. Now it will be a community centre for the Ladywell Flats Tenants' Association.
(27.8.76)

September 1976

In their Diamond Jubilee year Salford Players are opening their new theatre in Liverpool Street. The society was formed in 1916 and their first Playhouse was in the old "tin" library in Cemetery Road, Weaste. They lost this in 1939, but played in various schools and halls after the war until they acquired a former Sunday school in Nursery Street, Pendleton, and transformed it into a theatre. Here they stayed until 1970, when the building was compulsorily purchased, and they have been nomadic again until now. The building of a new theatre is a rare event in this country since the war, and a credit to the devotion and determination of all the people involved.
(3.9.76)

The Evasholme elderly persons' home in Park Road, Pendleton, is to be phased out and closed down by the end of 1977.
(3.9.76)

A plan to preserve a group of six old workmen's cottages facing Ordsall Hall as a "housing museum" has been rejected. The cottages, in a clearance area, have no amenities at all and it was thought that people would be interested in a reminder of the crude and comfortless conditions in which thousands of families had lived. The scheme would have cost £3,000, most

of it for fencing the cottages in, and the decision not to go ahead, deferred since July, has been taken because of restrictions on Council spending.
(17.9.76)

Included in the Brindleheath industrial site is a long-disused Jewish Cemetery that the Council acquired on lease. It is to be tidied up and incorporated in a planned open space.
(17.9.76)

Beau the organist beat his own world record for continuous playing at the Racecourse Hotel, Littleton Road, on Friday night. He began at 4.00pm on Saturday 11 September and improved on his previous time by three hours, making money for charities in the process.
(24.9.76)

The new St George's Primary School on Enys Street, Charlestown, will be opened officially on Friday 1 October by the Minister for Social Security, Stan Orme. Earlier this month St Paul's Primary School, Kersal, was opened by the Prime Minister, Jim Callaghan.
(24.9.76)

October 1976

A new alcoholism unit has opened in Pendleton. Anyone with a problem can get help at Duchy House, Duchy Road, Brindleheath.
(1.10.76)

Regent Road is slowly vanishing, as pubs, banks, clubs and shops of all kinds are demolished. Among the shops to go this week was the tobacconist's just before Cross Lane,

where television personality Tony Wilson once lived.
(8.10.76)

The renovation of the century-old black-and-white clubhouse in Yew Street, Lower Broughton, which is the home of the Broughton Cricket and Rugby Union Club, has just been completed. Work has been going on since the end of May.
(15.10.76)

St Thomas's Church, Pendleton, is celebrating its 200th anniversary this week.
(22.10.76)

Rugby player David Watkins reached another milestone in his career when he kicked his 1,000th goal for Salford, a club record.
(22.10.76)

A distinction which the old Salford won in 1972 will be achieved by the new city after five more years campaigning. It is that of being the first industrial city in Europe to be covered 100 per cent by smoke control orders. The final order, which is for the Worsley area, becomes effective next July.
(29.10.76)

November 1976

Swinton Rugby Club's plans to introduce greyhound racing to Station Road have met with opposition from local residents.
(12.11.76)

December 1976

Salford's Windsor Band are hoping soon to have a home of their own; meanwhile, they practise in Hodge Lane Wash House.
(10.12.76)

A Davies & Co, drapers and corsetiers of Great Clowes Street, are to cease trading when their premises are bulldozed shortly. The business was founded in 1915 and moved to its present address from Blackfriars Road around the end of the First World War. Mrs Alyce Davies, the present owner, took over in 1936. Herself a national beauty queen, she decided to make a speciality of rigid (boned) corsets which were almost universally in use at that time. Being near the Victoria Theatre, she built up a clientèle among the stage folk, including some of the "drag" boys. Among the sales registered in the books is one for a corset for a Salford lady with 60-inch hips.
(10.12.76)

After many years in Salford, chemist Mr Julius Cohen has decided to close down his Silk Street shop and retire. He came here from Blackburn in 1940 and despite having his Liverpool Street shop bombed just a week after moving in, he stayed there for twenty-four years. After a short spell managing a Flixton shop, he moved to the Silk Street premises.
(10.12.76)

A special Christmas appeal has gone out for help to furnish a new dormitory block at the Salford Children's Holiday Camp in Prestatyn. The Variety Club of Great Britain has agreed to spend £12,000 building the new block, but

More goodbyes: Hartington Street in the summer of 1976

before it can be used next summer it has to be furnished. (10.12.76)

This year Salford City Council Parks Department has raised about a hundred turkeys from six- and seven-week-old chicks. By the time they were ready for slaughter they weighed between 15 and 24lb each. The location was kept secret for fear of "rustling". Most of the birds will end up with the Social Services and Catering Departments. (17.12.76)

The Co-op Store in the new Ordsall Shopping Centre was opened on Thursday 9 December. (17.12.76)

Salford's latest public house, The Mariner in Liverpool Street, opened this week. (17.12.76)

W W Hill, Son & Wallace, the Broughton paint and wood finish manufacturers, are building a new factory next to their existing one in Elton Street. The work will involve the demolition of a 150-foot incinerator chimney which was originally used by the Salford Corporation Cleansing Department for burning rubbish. The new premises will enable them to transfer forty employees from their works in Whit Lane, which is scheduled for demolition. The company was established in Salford in 1860. (17.12.76)

Jacko's Club and disco has opened in Broughton Lane in the former Wagon Wheels Club. (17.12.76)

Alec Goodall, the long-established Salford tailor, is retiring on Christmas Eve. His first shop was in Chapel Street, then he had one in Cross Lane, before moving to Broad Street nearly thirty years ago. Among his customers were artistes appearing at the Salford Hippodrome, including dwarfs, and he once made a suit for a man 7 feet 3 inches tall.

Alec is a lover of football, cricket and fishing, but he and his brother recently sold their lake in Bury, after plans to raffle it fell foul of the law. (24.12.76)

1977

January 1977

The former Condren Club in Broughton Road is under new management and renamed The Merry Go Round. (4.1.77)

Pinky's Disco-Bar-Diner is reopening on 10 February in Hilton Street (Rialto Corner), Broughton. It closed last Christmas Eve because of a licensing problem. (4.1.77)

Salford City Council is to buy a collection of personal effects of the artist L S Lowry, including fifty more paintings and 260 other items. The cost could be up to £30,000. (25.1.77)

Fieldsend's, the coach firm, is fifty years old. Mr J W Fieldsend established the business in Salford in 1926 and built it up until it was acquired by Mr Jim Hackett in 1948. Since then other licensed operators have been assimilated into the company, and when Salford Shopping Precinct opened, Fieldsend's established a travel bureau there. (25.1.77)

February 1977

The Miller brothers, Erwin and Louis, are retiring from their Eccles New Road dental practice this week. Before moving there they operated in Church Street and later in Regent Street, Eccles. (4.2.77)

The old school buildings at St Augustine's, Pendlebury, which are listed Grade II by the Department of the Environment as being of

architectural interest, have recently taken on a new rôle as the Environmental Institute of the University. (11.2.77)

As demolition in the Ordsall area is now going ahead quickly, the staff of the Salford museums have been busy trying to save some items of interest. They have collected many decorative brackets and plaster cornices from shop fronts, and were able to save the shelving and fittings from the corner shop owned by Miss M Barber on the day she moved out; unfortunately, the counter proved immovable. (18.2.77)

March 1977

There was beer at 2p a pint at the Welcome Inn on Ordsall Lane this week. The pub is the subject of a campaign to keep it open, after the Council put a Compulsory Purchase Order on it, saying the land was needed for a children's playground. (4.3.77)

The second phase of Broughton RUFC's development scheme began this week, when work started on the restoration of the house adjoining the club at Yew Street. (4.3.77)

On Sunday 13 March the new building of the Pendleton Unitarian Free Church in Cross Lane was dedicated. The old church has stood at the Windsor roundabout, where Cross Lane joins Broad Street, for over a hundred years. The Unitarians, a sect founded on absolute liberty of thought, first decided to build a church in Salford in 1858. By 1860 the members were meeting in the hall of the Pendleton Mechanics' Institute, but in the face of bitter resentment they moved into a small disused chapel in Ford Street. In 1871 these premises were sold and they moved again to a room in West George Street, having bought the site at the corner of Cross Lane and Broad Street for £1,500. The foundation stone was laid on 27 May 1873 and the completed church dedicated on 2 June the following year. It had cost £2,500 to build and there were 123 members. (18.3.77)

After more than 160 years of Methodist worship in Broad Street, Pendleton, Brunswick Church will close this weekend. Although John Wesley preached at Sacred Trinity in 1733, and at Salford Cross in 1747, it is probable that the beginning of Methodism in the Pendleton district followed his preaching at St Thomas's Chapel in Brindleheath on 6 April 1774. The foundation stone of the present Brunswick Church was laid on New Year's Day 1880, and the opening and dedication services were on Good Friday, 15 April 1881, but smaller chapels had been on the site since 1814.

On 27 March the final services will be held at St John's Methodist Church,

Alec Goodall's tailor's shop (right), the Wheatsheaf (centre) and Berry's on Broad Street

Seedley, and the following week will see the two Methodist congregations joining forces at the new Methodist Community Church, Fitzwarren Street, near the shopping precinct. (18.3.77)

Salford's new, nine-hole Brackley municipal golf course on the Little Hulton overspill estate opens on Saturday. It has taken three years to build, at a cost of £108,000. (25.3.77)

History was made on Wednesday 16 March when the Salford Table Tennis Team took on the Israeli national team at Littleton Road Recreation Centre. For the Israelis, this was a warm-up game before they competed in the World Championships and their class stood out in a 10-0 victory over Salford. (25.3.77)

April 1977

Although it is called the Manchester Ski School, the 120-foot-long plastic training slope is well inside Salford. It is located under the railway arches, enclosed by two large wooden doors and is next to Victoria Bus Station. (8.4.77)

Brunswick, the part of Pendleton bounded by Broad Street, Cheltenham Street, Frederick Road and Broughton Road and one of Salford's oldest residential districts, is to have the worst of its homes demolished and the rest of the area developed as far as possible in accordance with residents' wishes. At present many of the houses are bricked up or abandoned and there are serious problems with damp and decay in most of the properties. (8.4.77)

Four sixth-formers from De La Salle College shattered the world record for continuous table tennis this weekend.

They notched up 100 hours, beating the previous record of 89 hours, 18 minutes. The four lads, Gary Bates (16), Brendan Hanley (16), Steve Hassall (17) and Duncan Greig (17), hope to raise £400 for charity. (22.4.77)

Pendleton Unitarian Church, near the Windsor roundabout, is almost completely demolished and soon to follow are St John's Methodist Church, Seedley and Brunswick Methodist Church, Broad Street. (29.4.77)

May 1977

Four Greenall Whitley pubs closed within the last year are the Alexandra, Lower Broughton Road; the Brunswick, Ordsall Lane; the Pickwick, Oldfield Road and the St James, Markendale Street. (4.5.77)

June 1977

Bunting was out and flags were flying, pubs had extended drinking hours and street parties were held throughout the city this week to celebrate Queen Elizabeth II's Silver Jubilee. (10.6.77)

The Regency Club over Burton's tailors on Regent Road has just reopened. The club had been closed following a fire in the early morning of Sunday 22 May. (17.6.77)

The Secretary of State for Social Services, the Rt Hon David Ennals, was at Hope Hospital on Thursday to open the Frank Rifkin postgraduate medical centre, which is built on the site of the former Broomhouse Lane Junior School. He also opened Ellen Webb House and Leslie Worthington House, two staff residences. (17.6.77)

The owner of Salford's oldest boxing gymnasium, Mr Albert Marchant, has died at the age of 73. Born in Salford

on 10 September 1903, he attended St James' School, Pendleton and was one of the six famous Marchant brothers brought up in Regent Road. After fighting all the top featherweights in England, he turned his hand to boxing management and his famous gym was established in Hulme Street some fifty-five years ago. It was later moved to Gardner Street, Pendleton. (17.6.77)

July 1977

John Binns Ltd of Eccles Old Road are celebrating their 50th anniversary. The Victoria Café and shop next door were opened in 1927 by Mr John Binns senior. (8.7.77)

There is a campaign to save the Grey Mare pub on Eccles New Road, which is subject to a Compulsory Purchase Order. Brewers Greenall Whitley, backed by CAMRA, are opposing the order. (8.7.77)

A crowd of 12,000 turned up at the Willows, Salford's rugby ground, on Sunday 3 July, but sadly, they weren't there to cheer on the "Reds". The attraction was an "It's a Knockout" competition organised for charity. (8.7.77)

After 125 years, Adelphi House School has closed. It has been merged with Sacred Heart to form a new school, Cathedral High. (15.7.77)

Another pub threatened by the bulldozer is the Old Veteran, Weaste. Owners Greenall Whitley are fighting to get it excluded from a Compulsory Purchase Order issued by Salford Council. (22.7.77)

Eight years of work by Dr J T Henshaw of Salford University, working closely with the noted orthopaedic surgeon Mr J Griffiths at Salford Royal Hospital, has resulted in a new aid for the handicapped. The device, called a swivel walker, involves a frame containing leg and body supports which enables children who have been confined to a wheelchair to be held in an upright position. They can then walk away unaided. The walker has had successful trials for some time at Oaklands School in Kersal, and puts Salford at the forefront of this type of development. (29.7.77)

August 1977

Salford schoolboy David Burchill has broken the world 5,000 metre record for a twelve-year-old. In a special race for under-20s at Stretford, he achieved a time of 17 minutes, 39 seconds, five seconds faster than the record for a boy of his age. (5.8.77)

The Liverpool Street Industrial Estate is nearing completion and many firms are already operating in this modern working environment. (5.8.77)

The Rector of St Paul's Church, Pendleton, has discovered a large

Gardner Street gym, photographed in 1978

plaque, five feet high by two feet wide, in the cellar of the church. After cleaning it became recognisable as a memorial to John Charles Blake, Esq, RN, London. Who he actually was remains a mystery. (12.8.77)

September 1977

Next week Salford Royal Hospital celebrates its 150th anniversary. On 2 May 1827 a public meeting was called at the Town Hall to consider the problem of lack of medical facilities in the area. A committee was formed, subscriptions guaranteed and a building obtained at 23 Broken Bank. By 10 September the Salford and Pendleton Dispensary was opened. In addition to a matron, honorary physicians, surgeons and apothecaries, there were three lady leechers and bleeders.

Soon it was obvious that larger premises were required and work began in 1830; the official opening was on 25 March 1831. King William IV consented to support the charity, donating 25 guineas annually, and it became known as Salford and Pendleton Royal Dispensary. (2.9.77)

Nigel Pivaro, aged 17, of Bridlington Avenue, Weaste, has just been accepted by the Manchester Youth Theatre Company and is currently playing Barnardo in "Hamlet" at the Royal Exchange Theatre. (9.9.77)

When the City Council bought the former Coal Board Regional Headquarters in Worsley, it was intended to save the beautiful "White House" premises and convert them into two flats. However, the Housing Committee has just learned that the building has been seriously vandalised and has agreed that it should be demolished. (9.9.77)

A battle scene from the American Civil War was re-enacted on Sunday 4 September in Buile Hill Park. Cannon, muskets and authentic costumes all helped to make the spectacle look true to life. (9.9.77)

The Rovers Return, Salford's newest pub, opens its doors on Tuesday 27 September. The pub is in Guy Fawkes Street, Ordsall. (23.9.77)

October 1977

Mr Julius Holmar of Pendleton has patented an invention which will produce electricity from sea waves. Since he first put forward his ideas two years ago, the Government has shown a keen interest in his work and now he has been invited to join a conference of British "wave power" experts. (7.10.77)

Two Salford brothers who started their engineering business with £100 six years ago have won an award worth £10,000. The Technical Development Capital Innovator Award goes to Mike and Peter Connett of Beaconet, for machinery for injecting foam into building blocks and cavity walls. (21.10.77)

Salford may become the first noise-controlled city in Britain if a pilot scheme in the Docks area is a success. It is still in the early stages and has Government approval. (28.10.77)

November 1977

St John's Primary School, the Height, was officially opened today by Mrs Marie Patterson, OBE. The Mayor, Councillor Stan Martin, presided. (11.11.77)

This year, for the first time, Salford Corporation had its own bonfires on 5 November, in a concerted effort to

eliminate the number of firework casualties and damage caused by fires in back alleys and on crofts and verges. The bonfires, organised by the Council's Recreational Services Department aided by the Salford and Worsley Round Tables, went off without a single firework or burns injury. (11.11.77)

Students from Salford College of Technology beat students from four other colleges from the North West when they took the first four prizes in the Bolton Black Pudding Competition. (18.11.77)

Mrs Mary Callison, of Callison's furniture store on Eccles New Road, celebrated her 103rd birthday on Friday 11 November. The business is only 98 years old. (18.11.77)

At St George's Church, Charlestown, on Saturday 19 November a ceremony was held to re-dedicate the stained glass window from St Barnabas's Church, Pendleton, which was closed for public worship in 1973 and demolished a few months ago. The window was first installed in St Barnabas's in 1902 and shattered in 1940, when a bomb exploded in Frederick Road and blew in all the windows of the church. The broken pieces of glass were carefully collected and twelve years later the window was restored. (25.11.77)

His Royal Highness the Duke of Kent officially opened the Ecclesholme old people's home in Bindloss Avenue, Eccles, yesterday. (25.11.77)

A unique group who specialise in translating official jargon into plain English have just won a notable victory in their fight against gobbledegook. The group, based at the Salford Form Market in Great Cheetham Street East, have been called in by the Supplementary Benefits Commission to redesign and reword one of the SBC's most important leaflets. (25.11.77)

Many of the terraced houses on White Street and end properties on Ashley Street, Rostherne Street, Cardigan Street and Pembroke Street, Seedley, are being demolished to make way for the M602 Salford/Eccles motorway. (25.11.77)

December 1977

A three-reel film of the city's 1930 Charter celebrations has been found at Salford Central Library. As the film is on 35mm nitrate stock, which is potentially inflammable, it will have to be copied on to 16mm film. (2.12.77)

Salford Rugby Club's flying winger, Keith Fielding, has won one of the European heats of the television "Superstars" competition and goes on to contest the European Final. (2.12.77)

Persona Textiles Ltd of Cobden Street,

White Street in the 1970s, with children on the railway observation platform

Pendleton, have announced the closure of their firm, with the loss of sixty jobs. (2.12.77)

Salford has been invited to exhibit at next year's Motor Show the first completed model of its Disabled Driver's Car, which is being developed jointly by the city and Manchester Polytechnic. (9.12.77)

The editor of the Salford City Reporter, Mr Tom Bergin, has announced his retirement at the end of the year. He joined the paper as a junior reporter in 1929. (9.12.77)

A new pub on Bank Lane opened on Wednesday 7 December. There was a local competition to choose a name for it, but in the end it was decided to call it Britannia, after one of the old pubs recently demolished for the Height roundabout scheme. However, it has already acquired a nickname, "the upside down pub", because the bars are upstairs and the living accommodation is down below. (9.12.77)

The organ recently installed in St Paul's Church, Pendleton, at a cost of £3,500 has quite a history. It was built for St Thomas's Church, Ardwick, in 1787 by Samuel Green of Isleworth, Middlesex, who was organ builder to King George III. According to records, it was the first to be made with horizontal bellows and the first to have a keyboard with white naturals and black sharps. The previous instrument was a small manual one and the Rector has been hoping to find a new organ for some years. This is another success for the hard-working Rev David Wyatt and his congregation. (9.12.77)

1978

January 1978

Holy Angels Church, Claremont, is celebrating its 50th anniversary. (6.1.78)

Former St Lawrence's School pupil, Mary Burchill of the Height, has been chosen to play in England's netball team. (13.1.78)

Salford actor Robert Powell is to play the lead in a new film production of the classic thriller "The Thirty-nine Steps". (20.1.78)

February 1978

Throwers at the Church Inn, Pendleton, have set a new darts marathon world record and raised £1,000 for charity. During the twelve-hour slog they scored 2,673 treble twenties, beating the old record by 450. The money will go to the Pat Seed appeal for a scanner for Christie's Hospital. (3.2.78)

Salford railway station is undergoing a £140,000 facelift, which will be finished in May. The upgrading is being carried out in anticipation of a large increase in passenger traffic by 1984. (17.2.78)

In the news at the moment is Salford-born racing tipster Mr Ken Hussey, who writes under the pen-name of "Split Second" in the Sporting Chronicle and in the paper's Handicap Book. He became nationally famous this week when a Bury St Edmunds man won more than £90,000 using Ken's selections. (24.2.78)

Keeping up with the skateboarding craze that is sweeping the country, Salford has its own indoor skateboard rink. The owners of Potters snooker club on Great Cheetham Street, Broughton, have converted the former nightclub next door. (24.2.78)

The Peeping Tom on Regent Road closed recently and will be demolished. The pub will be remembered for its fine tiled front. (24.2.78)

The Flying Angel Mission premises in Trafford Road are up for sale. (24.2.78)

March 1978

During a visit to Salford University on Friday, Prince Philip, Duke of Edinburgh, made a ten-minute recording to launch the Students' Union Radio, which goes on air shortly. (3.3.78)

The Green Shield Stamp distribution centre and shop on Salford Shopping Precinct has closed. (17.3.78)

The Peter Green Youth Centre has been bought by the Council for £6,000. The centre had been losing money since it opened and was affected by vandalism. (17.3.78)

In last week's British Academy of Film and Television Arts presentations, the television show "Rising Damp" was voted "best situation comedy" and it was a Salford lad who went up to receive the award from Princess Anne. Ronald Baxter, the producer and director of the show, was a pupil of Grecian Street and Broughton Modern Schools. His delighted parents, now living in Eastham Way, Little Hulton, watched the BAFTA ceremony on television. (24.3.78)

Hope High School's fifth year rugby team completed a unique record on Thursday 16 March. They have been undefeated in both thirteen- and seven-a-side games since 1973, a total of more than 150 matches. (24.3.78)

Mount Carmel Church, Oldfield Road, is to close. The last Mass will be on 9 April, after which the church will merge with St Joseph's nearby. The foundation stone of the present Mount Carmel Church was laid on 9 August 1879 and the building opened on 29 September 1880. (31.3.78)

April 1978

This week Salford became the first city

Robert Powell in "The Thirty-Nine Steps"

in Britain to get Government help in the battle against vandalism. It is to receive £42,000 from the Manpower Services Commission towards the £50,000 cost of launching anti-vandal patrols. (7.4.78)

A Compulsory Purchase Order served on the property in the Hulme Street area, which the Council wants to develop, affects the coal yard business of Mr Charles Slater. The firm has been in operation on this site since the time of the First World War. (7.4.78)

Harold Williams, who attended St Ambrose School, Seedley, has just won a world professional skating championship. His twenty-year ambition was not achieved without a great deal of hard work. He has previously won a gold medal in the Commonwealth Games and was reserve for the Winter Olympic games twice. (14.4.78)

Martyn Hesford (18), who attended Buile Hill High School and lives in Moss Bank Road, Swinton, has won a part in the film "Absolution", starring Richard Burton. The story is about the relationship between a priest at a public school and twelve of his pupils, one of whom is played by Martyn. (21.4.78)

May 1978

Salford held its very first May Day Gala in Buile Hill Park on Monday. A beer tent, Morris dancing, side shows and stalls attracted around 20,000 people. (5.5.78)

After forty-three years behind the bar at the Wellington, Regent Road, Mrs Jessie Valentine retired on Tuesday 9 May. The new landlord will be Len McMullen. (12.5.78)

Eccles councillor David Dow was installed as Salford's new Mayor on Wednesday 17 May. (19.5.78)

A company is to be formed to market the Disabled People's Vehicles designed by the City of Salford and Manchester Polytechnic. The company is to be known as Salford DPV Charity Limited. (19.5.78)

The £50,000 transformation of the Holland Street Laundry into Charlestown Neighbourhood Centre is almost complete. It is the first of three such projects to provide sporting and social facilities in Salford. The two others, to be finished later this year, are the Clarendon Centre and Broughton Hall.

Among the attractions at the three centres will be indoor skateboard rinks. Another is being provided at Princes Park, Irlam and eight more sites are under consideration. (26.5.78)

Alex Murphy, appointed as Salford Rugby Club's new coach on Monday 22 May, has raised hopes that next season could see the team at Wembley again. Echoing his sentiments, the headline in the Reporter was, "Exit the Quality St. Gang. Enter the professionals." (26.5.78)

June 1978

Former Pendleton College pupil Nigel Pivaro (18), who has been getting recognition for his acting, has been accepted by the Royal Academy of Dramatic Art. (2.6.78)

The Royal Archer pub on Lower Broughton Road has just reopened after being closed for eight weeks for extensive renovations. (2.6.78)

Two Salford-born people have

received the MBE in the Queen's Birthday Honours list. They are Pat Seed, whose courage in the face of cancer has been an inspiration to thousands and Rowland ("Ron") Waite, who has served as the Mayor's secretary for the past twelve years. (9.6.78)

The Agecroft Regatta, cancelled last year because of lack of entries, will be held on Saturday 10 June. (9.6.78)

Amateur rugby player Bernard Southern, who plays for Folly Borough, returned home this week. He has been with the British Amateur Rugby League Association touring squad, playing in Papua New Guinea, Australia and New Zealand. (9.6.78)

Salford's new instant lottery was launched on Thursday 8 June by comedian Bernard Manning, who bought the first of the 40,000 tickets. Prizes range from 50p to the £1,000 jackpot. (16.6.78)

Spending plans of £100,000 for the first section of the Irwell Valley improvement in Salford have been approved by Greater Manchester Council. The work will include fencing, creation of footpaths, clearance of debris, tree planting and grass seeding. (16.6.78)

Work has begun on a pair of semi-detached, low-energy houses in Strawberry Hill, Wallness. They are part of a joint project between Salford City Council and the University of Salford. (16.6.78)

An ambitious new project based at the hostel next to the Margaret Whitehead School in Fitzwarren Street, Seedley, was launched last week, when the Mayor, Councillor David Dow, opened the new toy library. The scheme, which works just like a book library, means that toys and play materials, specially adapted for the disabled, will be available on loan to the handicapped, each toy taken home for a maximum of three weeks at a cost of 10p per toy. (23.6.78)

The five Salford Jets, four of whom live in Salford, are making their name in the pop music world. They have just secured a recording contract and have released a record, "Walking Round the Town Town Looking at the Squares". (23.6.78)

A former Salford policeman has just been made a deacon. Stanley Horrocks left the police force in 1972 after thirty years' service. In 1973 he began a three-year course at Manchester University leading to a BA in theology, and has just finished a year at theological college at Mirfield, Yorkshire. He is a lifelong member of St James Church of England, Higher Broughton. (30.6.78)

July 1978

Salford's first Woman Police Officer

Len McMullen behind the bar of the Wellington, Regent Road

retired this week after thirty-seven years with the force. Miss Lilian Hall joined the Salford City Police as an auxiliary in 1941, in the scheme designed to replace the men at the Front. (7.7.78)

Permission has been given to Greater Manchester Archaeological Unit to carry out excavations on two sites in the Ordsall area. The first is in Rixton Street, where it is believed a seventeenth century cottage and barn stood near to Ordsall Hall. The second site is the area thought to contain the remains of "Woden's Cave" or "Den". Drawings made in 1780 and 1875 provide evidence for the existence of these sites. (7.7.78)

Salford Rugby League player David Watkins received an honorary degree from Salford University today. (14.7.78)

August 1978

The Brass Tally public house on Liverpool Street opened last week. The name for the pub was chosen as the result of a competition, which was won by Mr Charles Wright of Old Trafford. It derives from a system of work allocation on Salford Docks, in which brass tallies were handed out to waiting dockers, entitling them to a day's work. (18.8.78)

The construction of the new Clarendon Sports Complex came to a halt this week, when it was announced that the contractors, Bracegirdle, had crashed and around two hundred workers had been laid off.

Four hundred jobs will be affected by the news that Ward & Goldstone, Salford's largest employer, is to move its accessories division from Frederick Road to Worsley. The union is opposing the move. (18.8.78)

BBC cameras were in Weaste on Thursday 10 August to film a scene in Robertson Street for the new television series based on the Howard Spring novel, "My Son, My Son!". The lead actor, Michael Williams, was born in Salford and many of his relatives still live in the city. His uncle, Harry Williams, was the last Mayor of Salford before local government reorganisation in 1974. (18.8.78)

September 1978

Regulars of the Welcome Inn on Ordsall Lane drank their last pints in Salford's only John Willie Lees pub before it closed on Wednesday 30 August, despite a hard-fought campaign to keep it open.

There was better news a couple of miles away, as regulars of the Old Veteran, off Eccles New Road, celebrated the fact that their pub had been saved from a Compulsory Purchase Order. (1.9.78)

Harold and Alice Birchall, who have been local newsagents for almost fifty years, and have been in their "new" shop on Silk Street for the last sixteen years, are retiring. They can remember when horses and carts used to line up outside the Raven public house, where Victoria Bus Station was later built, and all set off at the same time to deliver newspapers to the various parts of Salford. It was a beautiful sight, they said. (1.9.78)

Seedley Swimming Baths did not reopen after the Bank Holiday weekend. It is claimed that work to make the baths safe would cost £500,000. There was much anger about the decision, as Salford has now closed three public baths in the last ten years and the one designed to replace them, Clarendon, is not yet open. (8.9.78)

The demolition of Brunswick Methodist Church, Broad Street, has begun. (8.9.78)

The Salford Docks branch of the National Westminster Bank at no.1 Trafford Road closes today. (15.9.78)

Making a name for himself in the pop scene is Salford-born punk poet, John Cooper Clarke. (15.9.78)

The leader of the Conservative Party, Mrs Margaret Thatcher, lunched at the Kersal Cell Restaurant when she passed through Salford last week. (22.9.78)

October 1978

Two districts of the city bordering on Chapel Street were this week declared Conservation Areas. This will protect worthwhile buildings and put development under Council control. The buildings involved include Salford Cathedral, Salford Royal Hospital, St Philip's Church, the County Court, the former Adelphi House Grammar School, the Education Offices, the old Town Hall and Sacred Trinity Church. (27.10.78)

Albert Finney was back home this week and took time off to open the new Barton Moss County Primary School on Trippier Road, Peel Green. (27.10.78)

November 1978

The Duchess of Gloucester officially opened Gloucester House, the new home for children with severe emotional difficulties, on Tuesday 31 October. (3.11.78)

Salford's Civic Lottery has become a popular weekly event. More than £30,000 has been raised so far, and a decision is expected soon on how the first of it will be spent. (17.11.78)

In Salford's Rugby match against Barrow on the night of Friday 17 November, a young trialist stole the show, winning the Man of the Match award. He was Andrew Gregory, son of Arthur Gregory, who used to play for Salford at full-back; his uncle Harold also played, at scrum half. Andy is considering the terms offered by Salford. (24.11.78)

1979

January 1979

On Monday 22 January Pat Seed laid the foundation stone of the building at Christie's Hospital which will house the "magic eye" body scanner for which she is campaigning to raise funds. (26.1.79)

February 1979

The Salford Arts and Media Education Trust was launched this week. Awards will be made each year to needy Salfordians entering the professions of "communication, arts and the media" and ranging from ice dancers to journalists. The fund will honour the

The Salford Jets

work of Mr Eric Simm, former headmaster of Salford Grammar School, who helped so many young boys and girls to pursue their chosen careers. Among those he encouraged were Albert Finney, President of the Trust and artist Harold Riley, its Chairman. (2.2.79)

Awarded an OBE in the New Year's Honours list was Mr Joe Batty, born in Tarbuck Street, off Regent Street. Joe left Salford with nothing more than his tool-bag and £25. He is now head of four multinational companies. He lives in Toronto, but as Vice-president of Adelphi Lads' Club maintains strong links with Salford. (2.2.79)

Local bookmaker Jim Ramsbottom has been granted a licence for a new public house which he wants to build on the bank of the River Irwell at the old New Bailey landing stage, below the Albert Bridge, New Bailey Street. The pub is to be called "The Mark Addy" after the famous Salfordian. (2.2.79)

Pensioners living in sheltered housing in Salford are to have a round-the-clock link between the Town Hall and their homes, the first of its type in Greater Manchester. (2.2.79)

Building work is going ahead on the extension to Salford Royal Hospital, replacing the wing destroyed during the war. (9.2.79)

Manchester Liners are celebrating eighty years of business with the introduction of two new vessels to their fleet. The "Manchester Reward" and the "Manchester Renown" are to replace the "Manchester Courage" and the "Manchester Challenge". (9.2.79)

On Saturday a two-and-a-half-year-old Dalmatian named Lyndora Golden Wedding (Bryn to his friends) won first prize in his class at Crufts on his first visit to the show. He is owned by Mr Brian Williams of Beech Avenue, the Height. (16.2.79)

The Clarendon Recreation Centre was officially opened on Thursday 15 February by Mr Reg Freeson, MP, the Minister for Housing. It will not be opened to the public for some weeks. (23.2.79)

A tubular steel rocking horse, which has been in use at Seedley Infants' School since the 1930s, has been given to Monks Hall Museum for the toy collection. At first the toy was thought to be a one-off of unknown origin, but it has since been discovered that it was made by a Monton firm, R W Whittle, who are specialists in tubular steel toys and equipment. (23.2.79)

March 1979

The disused Astor Bingo Hall in St James's Road, Higher Broughton was virtually destroyed by fire on the night of Tuesday 27 February. Built at the end of the last century, it was the home of the North Salford Independent Labour Party, proudly bearing the name "Pankhurst Hall". For some years lectures and social events were held there, but by the time of the First World War it had become the Hightown Picture Pavilion. In the 1920s it became the New Marlborough, later the Astor Cinema and finally the Astor Bingo Hall. More recently an application was made to feature Indian films there to accommodate the needs of the growing immigrant population, but the building was found to be unsafe. Emmeline Pankhurst is said to have contributed towards the construction and now local historians are searching the debris in the hope of finding the foundation stone bearing her name. (2.3.79)

Two new low-energy houses in Strawberry Hill are complete. For the first year they will be lived in by the families of two university students while tests are conducted. (2.3.79)

Mr Harry Ratcliffe of Riverside, Lower Broughton, has come up with an idea which he thinks could solve all the country's problems. First mooted four years ago, his plan to replace Sunday with "Orday" (ordinary day) and introduce a countrywide system of shift work has attracted a lot of interest. Now he has released details of the scheme, which would mean introducing a 366-day, 61-week year with six days in each week. Everyone would work on a shift system of four days on and two off. The nine extra pay days in the year would bring an overall pay rise of 18 per cent as well as many benefits to employers and the Government. Many people, including the Prime Minister and top businessmen, are said to have shown interest. (2.3.79)

A device to replace the complex electronic wiring in cars has been developed at Salford University. The new system, "Salplex", consists of a single cable and five boxes containing silicon chips which are fitted to the four corners of the car and the dashboard. More boxes can be added if required. It was developed by Professor Michael Hampshire after an approach by Ward & Goldstone. (2.3.79)

A cigarette and sweets wholesaler's in Weaste is to close down after nearly sixty years trading in Salford. S O Lloyd of Cemetery Road was founded by Mr Oliver Lloyd in Regent Road and has been in the present premises for more than twenty-two years. The building is under a Compulsory Purchase Order. (2.3.79)

This year marks the centenary of the Salford City Reporter, to be celebrated officially in April. (9.3.79)

St John's Methodist Church, Seedley, has just been demolished, two years after it closed. (16.3.79)

The dancing school in Pendleton where Ena Adams has lived and taught for over forty years was burnt down on Sunday. The building was under a Compulsory Purchase Order and due to be demolished. (23.3.79)

Clarendon Recreation Centre becomes available to the public from Monday 26 March. (23.3.79)

Salford's first ever car registration number, "BA 1", has returned to the local scene. When it became law in 1904 that motor vehicles should be licensed and show their registration numbers, the prefix BA was allotted to Salford. "BA 1" went to a De Dion Bouton which had been purchased by a colonel living in Broughton for his wife. While on an excursion with the chauffeur the vehicle collided with a bale of hay, and it is said that the lady vowed never to ride in a car again, preferring her pony and trap.

The Welcome, Ordsall Lane

The vehicle was sold to a Dr Taylor of Eccles Old Road, whose home eventually became the Toc H house Mark XIV. Then the number was acquired by Salford Corporation for the Mayor's car, but replaced in the early 1930s with "RJ 1" when the new prefix came into use.

After being transferred to various vehicles, the original number was acquired by Tom Bergin, Editor of the City Reporter, who passed it from car to car. The last, an Austin 1100, was laid up because of MOT requirements, but it has now been restored by its new owner, Jens Bollerod of Pendlebury, a former City Reporter advertising representative. After passing its MOT, "BA 1" is once again travelling the roads its predecessor knew seventy-five years ago. (30.3.79)

Salford has adopted a ship, "HMS Minerva" but she won't be able to reach the city because the radio aerial is too high to pass under Warburton Bridge. The ship is docked at Liverpool and was visited by the Mayor and Mayoress on Friday 23 March. (30.3.79)

April 1979

Following the fire at the Beechwood Studios, Eccles Old Road, Mrs Ena Adams is holding dance classes at Hope Church Hall. Lessons have also been held at St Thomas's Church, Pendleton and at the Scouts' Recreation Centre in Odessa Avenue. (6.4.79)

St James's Church, Higher Broughton, is celebrating its centenary. It opened on 31 March 1879. (13.4.79)

Elton John was at Salford's Rugby ground, the Willows, on Sunday. He came to kick off a charity football match between Bobby Charlton's Lancashire lads and Jackie Charlton's Yorkshire team, in aid of the Elizabeth Fitzroy Home for mentally handicapped children. (13.4.79)

The thousand pitmen at Agecroft Colliery have hit a new productivity peak. Output per manshift in the financial year just ended reached 2.4 tonnes. During the year they produced 564,401 tonnes of coal, principally from the Doe seam. (27.4.79)

May 1979

Salford's new eight-and-a-half-million pound Blackfriars Telephone Exchange was officially opened on Wednesday 2 May by the Mayor, Councillor David Dow. (4.5.79)

Broughton Sports and Community Centre next to Broughton High School was officially opened on Friday 27 April by Mr Frank Allaun, Labour Party Chairman. The centre, which cost £420,000, was built with the aid of a 75 per cent inner city grant. (4.5.79)

The Weaste furniture firm, J Callison & Co, celebrates its centenary this year. Their first shop in Salford was opened in Ordsall Lane by Thomas Callison, the father of John, the present owner. They then moved to numbers 170 and 188 Eccles New Road before taking over their current shop at number 192. John's mother, Mrs Mary Ann Callison, is Salford's oldest citizen and celebrated her 104th birthday last November. (18.5.79)

On Friday Mr Stan Orme, MP for Salford West, officially opened the new Humphrey Booth Day Care Centre and the Harry Hall Gardens Sheltered Housing Estate in Lower Broughton. (18.5.79)

The Pat Seed fund to provide a special scanner for the Christie Hospital in Manchester has reached £1,712,000. Pat handed over a cheque for £750,000 on Saturday 19 May. (25.5.79)

June 1979

Following a public enquiry, the Priory Arms pub in Gardner Street, Brunswick, has been saved from demolition. Brewers Boddingtons now hope to extend the pub by adapting a small cottage next door. (8.6.79)

Salford has just taken delivery of the new Mayoral car, a £16,000 black Daimler limousine. Councillor J Burrows, the new Mayor for 1979-80, will be using it. (8.6.79)

Building work on a Booth's Charities old people's housing estate in Ordsall has been delayed because of an archaeological dig near Ordsall Hall. The dig has revealed a 400-year-old farmyard. (15.6.79)

The Griffin Hotel on Chapel Street, one of Salford's oldest public houses, closed on Tuesday 19 June and is unlikely to open as a pub again. (22.6.79)

July 1979

The new British Legion Club in Ordsall Precinct opens next Saturday. It replaces the old club on Trafford Road, which was in premises once used as the Empire Cinema. (6.7.79)

Done Brothers opened their newest and biggest bookmaker's shop in Chapel Street on Monday. The building is in the former North Western Electricity Board showrooms, and was used more recently as a pram and cycle exchange. (6.7.79)

Mr Tom Bergin, former Editor of the Salford Reporter, has been awarded an honorary Master of Arts degree by Salford University. (20.7.79)

Mike Wooley, a member of the Salford Triple S Club, has been chosen to swim for his country in a match between Britain, Germany and Holland to be held on 10 August. Mike is aged thirteen and lives in Irlam. (20.7.79)

In a BBC television programme to be shown on Monday evening famous Salfordians will invite viewers to share the sights and sounds that make Salford special for them. Among the contributors to "Good Evening, Salford" will be Freddy ("Parrot Face") Davies, Arlene Philips and Tony Warren. (27.7.79)

Martin Cutts and Chrissie Maher, who ran the Form Market in Broughton until it closed in December, have been trying to get official forms and leaflets simplified for years. Now they have organised a "plain English campaign", to start with a public shredding of forms and letters full of gobbledegook outside the Houses of Parliament. (27.7.79)

The new wing at Salford Royal Hospital, photographed in 1985

August 1979

Radio Rentals have announced that their central refurbishment works at Pendleton will close at the end of the year. More than a hundred jobs will be lost. (10.8.79)

The closure of the Manchester Dry Docks Company, owned jointly by Manchester Liners, Morrell Mills and Container Workshops Ltd, was announced this week. Four hundred and fifty-two workers were made redundant. (10.8.79)

Salford's last beerhouse, the Red Cow in Albion Street, is to close to make way for roadworks. The city is losing some of its fully licensed public houses as well. On Cross Lane, the Railway closed on Monday, the Church Inn will shut at the end of the month and the Falcon, the Wellington and the Station will go soon after that. The Grove, Eccles New Road and the Windsor Bridge Tavern, Broad Street, are also scheduled for demolition. (10.8.79)

"Bogies", Salford's latest disco, restaurant and nightclub, opens tonight in the old Seamen's Mission in Trafford Road, facing the Docks. There are twenty students' flats above the club. (17.8.79)

The new business premises of UBM Armstrong Glass have opened in Cromwell Road. (17.8.79)

After a brief retirement from Rugby League, David Watkins has returned to play for Swinton. (31.8.79)

September 1979

Prime Minister Margaret Thatcher came to Salford last week, visiting, among other places, the two low-energy houses at Strawberry Hill. Her reception by the general public was not always welcoming. (7.9.79)

Major alterations costing £50,000 have just been completed at the Bridge Inn, Lower Broughton Road. It is decorated in Victorian style with old photographs showing the area at the time the original pub was built in the nineteenth century. (14.9.79)

Longworth's outfitter's, now based in Swinton, is to close down after seventy-five years when the owner, Mr Frank Longworth, retires. The first shop in Pendlebury was opened by his father in 1904. A few years later the family opened another in Station Road, Swinton, where they stayed until 1966, when the business moved to its present address on The Parade, Swinton. (14.9.79)

The Gloucester Arms pub in Regent Road has been taken over by Mr David Pollard, owner of Pollard's Brewery in Stockport. It opened with a sing-song last weekend, selling Pollard's beer at 25p a pint, and is the first house in the city to be acquired by the brewery. Former Salford Rugby League star Billy Watkins once managed the Gloucester. (21.9.79)

October 1979

A farewell street party with plenty to eat and drink was held on Sunday in Elizabeth Street, Ordsall, which is soon to be knocked down as part of the general clearances in the area. (5.10.79)

A fire swept through the lounge and vault of the Duchy Inn, Brindleheath Road, on Saturday afternoon. The pub will be closed for a couple of weeks while it is renovated. (5.10.79)

A part of Salford's history, Hodge Lane Wash House, is to be pulled down for the extension to the M602. Local residents are not very happy and protests are to be made. (5.10.79)

Mr Sidney Hamburger, Chairman of the North West Regional Health Authority, cut the first sod to start the £18.3 million redevelopment at Hope Hospital this week. (12.10.79)

The Salford Mining Museum in Buile Hill Park has reopened to the public. (12.10.79)

Salford-born Mr Peter Craig is leading a team of surgeons at Withington Hospital who are pioneering ways of joining minute blood vessels, tendons, nerves and muscles with the aid of a special microscope. "Microsurgery" of this kind is expected to be especially useful in operations such as those to replace severed limbs. Mr Craig lived in Lullington Road, Pendleton, when he was a boy and attended St Sebastian School and De La Salle College. (19.10.79)

It is Salford Rugby Club's centenary this month, and on Sunday the team drew 16-16 against Widnes in a celebration match. The original Salford team was amalgamated from the old Cavendish Football Club and Crescent Rugby Union Club, and played its first match on 4 October 1879, visiting Dewsbury. The following Saturday the players made their début on their home ground at New Barns (now part of the Salford Docks), when they entertained Widnes. (19.10.79)

Mrs Mary Ann Callison, Salford's oldest citizen, died on Tuesday 23 October, three weeks before her 105th birthday. (26.10.79)

The Red Dragon, the Crescent, holds its grand reopening today. (26.10.79)

November 1979

Cargas Ltd, Lissadel Street, Pendleton, is one of the few companies in the North West to offer motorists the chance to convert their vehicle from petrol to natural gas. It is possible to change from one fuel to the other at the flick of a switch, even as you travel. A spare tank held in the boot of the car can hold enough gas for an extra 500

Callison's shop at 170 Eccles New Road before the First World War

miles travelling. Conversion costs £275 for an average family car. (2.11.79)

Salford gymnast Jackie Bevan has been selected to represent Britain in the Moscow Olympics next year. She lives in Broughton and is a former pupil of North Salford High School. (2.11.79)

Sir Matt Busby opened a new Dr Barnardo's Home yesterday, in Matt Busby Close, Pendlebury. The home will accommodate mentally handicapped children. (7.11.79)

Manchester Liners are to introduce their container ship "Lindo" on services from Salford Docks. It will replace the smaller vessel "Frontier". (30.11.79)

Prince Charles came to Salford yesterday, arriving at Swinton Station and going on to open the new Greater Manchester Fire Brigade Headquarters in Bolton Road, Pendlebury. The station has the first computerised mobilisation system in Great Britain, claimed to be the most effective currently in operation anywhere in the world. (30.11.79)

December 1979

"Plain English" campaigners Chrissie Maher and Martin Cutts recruited a gobbledygook monster (one of the workers dressed in a gruesome gorilla costume) to deliver a letter to Mrs Thatcher, asking her to direct civil servants to communicate with people in Plain English. Chrissie and Martin, who work from a house in Wiltshire Street, Higher Broughton, have met with considerable success since they

started their campaign in July this year. (7.12.79)

1980

January 1980

A blaze gutted the factory of Nab Quilters in Flax Street on Wednesday evening. Firemen stopped the flames spreading to three other firms in Adelphi Mill. (18.1.80)

Adelphi Lads' Club was officially reopened on Saturday night by the Chief Constable of Manchester, Mr James Anderton. The club has undergone a reconstruction programme financed by an inner city grant. (18.1.80)

This year is the 750th anniversary of Salford's being given its charter, and as part of the celebrations a new maypole is to be erected in Pendleton. A maypole stood at Pendleton Green from at least 1373 and one was mentioned by John Wesley in his diaries. In 1831 it was moved near to the Maypole pub and from 1887 until 1920, when it was blown down, it stood in Station Street, close to the old Pendleton Railway Station. (25.1.80)

February 1980

The archaeological dig at Ordsall Hall has been filled in to protect the site from the elements. The soft sandstone had begun to deteriorate because of frost, but it can easily be revealed at a later date. (1.2.80)

The old County Bingo Hall on Great

Cheetham Street East is to be pulled down. An application to turn it into a nightclub was rejected this week. (1.2.80)

Salford's prize-winning Dalmatian Lyndora Golden Wedding knocked spots off the opposition at Crufts last week. The three-year-old repeated last year's success by winning "Best in Class" and added to it the title "Best of Breed", which puts him among the ten top dogs at the show. (15.2.80)

Anderton's chip shop on St James's Road, Higher Broughton, has been saved from demolition. When local residents heard that a Compulsory Purchase Order had been served on the shop, they launched a "Save Our Chippy" petition, forcing planning officials to reconsider. Now it has been decided that as the shop is on a corner and does not interfere with development plans, it can stay. (15.2.80)

An L S Lowry painting was stolen from the walls of Salford Art Gallery this week in a daring daylight raid. The painting - "Two People" - shows a man and a woman and measures 29.5 by 24.5 centimetres. (15.2.80)

Eight hundred people packed Broughton Recreation Centre last week to watch the world-famous Chinese table tennis players compete in an eight-match demonstration against a select Salford team. (22.2.80)

The Merry Go Round Club on Broughton Road was closed down last week, after an appeal to renew its licence was rejected by the court. (29.2.80)

March 1980

Plans to turn the vacant British Home Stores shop (later the Queens Supermarket) in Regent Road into a nightclub have failed, owing to residents' disapproval. The Regency club, which closed suddenly in October, had hoped to reopen in the premises as the New Regency Club. (21.3.80)

April 1980

A grant from the Greater Manchester Council's Lottery Fund will help to pay for the Salford Sea Cadets' new headquarters. The building in Oldfield Road, Ordsall, was completed in May last year. (4.4.80)

Poor audiences and expensive artistes at the Willows Variety Centre have forced the management into economy measures. From the beginning of July the Variety Centre will open three nights a week instead of five, and the restaurant will only be open on Saturdays. (18.4.80)

The last wedding at Salford Register Office in Pendleton House before it closed on Saturday 12 April was that of

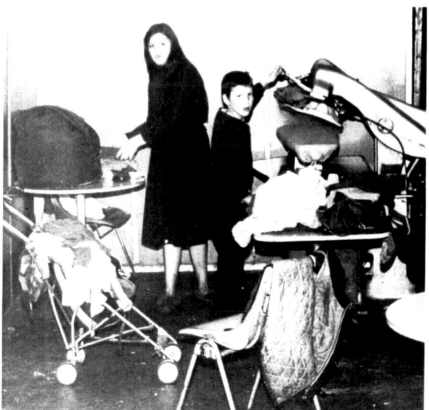

In Hodge Lane Wash House, November 1979

nineteen-year-old Debbie Leonard and Mike McLean, both of Kersal.

Before 1934 Salford had three registry offices, one in Pendleton Town Hall, one in Broughton Town Hall and one just off Bexley Square, near the old Salford Town Hall. All except the Pendleton one closed and that was moved to Pendleton House, which was built as a waiting room for the Civic Welfare Department in 1948.

The new office in Barton Road, Swinton, will serve the whole of the Salford Metropolitan area. The first wedding there was of Vincent Morris and Catherine McCall, both from Salford. The ceremony was attended by the Mayor and Mayoress, who presented them with goblets, a civic scroll and a bouquet to mark the occasion. (18.4.80)

May 1980

There will be no eleventh-hour reprieve for a two-hundred-year old cottage in Wallness, Pendleton. Whitehall officials have ruled that Salford Council can buy and demolish the cottage, 25 Wallness Lane, and two other properties, numbers 21 and 23. It is planned to build a car park on the land, or leave it as an open space.
(16.5.80)

Scenes of long ago were recreated for the May Day Gala in Pendleton, when the maypole was erected on its old site in Broughton Road and entertainment was provided for local people.
(16.5.80)

The new Miss Great Britain is Mrs Sue Berger, who can be seen most days working in her husband's DIY stores on Eccles New Road. She is the first married woman to win the contest, and the oldest at twenty-eight.
(16.5.80)

Seventy-four-year old Mr William Starkie has won his fight to save Knolls House in Higher Broughton, a listed building said to have been erected in 1822 by local antiquarian William Yates, out of materials from old shops on Market Street, Manchester. Some of the carving inside the house is said to have come from Manchester Parish Church (later the Cathedral) and the house has a Georgian staircase. (16.5.80)

Salford's Festival Queen was crowned recently at the Pembroke Halls, Walkden. The judges chose seventeen-year-old Ellen Hanlon of Ashbourne Road, Eccles, to represent the city. The runners-up were Bridget Curran, 19, from Irlam and Joan Drummond, 23, of Cross Lane, Salford. (16.5.80)

Maypole celebrations at Pendleton in May 1980

Councillor Tom Francis was officially installed as Salford's new Mayor in a ceremony on Wednesday 21 May. He is the first Tory to hold the position since Salford Council reorganised in 1974.
(23.5.80)

The Bradshaw Street Nursery Centre and later the Grosvenor Nursery Centre were officially opened by Princess Michael of Kent last Thursday.
(30.5.80)

June 1980

Salford's punk poet, John Cooper Clarke, is back home, filming for a Granada television programme, "Celebration". (6.6.80)

The Dooleys pop group was back in town recently, helping to raise money for a local children's home. (6.6.80)

Swinton Rugby Club is hoping for better things next season and has signed Danny Wilson, the Welsh Rugby Union back. (13.6.80)

Trafford Road School in Robert Hall Street, Ordsall, is to close shortly and the pupils and staff will move into new premises to be known as Radclyffe Primary School. The Trafford Road School has been part of the educational scene for 95 years and the school will hold an open day and a special reunion. (20.6.80)

The 350th anniversary of the founding of the famous Booth's Charities will be marked on Sunday 22 June. The father of founder Humphrey Booth owned a house and orchard near Salford Bridge and Humphrey, born about 1580, grew up to become a prosperous merchant. Concerned about those less fortunate than himself, he purchased land in Manchester and on 18 February 1630 signed a deed giving the land to trustees who were to ensure that the rents were "justly, truly, carefully, faithfully and wholly disposed of, distributed, converted and employed towards or for the Succour, Aid or Relief of such poor, aged, needy or impotent People, as, for the Time being should inhabit or dwell within the Borough or Town of Salford."

At that time the value of the land was £20, but by 1871 260 aged persons were receiving weekly amounts varying between 3 shillings and 5 shillings (15p and 25p). In 1891 the annual income of the Charities was some £9,000, by 1948 the trustees were building blocks of flats for the elderly and in 1971 the annual income had risen to £100,000. In 1980 the income is £350,000 and 1,600 aged people on the weekly list are receiving 75p.

The motto of the Charities is taken from words on Humphrey Booth's tombstone: "Love his Memory. Imitate his Devotion." (20.6.80)

The City Council has decided to ban the Collins family from holding fairs in

Salford for the first time since 1861. The fair at Easter this year was bigger than expected and vehicles damaged grass, kerbs and roadways in Buile Hill Park. However, a spokesman for the Showman's Guild (which was started in Salford) has asked to discuss the matter with the Recreation Department.

The present owner of Collins Fair is Michael, the fifth generation. His great-great-grandfather, John Collins, came to Salford from Ireland as a horse dealer and the family has lived in the city ever since. (20.6.80)

Salford has a star named after it. Charter Festival Co-ordinator Henny King wrote to the International Star Registry in America, who agreed to waive the fee in recognition of Salford's 750th anniversary. The result is that "Orion 39" is now "Salford Charter Festival", the city's own star. (20.6.80)

More than 1,000 people heard this week that they were to lose their jobs. 800 will go at the Burton clothing factory in Walkden, which is to shut. Also closing is Platt Clothiers in Greengate (340 jobs), and at Sir James Farmer Norton's 100 workers have already been laid off since Christmas. Other local firms which have been forced to slash their workforces are Winterbottom's and Cussons. (27.6.80)

July 1980

A 380lb unexploded bomb was uncovered in the scrap yard of George Cohen in Frederick Road, Pendleton, this week, causing a major alert. Cohen's scrap yard was opened in 1933 alongside the canal, which was used during the Second World War to transport ammunition. This is not the first bomb to have been found there, and it is believed that a few missiles may have been covered as they were delivered at the wharf and then forgotten. (4.7.80)

The "Salford 80" international photographic exhibition was opened on Monday 7 July by Prince Philip, Duke of Edinburgh. The brainchild of Salford's own Harold Riley, the show has been brought together after two years' work by Harold, his administrator Helena Srakocic and researcher Marianne Fern. This is the first such exhibition to be held anywhere in the world and will run for one month. (11.7.80)

On Wednesday 9 July Princess Alexandra visited Hope Hospital to open the Clinical Sciences building. (11.7.80)

The Red Lion on Chapel Street, first licensed in 1823, is being renovated and in June licensee Mrs Susan Dunnett wrote to the Reporter asking for information about the pub's history. One reader remembers when a donkey was regularly kept overnight in the vault, and another recalls the days when wedding receptions cost 2s6d (12.5p) per head. (11.7.80)

The 250-foot chimney stack at the old Seedley Bleach Works was being demolished this week, but not before two of the workmen had hauled a four-foot-high plaster of Paris mask to the top of the chimney, to get a few necks craning. (18.7.80)

Since opening in June, the new Galaxy Roller Disco in the Rialto Buildings, Great Cheetham Street, has become all the rage. It replaces the old skateboard rink. (18.7.80)

Two members of the Salford Triple S Swimming Club have won gold medals at the recent World Catholic Championships in Milan. Neil McCheyne (16) and Michael Lawlor (17) were chosen to swim for England. (18.7.80)

September 1980

Celebrations for the 750th anniversary of Salford's Charter began on 22 August. A replica of the Charter was handed over at the gates of Buckingham Palace to a team of relay runners, who brought it all the way to Swinton Civic Centre, to be handed over next day to the Mayor, Councillor Tom Francis.

Two weeks of festivities were brought to a climax with the grandest parade the city has seen: a mile-long procession of colourful floats of many different designs. (5.9.80)

Nine-year-old Warren O'Neill of Derby Road, Weaste, is Salford's newest television star. Next month, Warren will be seen in a leading rôle in an episode of "Minder", which stars George Cole and Dennis Waterman. He was chosen from a hundred boys to play the part of Dennis Waterman's son. (5.9.80)

At the official opening of Salford's Buile Hill Mining Museum on Thursday 4 September, Coal Board Chief Sir Derek Ezra said that a number of very old pits had been closed down, but there were others which still had valuable reserves and he could see a very long life for the Lancashire mines. (12.9.80)

Salford Rugby League Club's Willows Variety Centre is to be sold. New owners Greenall Whitley will take over at the end of September. The club has an overdraft of £135,000 and Chairman Keith Snape said that with such restricted finances it was proving difficult to run the Variety Centre. The squash courts, which made a £14,150

The Red Lion, Chapel Street

profit two years ago, are also being sold. (19.9.80)

A Height man has developed a unique way of engraving. Mr Richard Lewis uses a combination of photography and acid-etching techniques to get even the minutest details of a picture permanently embedded into glass. (19.9.80)

Salford's Fire Station on the Crescent is up for sale. Built in 1903, in the days of horse-drawn vehicles it was the envy of fire services all over the country, but has now become outdated. (26.9.80)

Collins' Fair is at the Eccles New Road/Cross Lane corner on 26 and 27 September. (26.9.80)

October 1980

Plans to rejuvenate the dockland area of Salford with the promise of thousands of new jobs were described as "ill-founded" this week in a blistering attack by a chartered surveyor. The plan to create Enterprise Zones in three hundred acres of derelict land between Weaste and Ordsall, with grants and rate-free premises as carrots to attract businesses, was said to be a waste of public resources and "positively harmful" to the area. (3.10.80)

A "serve yourself" Job Centre is being furnished in Hankinson Way on the Salford Shopping Precinct and should be open early in 1981. It will be manned by about ten staff from the Trafford Road Centre. The number of jobless in the city is now 3,518 men and 914 women. (3.10.80)

The former café in Light Oaks Park, which has been described as an "eyesore", is to be knocked down. (3.10.80)

Just opened on Mocha Parade, Salford, is Spencer's chemist's shop, owned by Mr and Mrs Blake, formerly of 109 Great Clowes Street. (3.10.80)

Hopes of saving the fifty remaining jobs at Sir James Farmer Norton's engineering works were raised this week. Salford City Council announced plans to buy the Adelphi Street factory, where 450 men have already lost their jobs, and to lease it back to the company to carry on business. (10.10.80)

The "Salamander", the Salford car for the disabled, should be ready by Christmas. There are plans to move manufacture from the present works in Muslin Street to Trafford Road. (10.10.80)

One of Salford's oldest firms is to make 170 people redundant before the New Year. The jobs will go from the rubber goods section of Greengate Industrial Polymers Ltd. (17.10 80)

It's happened again! After the spending of £1.5 million ten years ago, the cutting out of the Anaconda bend and many other preventative measures, the river still won. Two inches of rainfall in forty-eight hours caused the Irwell to burst its banks at Kersal, leaving many homes flooded with up to three feet of muddy water. (31.10.80)

November 1980

Alex Murphy, Salford Rugby Club's coach for the last three seasons, has resigned. (14.11.80)

Sacred Trinity Church on Chapel Street is to be re-hallowed and dedicated by the Bishop of Manchester, the Right Reverend Stanley Booth-Clibborn, for a new purpose. In future it will be open for members of every religion who wish to study there. As the congregation dwindled down the years, it seemed the church had outlived its usefulness, until several groups banded together to devise the new centre for religious studies. (14.11.80)

The Oaklands on Eccles Old Road, a home for blind men and women for more than fifty years, is to close down because of its dilapidated condition. Mr James Aspinall, Chairman of Henshaw's Society for the Blind, which merged with the Manchester & Salford Blind Aid Society earlier this year, said that the best solution would be to close the home because of the cost involved in maintaining it. (14.11.80)

David Brown Gear Industries Ltd, Hampson Street, are to make 128 workers redundant. Brown's, which took over the factory from P R Jackson in the 1930s, plan to transfer part of the operation to their main works at Huddersfield. (21.11.80)

December 1980

The son of a former licensee of the King William IV public house on Springfield Lane is making a name for himself in the engineering world. Twenty-nine-year-old Allan Robinson hopes to take his Amica sports car on a tour of Europe next year. The vehicle is designed to look like a 1928 Mercedes Benz but with a fibreglass body and Triumph engine, and he thinks it will sell well abroad. Allan is hoping to set up production in a Fallowfield garage in the near future to produce custom-made cars with engine capacities ranging from 1.5 to 3.5 litres and optional extras. Nine models have already been built in London to a rear-engine, two-seater design, but this has now been modified to allow for two extra passengers. (5.12.80)

Salford's maypole, erected as part of this year's Charter Festival celebrations, will be moved from near St Thomas's Church to another site in Pendleton, yet to be decided. In its place will be a commemorative plaque and a car park. (5.12.80)

The new Broadway Inn opens today on the site of the old pub which was demolished. Its nickname "11/9 Dock" refers to a non-existent shed - 11 shed, 9 dock - which was used to indicate where a docker was if he went missing. If he was in "11/9 Dock", it meant he was in the Broadway! (5.12.80)

"Caretaker" Kevin Ashcroft has been appointed as Salford Rugby Club's full time coach to succeed Alex Murphy. (19.12.80)

The Salford-based Plain English Campaign, which aims to stamp out over-elaborate language, is handing out the first "Plain English Awards" in London this week. Salford Council is in

Undaunted by the floods at Lower Kersal, 1980

the list of prize winners, but its entry is in the "failed miserably" category. (12.12.80)

Ranulph Court, the new sheltered housing scheme in King Street, the Height, was opened on Wednesday 24 December by Salford artist Harold Riley. Building work on the flats was completed in September. (26.12.80)

Demolition of Hodge Lane Wash House is almost complete, and the site will be landscaped and used for public open space. It will not now be required for the M602 extension. (26.12.80)

1981

January 1981

St Ambrose Church, Liverpool Street, celebrated its centenary on Tuesday. It began as a mission church of St Thomas, Pendleton, on the corner of Liverpool Street and Joseph Street. Thirty years later it became a parish in its own right and moved to the present building, which was gutted in the Blitz. When it was refitted in the 1950s, the east window was designed by Geoffrey Clarke, who was later responsible for three of the windows in Coventry Cathedral. Some of the vicars in recent years have had unusual accomplishments. The Reverend Allan Shaw (1958-62) collected works of art and gave harpsichord recitals in the vicarage, and the present incumbent, the Reverend Geoffrey Howard, travelled across the Sahara desert with a wind-assisted wheelbarrow in 1975. (9.1.81)

Salford Rugby League star Keith Fielding appeared on the television programme "Superstars". In a clash with eight former champions, he was already the winner before taking part in the final round, the steeplechase. (9.1.81)

Ward & Goldstone are proposing to make 250 men redundant from their Cable Division on Frederick Road. (16.1.81)

Nine-year-old Warren O'Neill, who attends Seedley Junior School, was on television again on Monday 19 January, when he made a brief appearance on "Coronation Street". (23.1.81)

Salford snooker player Paul Medati has been accepted on to the world professional players' list. This means that he is in the top sixty or eighty players and next year will be able to compete in the British and World Snooker Championships. (30.1.81)

A number of Vietnamese Boat People (refugees) moved into Salford to start a new life in Higher Broughton. (30.1.81)

February 1981

A new, regular, Monday night spot at the London & North Western pub on Cross Lane opened this week. It will star Salford's well-established pop group Sweet Chariot and take the form of a back-to-the-sixties disco. The group was approached by Whitbread's, the brewers, with the aim of reviving the music scene on "The Lane". (6.2.81)

Work on the M602 extension from Gilda Brook Road, Eccles, began on 2 February. (13.2.81)

A Pendleton girl has been selected to play netball for England when the team visits Sri Lanka in July. Barbara Green, of Light Oaks Road, will be one of the North West Senior Squad who will compete against the island's national team. (13.2.81)

Keith Fielding, Salford's international winger, was in action again this Friday when he won the British finals of "Superstars" in the recorded television programme. He thus qualified for the European finals, which will be held in Israel. (13.2.81)

Hot Gossip, "Britain's most controversial dance group" founded by Salford choreographer Arlene Philips, have just completed a four-night stand at The Willows. (20.2.81)

Salford Rugby Club's Keith Fielding sustained a foot injury in the European "Superstars" competition, but still managed to come third and qualify for the World finals. (20.2.81)

Members of the Salford Schools Rugby Association will have the great honour of playing in the "curtain raiser" to the Rugby League Challenge Cup Final on Saturday 2 May. Boys from the following junior schools will make up the 18-strong, under-elevens squad: St John's (Adrian Rollinson, Stuart Ellis, Robert Mulliner, Andrew Candlin); Seedley (Neil Clare, Tom Lydiate, Stephen Calderwood, Edward O'Hara); Worsley Boothstown (Paul Walker, James Whitehead, Anthony Law, Jason Holton); New Windsor (Denis Betts, Darren Betts); St Thomas's (Luke Adimora, Tim Stewart); St Philip's (Joel Kelly, Andrew Shepherd). (27.2.81)

March 1981

A new home for mentally handicapped adults was officially opened on Friday by the Mayor, Tom Francis. St Anne's Court, Brindleheath, cost £1.5 million to build and six of the residential places will be used for short-term care. (6.3.81)

The Manchester Ship Canal Company has decided to close the grain elevator at Salford Docks at the end of March. The elevator, which has a storage capacity of 40,000 tons, has been in use since the time of the First World War. The Company says there is no longer enough business to meet the expense of keeping it going. (13.3.81)

After some hundred years' service in the area, the chemist's John Jones of Eccles New Road is to close on 21 March because of a Compulsory Purchase Order. However, Mr Peter Jones, son of the retiring chemist Reginald Jones, plans to continue the photographic side of the business and open a shop in Langworthy Road.

Jones's was based on Cross Lane from the 1880s and has been in its present premises for the past seven years. The nearest chemist's shop left on Eccles New Road is Fletcher's, but that will also close soon because of a CPO. (13.3.81)

Victor International Plastics, one of Britain's biggest plastics firms, have this week closed their old factory in Cheltenham Street and moved to a

Langworthy Road in August 1988, with Jones's photographic shop on the left

new, larger factory in Langley Road South. (13.3.81)

The 250 job losses at Ward & Goldstone announced in January have been saved by a job-sharing scheme which involves 900 people in the Cable Division working a three-day week. (20.3.81)

The new Ladywell Community Centre opened officially on Friday. The centre was built with the aid of a grant from the inner cities' fund, using the shell of the derelict Smiley's Club at the corner of Eccles New Road and Stott Lane. (20.3.81)

Salford's toy library for the disabled has reopened after a twelve-month shut-down for building alterations. (20.3.81)

The war-damaged wing at Salford Royal Hospital, recently rebuilt at a cost of £537,000, was officially opened on Friday by Tom Bergin, former Chairman of the hospital and former editor of the Salford City Reporter. The new building was completed in July 1980. (27.3.81)

A Salford University team looking at Dutch Elm Disease has pioneered the first control programme in Europe. (27.3.81)

April 1981

The Lees Mission on Liverpool Street, which was founded by a Yorkshireman, James Lees, celebrated its 90th anniversary this weekend. The first service was held one Saturday afternoon in 1891, in Unwin Square, Salford, and from then on the group used a store room over a coal yard in Hodge Lane. Over the years the organisation became known as the Hodge Lane Mission and had its first

proper home in 1928, with James Lees as the Pastor. The Mission opened its Sunday School on 17 November 1956, but today attracts more adults than children to its services. On 15 May 1971 the present Lees Mission was opened. (3.4.81)

The new Pendleton telephone exchange was opened this week by the Mayor of Salford, Councillor Tom Francis. It was his last public engagement before retiring as Mayor. (10.4.81)

The end of a sad season for Salford Rugby Club came this week as the team was relegated to the second division, along with Oldham. Neighbours Swinton also failed to gain promotion from the second division, so at least local derbies will be possible next season. The teams promoted to the first division were York and Wigan. (24.4.81)

May 1981

Mother's Pride, the largest bakery in Salford, have announced the redundancy of 47 workers at their Fitzwarren Street premises. (1.5.81)

The Cambrian International Masters Trophy snooker finals were held at the Willows Variety Club this week. In the semi-finals Alex Higgins lost to Jimmy White and Salford-born John Virgo to Steve Davis; Davis won the final. (1.5.81)

Stowell Memorial Church may soon be demolished, but its spire will live on if the city's Planning and Development Committee have their way. The idea is to preserve the spire as a landmark when the Howard Street area is developed. (1.5.81)

Six-year-old Jill Dean of Ash Street, Seedley, a former pupil of West Liverpool Street School, is a rising star in the entertainment business. She has just been picked as an extra for Granada Television's detective serial "Cribb", and appears on screen for the first time on Sunday 10 May in the episode called "Invitation to a Dynamite Party". (8.5.81)

A Salford lad has recorded the best British performance in the standing long jump event whilst competing for his school, Irwell Valley High. Sixteen-year-old Steven Steele of Acresfield Road achieved 2 metres 70 centimetres (eight feet, ten-and-a-quarter inches). The current best performance for a senior man is 2 metres 81 centimetres. (8.5.81)

Despite protests from regulars since the news was first announced in January, brewers Whitbread have closed the Oakwood Hotel on Lancaster Road for conversion to a steakhouse. The closure marked the end of over forty years of service for 72-year-old Emma Burrows, who has been a barmaid there since the early days. (8.5.81)

Salford almost went red all over last Thursday with Labour winning eleven of the twelve County Council seats by huge margins. But for a Liberal victory in Worsley, it would have been a clean sweep. (15.5.81)

A piece of Salford's history was re-enacted last week in the Mayor's Parlour at the Civic Centre, Swinton. When the opening ceremony of the city's 750th Charter Celebration was recorded on film nine months ago, the cameraman missed the opening lines of the Mayor's historic speech. Now, nine months later, Mayor Tom Francis has made the speech again, complete with the line "I have just received this historic Charter", so that there is a full and complete record of the Charter celebration events on film. (15.5.81)

The Merry Go Round Club on Broughton Road, which had its licence withdrawn after complaints from residents, may open again by the end of the year. An application has been made for a drinks licence, and the intention is to open as a new pool and social club, to be known as the Condren Pool Club. (15.5.81)

Salford's oldest swimming baths could soon be demolished as part of a Council cost-cutting package, but not without a fight. Already a petition to save the 102-year-old Blackfriars Baths has been handed in at the Town Hall. It contains 1,230 signatures. (15.5.81)

Salford's new Mayor, Seedley councillor Ivor Zott, was installed in a ceremony on Wednesday. (22.5.81)

"A good idea, but too small," was the reaction from elderly residents in the Trinity area, when a new "Drop-In Shop" at Salisbury House, St Stephen

An anti-vandalism patrol car pictured at Salford Show in 1983

Street, was opened by actor Peter Dudley (Bert Tilsley of television's "Coronation Street"). Run by Age Concern and funded by an inner city grant, the shop is the first of five intended in Salford. The aim is to relieve the boredom and isolation felt by many pensioners by inviting them to drop in for a chat during the day and make friends over a cup of tea or coffee. (22.5.81)

Willshaw's bookshop has transferred to new £200,000 premises on Salford University campus. (22.5.81)

De La Salle College, Pendleton, founded in 1924, will cease to be a grammar school this summer. From next term it will be exclusively a sixth form college. (22.5.81)

Whitbread's Waverley pub on Eccles New Road is to re-open on Tuesday night, after a £25,000 facelift. (29.5.81)

Three dedicated Salfordians are running for Britain this week in an Olympic games that breaks fresh ground. For the first time, mentally handicapped adults from twelve European countries will compete at national level. Peter Craig of Walkden, Paul Pilling of Monton and Paul Holehouse of Eccles travelled to Belgium for the games on Wednesday and will compete in a stadium at Nivelles, twenty miles outside Brussels. Their events are the 5,000 metres, the 100 metres, the relay and softball. (29.5.81)

A new sheltered housing scheme, the first of its kind in the country, was opened in Eccles last week by Salford West MP, Stan Orme. The scheme at Monica Court, Half Edge Lane, provides independence and community care and can cater for a greater cross-section of elderly people needing support than the usual residential homes. (29.5.81)

June 1981

Dr Albert Edward Frankham is to

Salford's Salamander car for the disabled

retire this week after practising as a dentist in Murray Street since 1952. Born in Leningrad, he came to the city after the war and began work in a dental surgery in Regent Road in 1950, moving to Murray Street Clinic two years later.

The clinic itself is due to close next month, to be replaced by a new clinic at Higher Broughton Health Centre. The Georgian-style building will be preserved, although what it will be used for is not yet known. (12.6.81)

An anti-vandalism patrol is to be re-introduced to Salford to try to reduce the city's annual repair bill of more than £330,000. (12.6.81)

Salford's newest indoor shopping market, the County Market Hall, was opened on Monday by Brian Mosley ("Coronation Street's" Alf Roberts). The market is in what was the County Cinema building (later a bingo hall) on Great Cheetham Street East. (19.6.81)

July 1981

The first Salford pub to introduce betting alongside boozing (legally) may be the Paddock on Cross Lane. Done Brothers applied to the city's Planning Committee for permission to build a betting office in the rear yard of the pub. Also discussed at last Tuesday's meeting was Whitbread's application to convert the public bar of the Flemish Weaver into a betting shop. (3.7.81)

A new Salford newspaper will be launched in less than a month's time. The Salford City Reporter will become the Salford Reporter & Advertiser. (10.7.81)

A fire destroyed over 100 square feet of the sixty-year-old Townsend Road stand at the Swinton Rugby Ground. Police are treating it as arson. (17.7.81)

Salford's newest British Legion Club, in Ordsall Precinct, was officially inaugurated on Saturday by Colonel D

E Gibbs, CBE. However, the club first opened its doors to members two years ago. (24.7.81)

After being closed for a while, the Red Dragon on the Crescent will reopen on Wednesday 29 July with a Royal Wedding Celebration Night. The pub is owned by Gill Manton Catering Services and is their first public house in the Salford area. (24.7.81)

The historic Knolls House on Bury New Road has been in the Robinson family since 1895, but now the removal firm see it as a liability and would like to demolish it. Lead has been stripped from the roof and the house has been vandalised, but as it has been a listed building since 1973, permission to demolish has to be sought. (31.7.81)

August 1981

Mrs Sarah Halligan, Salford's oldest woman, celebrated her 103rd birthday on Thursday 6 August. (7.8.81)

The Salisbury Hotel, facing the dock gates on Trafford Road, opened yesterday after a complete refurbishment. Eight months ago the pub was badly damaged by fire. (7.8.81)

Within hours of closing for the summer term, and for the last time as a school, St Ambrose, Liverpool Street, was being prepared for a different rôle. The 68-year-old school has been bought by the Salford Playhouse and in future it will be used for rehearsals by the Salford Players, the Salford Youth Theatre, the Salford Children's Theatre and other local drama groups. Pop groups will also be able to practise there. (7.8.81)

Permanite Ltd, Britain's largest manufacturer of bitumen-based roof waterproofing materials, has opened a new mastic asphalt plant in Salford. Sited in Indigo Street, off Langley Road South, the plant is the first in the UK designed specifically to produce hot mastic asphalt for discharge directly into transport. (7.8.81)

Street parties were held throughout the city last week to celebrate the Royal Wedding of Prince Charles and Lady Diana Spencer on 29 July. (7.8.81)

Thursday 13 August was the official opening of the new Mark Addy pub, for invited guests only. The doors opened to the public at lunchtime the following day. (21.8.81)

Salford's Central Lending Library, the first unconditionally free public library in the country, will close on Saturday after more than 130 years' service. Most of the books will be transferred to the new district library at Broadwalk, Salford Precinct, which opens on 25 September. The Local History Library will remain open at Peel Park. (28.8.81)

The first Manchester "Pony Marathon" was run on Sunday 23 August, and thousands of people lined the streets as the runners passed through on their way to Bolton. The race was won by Salford Harrier Stan Curran.   (28.8.81)

September 1981

St John the Evangelist Church Hall in Broughton has been given a £62,000 facelift after being closed for three years. The hall was opened as a youth club and social centre by the Bishop of Manchester, the Right Reverend Stanley Booth-Clibborn and the Mayor, Councillor Ivor Zott, who unveiled a plaque.   (4.9.81)

Three steam locomotives which have hauled coal around Agecroft Power Station for thirty years are running out of puff. Built by Stephenson & Hawthorn in the late 1940s, two of the locos started life at the "B" station, which opened in 1950. The third came from Chadderton Power Station in 1954. The engines will be used less and less over the next twelve months and then probably sold to railway preservation societies. They will be replaced by a conveyor belt stretching the quarter of a mile from the colliery to the power station.   (4.9.81)

Regulars at the Dover Castle pub, Higher Broughton, held an old-fashioned party night to celebrate the pub's reopening this week. Among the old pictures hanging in the pub showing the area as it was is the old street sign of Charlotte Street, on which the pub used to stand. Its new address is Highclere Avenue.   (4.9.81)

An application to turn Kersal Cell into a motel and banqueting suite was refused by Salford's Planning Committee last Thursday. There has been local opposition to the scheme since the application was first made in July.   (4.9.81)

Salford Rugby League Club made

history on Sunday by becoming the first visitors to the new Cardiff Rugby League team, who are to play at Ninian Park, the home of Cardiff City Football Club. Salford came out winners 26-21.   (4.9.81)

Residents on the Langworthy estate, as well as local shopkeepers and schools, are furious about the loss of a bridge that was a vital link with the Eccles New Road estate and shops. The footbridge from Hodge Lane, which used to provide safe passage over the railway, has been demolished to make way for a new one when the M602 extension is complete.   (11.9.81)

Salford's revolutionary new car for the disabled has been given the seal of approval by those who know. A leading motoring magazine, "Drive and Trail", carried out a survey on the Salamander and the higher-priced Elswick Envoy, and after being tested by twenty disabled drivers, the Salamander was voted the better of the two.   (18.9.81)

Marchant's Gym, the home of boxing in Salford for over fifty years, is to be demolished on 28 September. Although the name is retained at the gym, the Marchant family "retired" from boxing about four years ago, after the death of Albert Marchant. The club is now leased from British Rail by another Salfordian, Jack Arrowsmith. Jack's son Russ is one of the twenty or so boxers who regularly use the Pendleton premises. Many famous boxers have trained at the gym over the years, including Joe Bugner. Rocky Marciano once brought an American fighter, Joe Brown, there to prepare for a fight with Britain's Terry Downes.   (18.9.81)

October 1981

Anyone in Clifton who can't get to

sleep tonight because they think they can hear haunting tunes drifting through the night air should not worry - it will only be Beau, playing at the Beehive in Rake Lane. He is trying to regain his organ marathon world record by playing for 420 hours non-stop. As with his previous attempts, this is being done to aid local charities. Beau, who changed his name by deed poll, will still not reveal his original name.   (2.10.81)

Broadwalk Library was opened on Friday 25 September by Alan Longworth, President of the Library Association.   (2.10.81)

The work of the astronomer William Crabtree is to be commemorated by a blue plaque at Scarr Wheel on Lower Broughton Road, which is near the site of his former home. The plaque will be unveiled by Salford don Dr Allan Chapman for the Salford Astronomical Society on 24 November, 342 years to the day in 1639 when Crabtree observed the Transit of Venus. (2.10.81)

A new venture in Rocky Lane, Monton, is the Legendary Lancashire Heroes shop dealing in real ales from around the world. A selection of 90 beers from 15 different countries is available.   (2.10.81)

Mrs Ada Weston of Pendlebury Road, Swinton, has just completed a tapestry of the Last Supper which took seven years to do. She is donating the tapestry to St Paul's Church, Broadwalk.   (9.10.81)

The Globe pub on Bury Street, Blackfriars, which has been closed for the past eighteen months, has been refurbished by Wilsons Brewery and has recently reopened.   (9.10.81)

A Darwen ironmonger wants to use the former Griffin pub on Chapel Street (closed two years ago) for storage purposes.   (9.10.81)

Beau's attempt at a new marathon organ playing record came to an end after just 178 hours. Doctors advised him to stop when he suffered acute stomach pains.   (16.10.81)

The new St Gilbert's Primary School in Winton was opened last week.   (16.10.81)

The London & North Western pub on Cross Lane has had a facelift, or some might call it "a smash in the face". All the fine wooden fittings, relics of its Threlfalls past, have been ripped out and the interior redesigned with a disco theme. There are wall paintings of trains and railway scenes to retain some links with its name. The pub reopens on 22 October.   (16.10.81)

The first Manchester Charity Marathon was won by Steve Kenyon of Salford Harriers. This is the second time in two months that a member of the Harriers has won a major marathon.   (23.10.81)

The Globe on Bury Street

A 12ft by 7ft painting housed in St James (Hope) Church, Pendleton, is something of a mystery. It is a reproduction of a work by the seventeenth century Spanish painter Murillo, "The Holy Family", but an expert from Manchester Art Gallery said of the Salford version, " I am afraid it is not a masterpiece and not a very good copy." The painting has been there for about fifty years according to the church rector, the Reverend Frank Bibby, but no-one knows where it came from. (23.10.81)

Salford looks set to become the North West's tourist centre. The latest brochure produced by Golden Circle, part of Global Holidays, describes the city as "a superb touring base from which to explore the Peak District and the Pennine Way, and see the areas which inspired Lowry and one of Britain's greatest novelists, Howard Spring." A week's holiday costs £89 and includes accommodation at Salford University. (23.10.81)

The traffic lights on two of the busiest routes in Salford - Bolton Road and Eccles New Road, which are used by thousands of motorists every day - are controlled by a £5 million computer system located in Magnum House, Piccadilly Gardens. More than half of the 1,000 traffic signals and Pelican crossings in Greater Manchester are controlled by the computer, which is connected to the system by telephone line. Closed circuit television cameras and other equipment monitor traffic flow and queues at about a hundred locations. In addition to parts of Bolton, Bury, Salford, Manchester and Oldham, areas in Trafford, Stockport and Tameside are also covered and it is possible to drive from Hazel Grove to Bolton under computer control, a distance of twenty miles. (30.10.81)

November 1981

A survey by Salford Corporation shows that a row of terraced houses in Alpha Street West is unfit and should be demolished, but most of the tenants want to stay and improve their homes. (6.11.81)

Next Monday, 9 November, C S Fletcher, dispensing chemists, open their new shop in Langworthy Road. Before the First World War the late Mr Charles Senior Fletcher came to Salford and acquired the business of C Whitfield, dispensing chemists. Whitfield's had started at the corner of Regent Road and Cross Lane and they stayed there until the site was required for the extension of a bank (now itself demolished to make way for the extension of the M602). In the mid-1890s they moved to Eccles New Road, where the firm has been ever since, and many of the fittings in the present pharmacy came from the Whitfield shop. The new premises in Langworthy Road will have a more

contemporary look, but some of the original items have been incorporated to provide a link with the past.
(6.11.81)

The statues of Queen Victoria and Prince Albert which stand in front of Salford Art Gallery are to receive an early spring clean. Queen Victoria's statue was erected in 1857 and that of the Prince Consort in 1864. Both are by sculptor Matthew Noble in Sicilian marble. (6.11.81)

The Stella Maris Seamen's Hostel and Club on Oldfield Road could close by the New Year, just fifteen years after it was built. The decline of the sea trade in the area is responsible. Salford City Council would like to buy the building and use it as a youth club, but can't afford it. (20.11.81)

December 1981

Houses off Eccles New Road, including those in Wynford Street, Thurlow Street, My Street, George Henry Street, Vere Street, Ward Street and West Ashton Street, are all in the course of demolition to make way for the new Enterprise Zone. (4.12.81)

A Salford pianist still tinkling the ivories after forty years is George Farrow, or "Georgie Farrer", as he is popularly known. George has played all over the world, including Australia, New Zealand and South Africa, and he

recalls when he was serving in submarines as a lad of nineteen and performed "People Will Say We're in Love" with Frank Sinatra in New York. His fondest memories are of playing around the pubs of Salford: he did sixteen years at the Ship on Cross Lane and has also been the star attraction at the Kersal Club, Regent Hotel, the Ordsall Hotel and the Osborne Hotel. He is currently playing at the Church Inn, Eccles, and has just recorded a tape of old favourites with his lifelong friend, Albert Rowbotham of Liverpool Street. (4.12.81)

Raffles wine bar in Regent Street, Eccles, opened in November. (4.12.81)

St Aidan's Church, Littleton Road, opens its new social club this weekend. The first pints will be pulled by Canon Geoffrey Cates and his wife Ann.
(4.12.81)

The Regent Community Centre in Huddart Street, Ordsall, a former school canteen, has been closed for a fortnight following a fire and may have to be pulled down. (11.12.81)

1982

January 1982

Salford City Council was presented with 2lb of tripe in December, as

The Live and Let Live, and shops on Regent Road

winners of the Plain English Campaign's gobbledygook prize. This is the second year running that the Council has won the uncoveted award. (1.1.82)

International table tennis came to Salford on Tuesday, when the sole test match between China and England was played at Ordsall Recreation Centre. The Chinese came out winners 5-2. (8.1.82)

John Wilkinson (36) became Salford Rugby Club's youngest ever Chairman on Sunday 3 January, succeeding Keith Snape, who will be the new Deputy Chairman. (8.1.82)

The recently reopened Salford Arms pub on Chapel Street features an ornate fireplace which it is claimed once belonged to Lord Pilkington, and a piano hanging from the ceiling. (8.1.82)

The Reverend Basil Buckley, one of Salford's longest-serving clergymen, is retiring after forty-three years at the same church, St Ignatius, Ordsall. (15.1.82)

Prime Minister Margaret Thatcher visited Salford University on Friday 15 January, with news that her son Mark had been found safe and well after he went missing in the Sahara desert while taking part in the Paris-Dakar rally. She was not, however, greeted with open arms by the students, who made a silent black flag protest about cash cuts. (22.1.82)

Mrs Harriet Rothwell, aged 86, of Milner Street, Swinton, was treated to tea with the Mayor, Councillor Ivor Zott, last Wednesday. The surprise engagement was to honour Harriet as the last surviving "pit brow lassie" at the Clifton Hall Colliery, where she started work in 1916, cleaning the coal as it emerged from the shaft on a conveyor belt. The hours in those days were from six in the morning until five at night. (22.1.82)

Local butcher Gordon Flaherty of Chandos Grove, Weaste, was taken into Harefield Hospital, Middlesex, for a heart transplant on 21 January. The operation was performed by Dr Magdi Yacoub and was a complete success. (22.1.82)

Approval has been given for an £8 million refuse treatment plant on the former goods station site at Brindleheath. Building will start in May. The giant plant will handle 600 tons of rubbish a day, reducing it to fine grains or manageable blocks in a six-hour process. The finished products will be shipped out to South Lancashire by special trains. (29.1.82)

February 1982

The Kersal Cell Country Club has submitted a plan for a motel, banqueting suite and car parking facilities similar to the one rejected in 1981. Local residents have renewed their opposition. (5.2.82)

Vandals were blamed for a fire at the Salford Playhouse in the early hours of Monday morning. It will cost £5,000 to replace carpets and bar fittings. (12.2.82)

Hepworth's tailor's shop in Salford Precinct will close on 27 February. (12.2.82)

On Saturday Albert and Doreen Tanner will close their ironmongery business on Gerald Road, Pendleton, for the last time, ending a sixty-year family connection. The shop, which overlooks the Cromwell roundabout, was opened by Mr Tanner's father, also called Albert and taken over by the present proprietor in 1961. There will be some reminders of the family, however, as the new owners have promised to retain the name A Tanner

The new Wellington, Regent Road

as well as carrying out a similar business. (26.2.82)

March 1982

Agecroft Power Station has been chosen for the development of Britain's first major combined district heat and power project. (5.3.82)

Eccles schoolboy Simon Radcliffe has been chosen to captain England schoolboys against Ireland schoolboys at Barnsley, the first Salford boy to win this honour. (5.3.82)

Ward & Goldstone have announced 286 redundancies in their Cable Manufacturing Division. They are also to sell the six-acre site at the corner of Lissadel Street and Broughton Road to Salford Council for £400,000. (12.3.82)

The Flemish Weaver pub has won an appeal against the refusal by Salford Licensing Justices to grant a betting office licence for the premises. In allowing the appeal, Judge Desmond Franks imposed the condition that the betting area must be completely sealed off from the rest of the building. (12.3.82)

The Brown Bull Hotel on Chapel Street is reopening on Monday after an £80,000 refit. To add a realistic touch to the occasion, Macclesfield farmer Alan Wood will be bringing his prize Hereford brown bull to the city for the day. (12.3.82)

Kevin Ashcroft has resigned as Salford Rugby Club coach to take up a position with Warrington. Alan McInnes has been appointed acting coach, with Mike Coulman as his assistant. (12.3.82)

Higher Broughton Health Centre was officially opened today by Mr Richard Roberts, Chairman of the Salford Area Health Authority. (12.3.82)

At last the Salford-based "Plain English Campaign", run by Chrissie Maher and Martin Cutts of Higher Broughton, has been given recognition. The Government has announced plans to save the public millions of pounds by simplifying Government forms, and Chrissie and Martin have been awarded an £11,500 contract, spread over two years, to travel to London to give advice on documents and to train those involved in writing the forms. (26.3.82)

April 1982

Salford's - and Britain's - only matador, Frank Evans, returns to Spain next week, after recovering from injury in the most intimate of parts, inflicted by a sharp-horned cow during training. (16.4.82)

Salford Council has won its battle to bulldoze seven of the few remaining pubs on Regent Road to make way for factory units. Despite opposition from the Campaign for Real Ale, the decision, made behind closed doors in

London, is that the Duke of York, Albert Inn, Spread Eagle, Grove Inn, Wellington Inn and the Gloucester Arms may be knocked down in the near future. The time scale for demolition varies between six weeks and two years. The seventh pub, the Live and Let Live, will be allowed to remain only until the road is widened in the 1990s.

Last Wednesday members of CAMRA, dressed in black and carrying a coffin down Regent Road, held a wake to mourn the loss of the pubs. (16.4.82)

May 1982

Princess Anne will officially open Radclyffe Primary School, Ordsall, next Thursday, 13 May. (7.5.82)

At 1.30pm tomorrow Kidd's chip shop on Bolton Road, the Height, closes. The shop was taken over by Mr and Mrs Harry Kidd in 1933 following their honeymoon. The couple retired to Lytham eleven years ago.

Mrs Stella Metcalfe, who now manages the shop with a staff of eight, joined the business in 1950 and, together with Mr Kidd, later opened another chippy in Langworthy Road. When that was sold, she and her husband Louis returned to the Height shop and in 1972 became business partners with Mr and Mrs Kidd. (7.5.82)

Salford girls Di and Julie Carter of Chartwell Close, Pendleton, were called to play for the England national

handball team on Monday. The match was a "friendly" against the Belgian under-21 national side, played in London. Also making her début in the game was Colette Squires of Buckingham Road, Cadishead. (7.5.82)

The Mayor of Salford, Ivor Zott, officially started the work on the Stowell Technical Park, a £2 million-plus development in the city's Enterprise Zone, this week. (7.5.82)

Salford's new fire station on Liverpool Street has just been opened. (7.5.82)

Dr Joe Jaffe was installed as Salford's 138th Mayor on Sunday 23 May. (28.5.82)

Work is about to begin on the new Co-op Shopping Giant store on the Height. It should be open in twelve months' time. (28.5.82)

Mal Aspey has taken over from Salford Rugby Club's caretaker coach, Alan McInnes. (28.5.82)

June 1982

The future of the Carlton Cinema is looking doubtful, with attendances in decline. Although films are still being shown in Studios 1 and 2, the management is considering other ways of attracting audiences; live music concerts might be one possibility. (4.6.82)

International Wrestling is advertised at the Beehive Hotel, Clifton (including two ladies' bouts). (11.6.82)

Local schoolboy Simon Radcliffe had to have his spleen removed, following a freak accident while skippering England's under-15 soccer side against Scotland at Wembley. (11.6.82)

Salford Rugby Club has announced a break from tradition. Since the late 1960s Friday has been Rugby night at the Willows, and before that games were played on Saturday afternoons, but now the club has opted to play regular home matches on a Sunday. (18.6.82)

The second Piccadilly Radio Charity Marathon hit the streets of Salford, Worsley and Manchester on Saturday and this year's winner was Worsley fireman Kevin Best. (18.6.82)

The Carlton Cinema, Cross Lane, played host to local bands in May, the first time a live show has been held there since 1960. The groups appearing were Forgotten Heroes, Vandoy, Paris, Dix-Step, Spiral Gold and Dead Giveaway. (25.6.82)

July 1982

The 1982 Great Salford Raft Race took place on Sunday 4 July. It was the second such race to be held, following the success last year. The winning raft finished the course from Littleton Road Bridge to Peel Park in 53 minutes, passing Charlestown Rapids, Kersal Swamps and avoiding the Peel Park Sharks with the greatest of ease. (9.7.82)

Regent Road Primary School will close its doors for the last time on 22 July, after nearly eighty years of educating Salford children. (16.7.82)

September 1982

Salford pub and club entertainer Klive Jaymes is making a pop record entitled "Salford Part One and Part Two". Whitbread, the brewers, have backed him to the tune of £7,000. (10.9.82)

In the first round of the Forshaw's Lancashire Cup on Saturday, Langworthy completely overran a game British Aerospace side to win 98-0. Edge scored five of the 22 tries and all 16 goals to set a highest individual points record of 47, beating the previous record which was set in 1955. (17.9.82)

October 1982

Oaklands School for the physically handicapped in Lower Kersal has been recommended for closure by the city's Education Department. (1.10.82)

There was a massive fire on Saturday night in the premises of B & R Hauliers in Silk Street. Two thousand people were evacuated from their homes as an explosion, which could be heard twelve miles away, ripped the heart out of the depot. A series of smaller bangs followed with fireballs leaping into the air, and the whole of the

After the explosion in Silk Street

surrounding area was bleached by chemical fall-out on the ground. The bill for repairing the damage is estimated at £1.5 million.   (1.10.82)

The Woodland Suite, a 70-seat extension to the Buile Hill Park Banqueting Suite, was opened this week.   (15.10.82)

A giant mural which can be seen when entering Salford has been erected on the side of a warehouse in Trafford Park. It depicts many local industrial and sporting scenes, is 72ft high by 63ft wide and was painted by Walter Kershaw, who was educated at De La Salle College, Pendleton.   (22.10.82)

Door-to-door rent collection is to be scrapped by Salford Council following a series of attacks on collectors. All Salford City Council tenants will pay their rent at offices.   (29.10.82)

The successful 1982 Canadian Mount Everest Expedition was led by Salfordian John Amatt.   (29.10.82)

A former De La Salle pupil is one of only seven people in America to be honoured by the massive MacDonald Douglas Corporation for "outstanding technical performance". John Mackey received his award for inventing a computer simulation system. He emigrated to the States eighteen years ago, but his mother still lives in Lower Broughton.   (29.10.82)

November 1982

There are more than eight thousand unemployed in Salford.   (5.11.82)

Salford's local lottery is to be scrapped at the end of the year and outstanding profits handed to selected voluntary groups. The ailing lottery is organised for Salford City Council by Greater Manchester Council, which is axing its own lottery on New Year's Eve.
    (12.11.82)

A plan for a new 700-metre link line

from Windsor Bridge to Ordsall Lane will provide a through route from Euxton Junction, near Preston, to Manchester Piccadilly, linking for the first time rail networks to the north and south of the city. The scheme was initially approved a year ago and now the Government inquiry team has also given it the green light.   (12.11.82)

Two buglers from the Windsor Band, Pendleton, played the "Last Post", a serenade of sadness, for the last time in the once-grand Light Oaks Park bandstand. A victim of time and vandalism, the bandstand will be demolished later this month. (12.11.82)

Salford girl Leanne Bryon, aged ten, has won a part in the Manchester version of the smash hit musical "Annie" which has swept Broadway and the West End. She will play the part of Duffy, one of thirteen orphans in the show.   (19.11.82)

December 1982

Opening today is Morrissey's club and disco on Trafford Road.   (10.12.82)

"Gandhi", acclaimed by many as the greatest film since "Gone with the Wind", seems destined to bring international fame to yet another Salford actor. Playing the lead rôle is Ben Kingsley, who in his years as a member of the Salford Players' Theatre acted under his real name of Krishna Bhanji.   (10.12.82)

A fire at St Paul's Church, Moor Lane, Kersal, last Friday night caused £20,000 worth of damage to the vestry roof.   (17.12.82)

The death occurred last week of Mark Marchant, one of the famous Salford boxing family. He was 76.   (17.12.82)

The new £22.5 million M602 extension from Eccles to Cross Lane will be officially opened on Monday by Government minister Mrs Lynda

Chalker. It is six months ahead of schedule. She will also be opening the Cross Lane to Windsor Bridge link, Albion Way.   (17.12.82)

1983

January 1983

A proposal by brewers Joseph Holt to build a pub at the corner of Ashley Street and Liverpool Street is meeting with local opposition.   (7.1.83)

Cussons, the Kersal soap company, has announced the loss of over 300 jobs.
    (21.1.83)

Mr Graham Atkinson, the Salford Rugby Club general manager and secretary, was made redundant this week.   (21.1.83)

Worsley residents have launched an appeal to save an old turret clock which is presently under lock and key in Council care and has not been seen for six years. Spearheading the campaign is local historian Frank Mullineux, who is trying to get local industry sponsorship and public subscriptions to help finance the cost of re-erecting the clock, which once surmounted the Bridgewater Trustees Offices on Bridgewater Road, Walkden. It was unveiled at one minute past midnight on 1 January 1901 by Mrs Bourke, wife of the Superintendent Trustee, and became affectionately known as "Lady Bourke" thereafter. Made by Messrs Smith of Derby, it struck thirteen at one o'clock, following an old tradition.

Local folklore has it that in the eighteenth century the Duke of Bridgewater found that some of his workmen were extending their lunchbreaks, claiming that they could not hear the clock strike 1pm. He gave instructions that the clock was to be adapted to strike thirteen instead, so that no-one had any excuse for taking more than an hour, and public clocks in Worsley still strike thirteen.   (21.1.83)

The last "House" was called at the Carlton Bingo Hall this week before it closed. Films are still being shown there.   (21.1.83)

Gordon Flaherty, the Salford butcher who had a heart transplant a year ago, returned to Harefield Hospital, Middlesex, for what he called "My twelve months MOT".   (28.1.83)

One of Salford's most famous boxers, Jack "Kid" Doyle, has died at the age of eighty-seven. He was a leading flyweight in the 1920s.   (28.1.83)

Television cameras were in Salford this week, filming in Derg Street, Seedley, for a new BBC2 play called "The Gathering Seed". It is set in 1930s Collyhurst, where in 1936 there were said to be 12,000 Catholics within a half mile radius. However, the Collyhurst

Taking up the tramlines at Cross Lane junction

of today bears little resemblance to that of the 1930s, so the BBC planners had to look around for their location shots and Derg Street fits the bill.

(28.1.83)

The Mother's Pride bakery in Fitzwarren Street, Pendleton, is to close down with the loss of 270 jobs. The management have given 30 April as the official closure date and are offering 111 jobs at bakeries in Stockport and Wigan. (28.1.83)

February 1983

Radio Four's "Any Questions" programme was staged at Hope High School last Friday. (11.2.83)

Salford's new Salvation Army Goodwill Centre on Eccles New Road was officially opened on Saturday by "Coronation Street" actress Thelma Barlow. (11.2.83)

A £15 million plan to redevelop part of Salford Docks was announced on Wednesday. The scheme to transform twenty acres of No.6 Dock with a 180-bedroom hotel, a leisure and sports complex, housing, business and office blocks was given the go-ahead by Environmental Secretary Mr Tom King, who has allocated £800,000 for land acquisition and environmental improvements. The first stage will involve filling in one of the docks and work will begin as soon as spending plans for the £800,000 are approved.

(18.2.83)

Salford's MP for twenty-eight years, Frank Allaun, has announced that he is to quit politics at the next general election. (25.2.83)

March 1983

A site has at last been found for the Salford maypole, after much argument as to where it should go. It will be erected in the three-quarter-acre Brunswick Park, Upper Gloucester Street, Pendleton, as near to a village green as you are likely to find in twentieth-century Salford. Before it was blown down in 1883, the maypole was 66 feet high. Its replacement was said to have measured over 78 feet, but this height seems to have been reduced, perhaps when it was moved to Station Street to make way for the railway, as the one which blew down in 1920 was a mere 60 feet tall. The new pole, which is made from a 25ft street lighting column, was last used to celebrate the Salford Charter Festival in 1980. It is hoped that its new home will be a permanent one. (4.3.83)

The city planners have rejected a proposal for a new pub at the corner of Ashley Street, Seedley. (4.3.83)

The Centurian Housing Association has applied to the City Council for permission to build houses on land at Seedley Bleach Works, off Nona Street. (4.3.83)

The former Mainstop store in Eccles Shopping Mall has reopened as Morrison's stores. (11.3.83)

On Saturday Irlam Hornets amateur Rugby League Club became the first from the North Western Counties League to play a Welsh Rugby League side home and away. They travelled to Aberavon earlier in the season and the trip was so successful that a return match was arranged. Irlam won Saturday's game by 43-21, with Dave Twist leading the way with five tries and eight goals, to collect 31 of Irlam's points. (25.3.83)

April 1983

The London & North Western pub on Cross Lane opens again on Monday. The new landlord, Salford-born Jackie Richmond, has introduced the sort of live entertainment familiar in the good old days. Monday night will be Talent Competition night, with darts and pool matches during the week and top class acts at weekends. (8.4.83)

Salford actor Ben Kingsley has won an Oscar for best actor in the film "Gandhi". At the British Academy Awards he won two titles, "Best Film Actor" and "Most Promising Newcomer". (15.4.83)

There was a fire at Regent Road Carpet Warehouse on Wednesday, in which an estimated 55 rolls of carpet were destroyed. The derelict Gas Tavern pub, which divides the premises, prevented the flames from spreading. (15.4.83)

A proposal to convert Morrissey's nightclub on Trafford Road into a hostel has been submitted to the city's Planning & Development Committee. (15.4.83)

Agecroft Rowing Club has applied for grants to help develop and clean the Irwell. The club, which has been using the river since 1861, would like to expand the rowing facilities available to the public. (15.4.83)

Mark Fletcher and Tony Horrocks win the Buile Hill Park Kart Race, 1983

May 1983

Old railway sidings at Brindleheath have been bought from British Rail by Salford City Council for £486,000.
(6.5.83)

The Norwest Co-operative Society opened their new "Shopping Giant" superstore at the Height on Wednesday 4 May.
(6.5.83)

Beverly Morris (22) of Grosvenor Drive, Walkden, is once again European Middleweight Karate Champion. She is the only karate exponent, male or female, ever to retain a European title. At the world championships held in Taiwan last November, she came third at her first attempt.
(6.5.83)

Salford are back in the First Division of Rugby League next season. They finished in third place in the Second Division, and so qualify for promotion.
(6.5.83)

Stafford House, Ellesmere Park, Eccles, opened four weeks ago as a private home for the elderly. The 90-year-old Victorian premises were converted and renovated to create accommodation for twenty-five people.
(6.5.83)

Salford policeman John Howard-Norman stopped a minibus designed to carry fourteen passengers, and to his astonishment found inside forty-nine people, plus the driver. Thirteen of the passengers were standing; the rest were sitting either on seats or on each other. The incident was reported in the spring issue of "On the Road", a Greater Manchester Police Traffic Department publication.
(13.5.83)

Only the tower and spire remain of the 114-year-old Stowell Memorial Church. The body of the church was demolished recently to make way for the Trafford Road/Eccles New Road junction.

Another victim of this development was the intricate tramline junction. This was of the "Grand Union" type, with two lines each way across the junction and double tracks round each of the four corners, so that a tram could approach the junction from, and depart to, any of four directions: Cross Lane, Regent Road, Trafford Road and Eccles New Road.
(13.5.83)

The investiture of Salford's new Mayor, Councillor John William Hincks, took place on Tuesday 17 May at the Civic Centre.
(20.5.83)

Salford Council has sold the old flats on the Regent Road/Ordsall Lane junction to Barratts, the builders.
(20.5.83)

There was tragedy at the Barton Air Show on Sunday 15 May, when a stunt pilot's aeroplane mysteriously nose-dived into a peat bog, killing him instantly.
(20.5.83)

June 1983

One of the founding members of the Suffragette movement, Hanna Carrier, was a hundred years old yesterday. Hanna has lived in Unwin Court old folks' home in Fitzwarren Street for the last eight years, since moving from nearby Sutton Flats.
(17.6.83)

The new wing at Pendlebury Children's Hospital opened last Thursday will provide overnight accommodation for fourteen visiting parents.
(17.6.83)

Salford's Enterprise Zone is already being praised. Ten-year "rate free" inducements have contributed a great deal to the success of the scheme.
(24.6.83)

July 1983

The Manchester Ship Canal Company is close to achieving its objective of chopping the dock labour force to just eighteen men. Redundancy schemes are on offer, and many have been taken up.
(8.7.83)

The Great Salford Raft Race held on Sunday 17 July started at Littleton Road Bridge and finished at Peel Park. Fifteen rafts of all types took part.
(22.7.83)

Next month Tetley Walker are introducing shuffleboard to five of their pubs, including the Kings Arms on Whit Lane and the Keystone in Salford Precinct, to see how Salfordians like the game. It is similar to curling, but played on a 9ft-long wooden board with a highly polished surface on which weights are slid towards scoring areas.
(29.7.83)

August 1983

A five-year plan to guarantee the long-term future of Agecroft Colliery, despite heavy losses and dwindling production, was put to miners at a special meeting on Monday. The management are seeking 120 volunteer redundancies, which will reduce the labour force to just over 700. It will also be necessary to shut down one of the two coal faces.
(5.8.83)

Members of Salford's Kenyukai Karate Club have achieved their biggest success to date by finishing runners-up in the North West League.
(5.8.83)

Salford's newest boxing gym opens for the first time on Monday night, at the St Boniface's Community Centre, Frederick Road.
(5.8.83)

The 140-year-old Peel Hall at Little Hulton is to be demolished to make way for a new hospital for elderly psychiatric patients.
(5.8.83)

The Salamander Company, which was set up five years ago by the City Council in conjunction with Manchester Polytechnic, has been put on the market. The company needs an "injection of working capital" to be able to compete with other motor manufacturers, otherwise it will close in September.
(12.8.83)

Mrs Sarah Halligan, who has lived at Ladywell Hospital for the last four years, celebrated her 105th birthday last weekend with an old-fashioned sing-song. One of the guests was her daughter, Emily, who is "only" eighty.
(12.8.83)

White collar workers at Salford's Docks have demanded talks with the Ship Canal Company management, to clear the air over speculation that the Docks are to close in November.
(12.8.83)

The first-ever Salford go-kart rally was held in Buile Hill Park at the weekend, and two twelve-year-olds from West Salford Youth Club were the stars of the show. Mark Fletcher and Tony Horrocks entered in all three events, winning the three trophies for obstacle, downhill and circuit sprints. (12.8.83)

Crisis talks are being held at Ward & Goldstone's this week in an attempt to save jobs in their Cable Division. It is

Engineers at Barlow & Chidlaw in its heyday

threatened with closure unless a buyer can be found. (19.8.83)

The Carlton Cinema is to have a £75,000 facelift in a bid to bring back customers. A plan to convert the former bingo hall into a snooker club is also being considered. (19.8.83)

The firm of Thomas Reynolds closed its Great Clowes Street workshop on Saturday after more than a hundred years of making brass band instruments. Several members of the Reynolds family played for the Hallé Orchestra and the company was started by Charles or Thomas Reynolds in the third quarter of the nineteenth century.

The current managing director, Fred Baxendale, can remember when they had eighty-two Royal Air Force bands on their books, and recalls how at the Coronation in 1953 the Royal Marines kept time with miniature metronomes made by Reynolds which they fitted in their gloves. The firm once had a shop on Chapel Street, and supplied comedian Jimmy Edwards with his euphonium. (19.8.83)

Pendleton Congregational Church, which for the past five years has been used as a china warehouse and an antiques store, has been demolished. (26.8.83)

September 1983

An attempt on the world water speed record by Salford businessman Tony Fahey, scheduled for next month, has been called off until next year because of problems with design and funding. Mr Fahey, who runs a haulage, shipping and storage company in Pendleton, hopes to beat the current

record of 319.627mph held by Australian Ken Warby. (2.9.83)

Thirteen-year-old Terry Breck of Roe Green, Worsley, has won a part in the musical "Oliver" at Manchester's Palace Theatre. He was one of those chosen from hundreds of youngsters who auditioned to play members of Fagin's gang. (9.9.83)

The five-year-old Salamander car firm on Muslin Street is being voluntarily wound up and is now in the hands of the liquidators. (9.9.83)

Only weeks after Pendleton engineering giants Ward & Goldstone decided to cut their workforce by 550, the Whit Lane firm of Barlow & Chidlaw, one of the oldest companies operating in the city, is to close with the loss of 80 jobs. (9.9.83)

The Gang of Four - Shirley Williams, Bill Rodgers, Roy Jenkins and David Owen - brought the SDP to Salford this week for a highly successful three-day party conference at Salford University. (16.9.83)

Salford-born Brenda Dean has been elected as president of SOGAT, Britain's biggest print union, representing 235,000 members nationwide. (16.9.83)

The new Albert Park pub in Great Clowes Street was opened last Thursday. The pub has been converted from a house next door to the Holm-Lee Hotel by John Kain, who has named it after the old local he used to frequent before it was pulled down. (16.9.83)

Former managing director of Ward & Goldstone, Michael Goldstone, is suing his old employers for wrongful

dismissal. He was opposed to the large scale job losses announced by the company recently, with the closure of three of its four factories in Salford. The decision led to a boardroom split and Mr Goldstone's eventual sacking. (23.9.83)

Neil Huddart, aged eight, travelled to Derby with his family last weekend to compete in the British BMX bike riding championships. He came out top, winning a gold-coloured helmet and a trophy almost as tall as himself. Neil lives in Grassfield Avenue and attends Grecian Street School. His brother Mark also competes in the sport. (23.9.83)

One of Salford's newest attractions is the Leaning Tower of Ordsall, the old grain silo on the Docks. Demolition work started in May on the seventy-year-old structure, which is proving a tough nut to crack. At the moment it is leaning over as though it has had a good night in the Broadway pub! (23.9.83)

A 125-year-old vertical engine from a Salford mill is to be given a new lease of life. It is of a type first developed in the 1840s to drive overhead line shafting in small workshops and, after being used in a mill at Crumpsall for many years, was transferred to the works of J Martin & Sons, Weaste Road South, in 1960. Two years later the owners, Simplex Circulume Ltd, presented it to Buile Hill Mining Museum, and it was later loaned to the North Western Museum of Science and Industry. Now restored, the engine will be one of the attractions in an exhibition at the Museum of Science and Industry which opens today. (23.9.83)

The Wallness Tavern in Wallness Lane reopened on Wednesday after refurbishment. The pub has been taken over by Salford University Students' Union, who hope to be able to knock at least 2p per pint off the beer price. The Wallness will also be one of the few Tetley pubs in the area to sell Walker's real ales. (30.9.83)

October 1983

The church of St George with St Barnabas celebrated its 125th anniversary this week. The church was built on land given by J P Fitzgerald and the present minister, the Reverend B Sagar, is only the twelfth incumbent since St George's was consecrated on 2 October 1858. In 1886 one of his predecessors, the Reverend S Rees, was responsible for installing the clock which is now retained in the new Church School. During the Second World War there were 250 people in the crypt when a bomb came through the roof, smashing glass and damaging the organ. More recently, one of Salford's most famous sons, Albert Finney, was baptised there. (7.10.83)

The Ambassador Cinema, photographed in 1984 when it was being used for bingo

Thirteen threatened jobs at the Salford car manufacturing company, Salamander, will not be lost after all, as the company has been taken over by Sandbach-based PK Manufacturing. Since 1981 PK has been making a two-seater runabout called the Jimp, and some work could be transferred to Salford. (28.10.83)

Eccles-based Frank Evans, Britain's only professional matador, wants bullfights to be staged at the "Plaza de Toros", Salford's Willows Rugby stadium. Frank, known in Spain as El Ingles, reckons he could pack 20,000 into the Willows without any trouble. The amazing idea was given the thumbs up by the Chairman of Salford Rugby Club, John Wilkinson, who said that they would have to look at the damage it might cause the turf. "But we live in an age when we've got to look at every way of making money and I would give this serious consideration," he said. (28.10.83)

November 1983

Plans to open up a stretch of the Duke of Bridgewater's largely eighteenth century underground canal system to the public have been dropped. The 52-mile system of underground canals was used to bring coal from the mines and, by means of the surface canal, direct to surrounding towns. Inspections by Salford Council and the National Coal Board ruled that the exercise would be unsafe because of a build-up of noxious gases. (4.11.83)

Langworthy Rugby Club will open its new headquarters and social club at Bank Lane, the Height, tonight. (4.11.83)

A "pop-in" police sub-station on Trafford Road, Ordsall, is to reopen

after being closed for two years. If successful, it will open twenty-four hours a day until a new, purpose-built sub-station is completed on Salford Precinct. It will be the only sub-station in the inner city . (11.11.83)

Following proposals by Eccles matador Frank Evans to bring bullfighting to Salford, and also to Belle Vue, the Home Office warned this week that bullfighting is illegal in Britain. (11.11.83)

This week saw a wedding which must be some sort of a record. Ninety-nine-year-old Jane Murphy and eighty-nine-year-old George Brearley were married at Swinton Registry Office. The couple live at Unwin Court, Pendleton. (18.11.83)

The future of Knolls House, the historic building on Bury New Road, will be finally settled in the New Year. Owned by Robinson's, furniture removers, the house has been vandalised and empty for some time and has recently suffered from fire. Salford Council wants to pull it down, but local preservationists have called for a public inquiry. (18.11.83)

The Narrow Boat, Salford's newest pub, opened on the East Lancashire Road, Swinton, last week. (25.11.83)

The Cross Keys, the oldest pub in Eccles, has been refurbished and reopens on 1 December. (25.11.83)

December 1983

The Rock House pub in Peel Green Road, Barton, was reopened last Friday after a £75,000 refit. (9.12.83)

The old projector, slide projector and spotlight from the Ambassador Cinema on Langworthy Road have been acquired, along with other

equipment, by the North West Cinema Preservation Society. The Society has been allocated space in the Museum of Science & Industry in Manchester to recreate a cinema of the 1950s. (9.12.83)

On 30 November Tom Bergin retired from the Salford City Reporter, which he joined way back in 1929. In the course of his time with the paper he has been a journalist, editor and sports editor. (9.12.83)

Today saw the official opening of the first four show apartments at the new development by Barratt Homes of the old Ordsall flats at the corner of Regent Road and Ordsall Lane. The new flats will be sold to first-time buyers at prices ranging from £13,950 to £19,750. (23.12.83)

1984

January 1984

The death occurred at Christmas of Mrs Marjorie Goodwin, aged 81, the former head of the giant Cussons soap and toiletries firm. The daughter of the company's founder Alexander Tom Cussons, Mrs Goodwin became president in the 1960s, retiring as a director in 1978. She also once played hockey for England. (6.1.84)

The Grove Inn, Bury New Road, reopened on Thursday 22 December after a £160,000 facelift which included removal of the top floor. (6.1.84)

Local residents are angry about plans to dump low-level radioactive waste at Lumns Lane tip. (13.1.84)

After fifty-two years in Salford, George Glass is closing down. The firm will continue trading from its shop in Cheetham, Manchester. (20.1.84)

A £10 million offer has been made for the defunct Cable Division of Ward & Goldstone, with the promise of 200 new jobs. The offer is from R & D Holdings Ltd and would involve the sale of Ward & Goldstone's Orchard Street factory and the transfer there of machinery from their Lissadel Street and Cheltenham Street factories. (27.1.84)

February 1984

Ward & Goldstone have decided to sell off machinery to a consortium of cable makers instead of the company which offered £10 million for their building and plant. As a result, the offer to buy has been dropped. (3.2.84)

The former Three Crowns on King Street reopened last night as "Buskers", a Whitbread theme pub. After two months' closure the traditional layout has gone and the inside has been transformed into a street scene with lamp posts, pillar box and other relics of the past. (17.2.84)

The Three Crowns, King Street, before it became Buskers

The massive grain silo on the Docks is still leaning over drunkenly. It has resisted three attempts to dynamite it and is yielding slowly to the iron ball. (17.2.84)

The latest dance craze is "break dancing" or "body popping", and quite a few youngsters have taken to doing displays in public. One group from Kersal, who have named themselves "Street Justice", can be seen performing on Salford Precinct and other venues in the city. The dancing involves much-contorted hand and leg movements, head spinning and other acrobatics demanding a high level of fitness. The only equipment needed is a mobile tape player and a good-sized piece of oilcloth. (17.2.84)

The Carlton Cinema closed at the end of January for urgent heating repairs, and seems unlikely to reopen. The last films shown were "Never Say Never Again" at Studio 1 and "Revenge of the Ninja" and "Enter the Ninja" at Studio 2. (24.2.84)

Swinton's eighty-year-old public swimming baths in Swinton Hall Road are to be demolished after gale force winds caused extensive damage which would cost more than £100,000 to repair. (24.2.84)

March 1984

Karate champion Bev Morris has just completed a hat trick of wins at middleweight in the European Championships. She notched up her latest victory in Rome. Bev is a member of the Broughton Kenyukai Club, lives in Walkden and trains at Ordsall Sports Centre. (9.3.84)

This year is the centenary of Salford Harriers. The club was formed in the

Swinton Baths on Swinton Hall Road

long-since-demolished Grapes Hotel on Cross Lane. (23.3.84)

Salford's 51-32 defeat at Hull Kingston Rovers sentenced them to second division Rugby again next season. (23.3.84)

Christine Hall of St Simon Street has just won the title of Miss European Bodybuilder, 1984. The competition was held in Holland. (30.3.84)

April 1984

The Manchester Ship Canal Company has announced that it is to close the canal between Runcorn and Salford within three years because the waterway has no commercial future. (13.4.84)

Salford Council has approved the sale, for £180,000, of the thirty homes for firemen behind the old fire station on the Crescent. The houses will be redeveloped by Barratts and then sold. (13.4.84)

Beau Furnishers, the last retail shop on Regent Road, closed its doors on Saturday after twelve years in the premises. All that is left is the Post Office, which is due to shut in the summer, when the whole row of elegant buildings will be demolished. (13.4.84)

A £70,000 refurbishment has been carried out at the Weaste Hotel, to create a Victorian atmosphere. (27.4.84)

The new £21 million development at Hope Hospital will receive its first patients on 8 May. (27.4.84)

May 1984

The premises of the Lancashire Refrigeration Company on the corner of New Bailey Street and Chapel Street

are to be knocked down. Salford Council was to buy them for offices, but has withdrawn after finding the building is structurally dangerous. (4.5.84)

Stowell Technical Park, part of the Eccles New Road Enterprise Zone, opened on Wednesday. (11.5.84)

Jim Thorpe of Buile Hill Drive, Salford's top snooker referee, took charge at the Crucible, Sheffield, last week in the World Final between Steve Davis and Jimmy White. (18.5.84)

Salford's new Mayor, Councillor Mrs Joan Bryans, took office in the traditional ceremony at the Civic Centre last week. (25.5.84)

June 1984

One of Salford's most familiar landmarks, the twelve-storey tower block wedged between the Library & Art Gallery and the Peel Building is to be demolished. The building houses the chemistry departments of Salford University. (1.6.84)

A new police section station was opened last Monday on Broadwalk, Salford Precinct. (1.6.84)

Jane Brearley, formerly Murphy, who married last November at the age of 99, celebrates her 100th birthday on Monday 25 June. (22.6.84)

A new record for the colliery was created at Agecroft last week, when 9,035 tonnes of coal were produced from one face. A Coal Board spokesman said, "It is achievements like this that will carve out a secure future for British Coal." (22.6.84)

July 1984

A replica of Sir Francis Drake's ship, the Golden Hind, docked at Salford on Monday. (6.7.84)

Sorbus Close Community Centre will be officially opened today by the Mayor, Councillor J Bryans. (20.7.84)

Hoping for a place in the Guinness Book of Records, members of Agecroft Rowing Club will next month attempt to row the length of Loch Ness in a time less than the current record of 2 hours, 35 minutes, 38 seconds. (27.7.84)

It was announced at last week's Council meeting that Salford will make a bid for the 1994 Commonwealth Games. (27.7.84)

August 1984

Conservationists have won a battle over the future of Knolls House on Bury New Road. It was announced on Tuesday that Environment Secretary Patrick Jenkin had refused permission to demolish the house, a Grade II listed building. (3.8.84)

The National Children's Home in Back Duncan Street will close in September after only six years. The closure may only be temporary, however. (3.8.84)

Swinton Rugby Club makes history on 22 August by becoming the first team to play League newcomers Mansfield at Station Road. (3.8.84)

The Regent Road Post Office has closed three weeks ahead of schedule because of vandalism. (10.8.84)

Salford's oldest resident, Mrs Sarah Halligan, celebrated her 106th birthday on Monday by singing some of her favourite songs. (10.8.84)

Pat Seed, who has raised three-and-a-half million pounds for Christie's Hospital over the last few years, has died from the illness that she fought against so bravely. The original target of her "One in a Million" campaign was one-and-a-half million pounds for a new body scanner. (10.8.84)

Just back from the Los Angeles Olympic Games are Salford's bronze medal winners, Neil Eckersley (Judo) and David Mercer (Weight Lifting). Both lads come from Walkden and live near each other. At a recent Council meeting the Mayor of Salford recognised their achievements, along with the outstanding success of Michael Kenny of Swinton, who won five individual gold medals and one silver medal as a member of the swimming relay team at the recently held Paraplegic Olympics in Stoke Mandeville. (14.8.84)

The site of the former Seedley Bleach Works is in demand again. The Royal British Legion Housing Association have applied for planning permission to build flats, wardens' houses and communal facilities there. (24.8.84)

September 1984

The Wallness Ultrasonic Unit at Pendlebury Children's Hospital was officially opened yesterday. (7.9.84)

Tonight customers at the Racecourse Hotel, Littleton Road, will be able to see the results of alterations costing £200,000. The vault has remained open throughout the work, which has involved refurbishing the pub in a "Country Manor" style, complete with a "men only" snooker room, a baby grand piano and ornate fireplace. (7.9.84)

The Grosvenor Hotel on Great Clowes Street has been refurbished as a theme pub and has had its name changed to the Hanky Park Hotel. (9.9.84)

Forty rafts took part in the Salford Raft Race on Saturday. The course began at Adelphi Weir and ended at the Mark Addy pub. (14.9.84)

A company which still holds salmon fishing rights for a stretch of the River Irwell celebrates its 200th anniversary this year. David Bentley Ltd, which makes calender bowls, occupies its original site on the river bank in Greengate, and within living memory the premises contained a cottage which was there in the seventeenth century, when there were outbreaks of plague in the district. The present Chairman and Managing Director, Mr Robert Oliver, is directly related to the founder. (14.9.84)

Once again Swinton Rugby Club's team has been the first to play a League newcomer. Sunday's fixture with Swinton was the inaugural match for Bridgend, apart from a brief introduction to the code some forty years ago. (14.9.84)

In the final round of the Cheshire League, Salford Mets male athletics team made history by becoming the first club ever to retain the championship. (21.9.84)

Back Roman Road, Higher Broughton, was split into two this month when a prohibition of driving order came into

Making calender bowls at David Bentley's (from their 150th anniversary booklet, produced in 1934)

force. Now the City Council has decided to rename the north section of the road, for 45 metres from Great Cheetham Street East, Leybourne Mews, after a former street in the area. (28.9.84)

October 1984

The three "Dale" houses - Ennerdale, Patterdale and Langdale - in the 25-year-old Regent Road flats are to be demolished in 1985. It is said that demolition will cost only £40,000, but £1.5 million would be required to make them habitable again. (12.10.84)

The Leaning Tower of Ordsall has finally been toppled. It took the specialist firm of demolition contractors, P P O'Connor & Sons, more than a year to demolish the 185-foot former grain silo. (12.10.84)

The Keystone pub on Salford Shopping Precinct has been refurbished to a 1940s theme and will reopen on Tuesday 16 October. (12.10.84)

The Salford Law Centre at 498 Liverpool Street will be officially opened today. (26.10.84)

The world famous folk music group, the Spinners, will play at De La Salle College, Pendleton, on 2 November as part of the college's Diamond Jubilee celebrations. This will be a homecoming for Mick Groves, guitarist with the group. Mick was born in Broughton and attended De La Salle, leaving in 1955. (26.10.84)

Water workers laying a new sewer along Irwell Street have found an old burial ground. Assorted bones have been unearthed by a mechanical digger while removing a hundred-year-old sewer. (26.10.84)

November 1984

Salford councillors have reacted angrily to a decision by the Secretary of State for the Environment to allow dumping of low-level radioactive waste on the Lumns Lane tip. (2.11.84)

The City Council has begun formal moves to bring the 1994 Commonwealth Games to Salford, and already a 70-acre site in Ordsall has been earmarked for a sports complex. (9.11.84)

Langworthy Rugby Club celebrates its 50th anniversary this month. (30.11.84)

December 1984

Two men were killed when a passenger train and a freight train collided at Weaste on Tuesday 4 December. The last major disaster in Salford was the Silk Street explosion two years ago. (7.12.84)

Work started this week on a £6 million, four-star hotel in Salford's former dockland. The four-storey, 330-bed hotel will be ready by summer 1986. (21.12.84)

Salford girl Linda Wray, who had a life-saving heart and lung transplant at Harefield Hospital, Middlesex, last month, came home for Christmas last week. (21.12.84)

Another Salford business has given way to roadworks. After almost thirty years Mary and Ernst Baierl have had to stop serving bacon butties and traditional workmen's breakfasts at Mary's Café on Greengate. (28.12.84)

1985

January 1985

Salford opened its first Carr-Gomm home on Friday in Wellington Road, Eccles. The Carr-Gomm Society's aim is to provide accommodation for single, lonely people of all ages. (25.1.85)

Salford's Mayoral badge is being replaced at a cost of £1,668.95. The old Salford City chain and badge bearing the 1857 coat of arms was stolen fourteen months ago from the Mayor's Parlour in the Town Hall, and since then the Eccles chain and badge have been worn by the Mayor at civic functions. The new badge will be in the form of a pendant bearing the new coat of arms, dating from 1974. It will be designed by Thomas Fattorini Ltd and the cost will be met from the insurance payment received after the loss of the old chain. (25.1.85)

The black Daimler Mayoral car, which has served six mayors, is to be traded in for a Ford Granada Ghia. The official number plate, "RJ 1", will be transferred to the new car. (25.1.85)

February 1985

Salford & Manchester Licensed Victuallers' Association has voted narrowly to extend opening hours during the week. On 6 February the Association will apply to the Brewster Sessions at Eccles Magistrates' Court for drinking to be permitted until 11.00pm every night except Sunday. (1.2.85)

A house on Seedley Road, Seedley, which was occupied by students from Salford University, collapsed almost without warning. Noticing cracks appearing, floorboards creaking and his bedroom starting to sink, one of the occupiers, who was cooking his tea at the time, ran back in to turn off the gas just before the building fell down. (8.2.85)

Local businessman Richard Everton is to spend £2 million developing the site of the former Adelphi Convent School. The plans include a riverside pub and restaurant, prestige offices, a conference centre, dance and television studios, saunas and a squash centre. (15.2.85)

The former Globe pub on Regent Road reopened after refurbishment as the Park Royal. The official ceremony on Thursday 14 April was performed by comedian Jim Bowen, although the pub has been open unofficially for four weeks. (15.2.85)

Newens', the bakers and confectioners on Liverpool Street, celebrate sixty years of trading in the city this week. (22.2.85)

March 1985

Salford magistrates turned down the recent application to extend drinking hours to 11.00pm every night except Sunday. (8.3.85)

A Salford nursing sister who was first at the scene of the Weaste train crash in December has won a national award for bravery. Christine Grimshaw (29) received her Daily Star gold award in recognition of the "outstanding courage" she displayed in helping victims of the tragedy, which eventually claimed three lives. (8.3.85)

Salford referee Neil Midgeley has been given the honour of officiating at the Milk Cup Final at Wembley between Sunderland and Norwich on 24 March. (8.3.85)

The Old Priory Tavern, Priory Grove, Broughton is to undergo further extensions, including a new glass conservatory room and a pets' corner, with rabbits, goat, donkey and many other family attractions. The pub closed on 5 November and reopened at the end of December after a £190,000 facelift, which gave it an "olde worlde" look with panelling and bric à brac. (29.3.85)

April 1985

Carpetworld on Regent Road opens at 10.00am on Saturday 6 April. The official opening ceremony will be on Sunday 7 April and there will be two days of entertainment and fun, starring Ken Dodd. (5.4.85)

Cable television may be on its way to Salford. The Government's Cable Authority has given permission for tests to be carried out in Walkden and Little Hulton, and a pilot scheme could start later this year. (12.4.85)

Swinton Rugby Club beat Salford by 9 points to 5 in the Easter Monday Derby game, ensuring a return to Division One next season. Swinton need two more points to take the title of Second Division Champions. (12.4.85)

After three years of preparation, the Salford Women's Centre opens at the end of April. The centre is in a Rowan Close maisonette, where two flats have been knocked into one. (19.4.85)

Swinton have clinched the Second Division Championship by beating Bramley 18-10. (19.4.85)

Salford's pioneering Salamander Car Company has gone bust. Saved from the scrap heap only two years ago by a merger with a Cheshire firm, it was put into liquidation on Wednesday 17 April. (26.4.85)

Despite the efforts of an action group and many appeals against the tipping of low-level radioactive waste at Lumns Lane, Mr William Waldegrave, Parliamentary Under-Secretary of State for the Environment, has refused to rule against the practice. (26.4.85)

Pupils at Ordsall Primary School

Salford Rugby Club will join neighbours Swinton in the First Division, after clinching promotion by beating Wakefield Trinity 16-15.
(26.4.85)

May 1985

Heron Court, a new development of forty flats on Eccles Old Road, was officially opened last week by Lord Barnett of Heywood and Royton.
(3.5.85)

Brand Packaging in Langley Road South is to close its factory, with the loss of 234 jobs. The firm, which has been in Salford for the last fifty years, employed 1,000 in its heyday. (17.5.85)

Salford's new Mayor is Councillor Fred Brockbank. His wife Phyllis is the Mayoress. (17.5.85)

The Duchess of Westminster opened the new £500,000 screening laboratory at Pendlebury Children's Hospital on Friday 17 May. The laboratory will help to detect and prevent mental retardation in children. (24.5.85)

The Salford Men's Handball team has reached the final of the British Cup by beating East Kilbride 14-13 in the semi-final. Salford will meet Brentwood Handball Club from London. The Salford Ladies' Handball Club has been invited to represent England in Nigeria in September. (31.5.85)

The City Council has announced that Irlam Shopping Centre will be demolished and new shops provided on Liverpool Road and elsewhere. Empty ground will also be used for recreation and more houses will be built. A major part of the redevelopment concerns the

Northbank Industrial Estate, the site of the former British Steel Works, which closed in the 1970s. (31.5.85)

June 1985

The Salford Men's Handball team was beaten 20-14 by Brentwood in the British Cup Final. (14.6.85)

Jane Brearley, who lives in Unwin Court with her 90-year-old husband George, was 101 years old on Tuesday 25 June. (28.6.85)

Salford City Council has banned animal circuses from performing anywhere in the city . (28.6.85)

A record 109 crews entered the 99th Agecroft Rowing Regatta this month.
(28.6.85)

July 1985

The old horse tram terminus on the corner of Bury New Road and Knoll Street is to be demolished. Although it is a Grade II listed building, it is in such a bad state that it would take £1 million to repair. (5.7.85)

Ordsall Primary School celebrates its 100th anniversary this year. Former pupils include Allan Clarke and Graham Nash from the Hollies pop group, broadcaster and journalist Alistair Cooke and former "Busby babe" Eddie Colman. Sadly, the school in Stoneway, which once had 600 pupils but now has around 150, is to close in December. (12.7.85)

Agecroft Rowing Club won a bronze medal in the Queen Mother's Cup, for four scullers, at Henley Regatta. They were beaten by the No.1 seeds, the National Squad, in the semi-finals.
(19.7.85)

The Agecroft Regatta in the old days

L Rhodes & Sons Ltd, who have been baking in Salford for almost sixty years, have opened new premises at Russell Road and at Eccles New Road.
(19.7.85)

£20,000 has been spent on the Egerton Arms, Gore Street, which now has a steak-bar restaurant with a late licence. The hotel reopens on 22 July. (19.7.85)

Salford's Linda Wray was the first "double transplant" patient to take part in the Transplant Games at Edinburgh. Linda began the three-day event in grand style by winning the table tennis crown. She also took part in other activities, including darts. (26.7.85)

August 1985

The Salford Raft Race took place last Saturday, 27 July, and although it rained all day, there were plenty of entries and lots of spectators. (2.8.85)

The Townsend Road stand at Swinton Rugby Club will be demolished in the next few days. (2.8.85)

Salford's Bev Morris, a four-times European champion, won the World Middleweight Karate crown at the weekend. In the heats at Crystal Palace, London, she beat a Chinese girl, then the reigning World Middleweight champion (a Japanese), then a Finn, to reach the final, in which she beat an American. (2.8.85)

Salford's Grand Old Lady, Mrs Sarah Halligan, celebrated her 107th birthday on Tuesday 6 August. (9.8.85)

The Manchester All Stars American Football team, who have completed a season at Swinton's Station Road Rugby ground, have opened negotiations to play on Salford's Rugby ground in 1986. (9.8.85)

Robinson's Removals Ltd have sold Knolls House on Bury New Road to Mr Fred Fielder for just £18.22p. Fred lived the first twenty-two years of his life only two doors away from the building and now hopes to restore it to its former glory. (16.8.85)

September 1985

The Prince of Wales on Oldfield Road has reopened as a free house after being refurbished. The new licensees are Dave and Jenny Brightman. Part of the pub used to be an undertaker's and was incorporated into the Prince of Wales during a previous refurbishment in the 1960s. (6.9.85)

A Salford company in which more than £1 million was invested in 1983 is to close down, with the loss of 500 jobs. Venesta International Packaging in Langley Road, Pendleton, will lay off 385 by Christmas and the remaining 112 will go next year. (13.9.85)

Of the three high rise blocks of flats on Regent Road which are being demolished, Patterdale has almost gone and Ennerdale is next. (13.9.85)

History has caught up with the Rex Cinema on Chapel Street. The building was originally the English Presbyterian Church, which had a spire almost as high as St John's Cathedral when it opened in October 1847. It became a cinema in 1912, when it was known as the Salford Cinema and also "Raymond's New Home of Entertainment". The name was changed to the Rex in 1938 and by 1967 the cinema had become a bingo hall. Now it has gone full circle, with the decision by Salford Council to allow the Victory Chapel New Life Fellowship to turn it back into a church. (13.9.85)

The Old Veteran pub, Weaste, is surrounded by fencing and is in the process of being refurbished and extended. (13.9.85)

Frank Foo Foo Lamarr, the popular drag artiste, is interested in taking over the old London & North Western Hotel on Cross Lane. (20.9.85)

The Langworthy Hotel, Langworthy Road, reopened on Thursday 12 September after a £200,000 refit. (20.9.85)

October 1985

Wakefield's snooker and leisure club on Fitzwarren Street opened on Tuesday 1 October. The club has been created through a £200,000 refurbishment of the former bakery, and has nineteen snooker and eight pool tables. (4.10.85)

Following the first ever American Football match at the Willows (between Manchester All Stars and Leeds Cougars on Sunday 22 September), Salford have said no to the All Stars playing at the Willows on a permanent basis, because the pitch was cut up badly. (4.10.85)

The old Carlton Cinema on Cross Lane has reopened as the Carlton snooker and leisure club, with fifteen tables and a full darts exhibition area. (11.10.85)

Carl Allen furnishings has just opened on Langworthy Road. (18.10.85)

November 1985

The Mark Addy bridge over the River Irwell, which had been closed because the old stone steps had been vandalised, is being renovated by Greater Manchester Council, with a ramp replacing the steps. (1.11.85)

Salford Council has accepted a £1 million bid for the Langworthy Estate. The offer by Regalian Properties for the estate off Eccles New Road, plus two neighbouring blocks of flats, Chadesworth and Shoresworth Houses, provides for the refurbishment of the flats, which are now derelict. (1.11.85)

The leader of Salford Council is to make a passionate plea to the Home Secretary to give back the day-to-day policing of the city. Councillor Les Hough is recommending that, when the Greater Manchester Council is abolished in April 1986, each of the ten Metropolitan Districts should handle its own policing. (8.11.85)

Salford cabaret group "Lemon Tree" will perform at the famous London Palladium on Sunday 10 November. They are among the sixteen acts selected from more than two thousand entries for a national talent contest, to be introduced by magician Paul Daniels. (8.11.85)

The unique bond between Salford and the Royal Regiment of Fusiliers was strengthened on Sunday when a freedom parade was held in the city. It was the first time that the soldiers had exercised their Freedom of the City since the privilege was granted in 1975. The occasion coincided with the rededication of the colours, now laid up in Sacred Trinity Church, of six battalions of the former Lancashire Fusiliers, the 1/7th and 1/8th (laid up in 1957) and the 15th, 16th, 19th and 20th, which comprised the famous Salford Brigade during the First World War. (8.11.85)

Former Salford Harrier Frank Handley died last week on his 75th birthday. Mr Handley, of Gore Crescent, Weaste, gained a silver medal in the Empire Games before the Second World War, and said that one of his greatest memories was meeting the legendary Jesse Owens at the Berlin Olympics in 1936. (8.11.85)

The Accident and Emergency Department at Salford Royal Hospital is to be closed any day now; all its services will be transferred to Hope Hospital. (15.11.85)

The lake at Light Oaks Park has been dredged and cleared of all its rubbish, and this weekend the summer-house will be painted. All the work is being carried out voluntarily by local residents, who want to see the park restored to its former glory. (29.11.85)

A unique record of Salford's past has been presented to the city by local historian Frank Mullineux. Hundreds of photographs, prints and glass negatives taken by Worsley man Samuel Lawrence Coulthurst late last century are now with the city's Archive Department in Irlam. (29.11.85)

December 1985

The bell of the historic clock which Worsley residents campaigned to save has been stolen from a Council store. The "Lady Bourke" clock, which struck thirteen instead of one, was part of the National Coal Board offices in Bridgewater Road, Walkden, before they were demolished several years ago. (13.12.85)

The former London & North Western pub (the Norwest) has reopened as "The End". (20.12.85)

Venesta International Packaging (formerly UMP), of Langley Road, closed down on Friday 20 December. (27.12.85)

1986

January 1986

Salford's Grand Old Lady, Mrs Sarah Halligan, died just before Christmas. She celebrated her 107th birthday on Tuesday 6 August last year. (3.1.86)

Langworthy Library, next to the Langworthy Estate flats, Eccles New Road, is to close in March. (3.1.86)

The Grosvenor Hotel, Great Clowes Street

Sixteen-year-old Denis Betts of Eddystone Close, Pendleton, has been selected to play for the Great Britain Under-16s Rugby team during its tour of France at Easter. Denis is an all-round sportsman and recently signed schoolboy soccer forms with Manchester United. (24.1.86)

Weaste bus depot on Eccles New Road closed on Sunday night, as part of a cost-cutting exercise by Greater Manchester Transport. The depot was built in 1929 to house both trams and buses, and the old tram lines are still visible at the side and back of the building. (31.1.86)

The former Salford Fire Station on the Crescent is to be renamed Vulcan House. A photographic exhibition is to be housed in part of the building. (31.1.86)

The Lowry Hotel on Langley Road has reopened after a refit. (31.1.86)

February 1986

Australian Rugby star Neil Baker flies home to Sydney on Sunday, two weeks earlier than expected after suffering a cracked thumb. In his nineteen games for Salford Rugby Club he scored 11 tries and 11 goals, plus 7 drop goals. He will certainly be missed by most supporters for his entertaining play. (14.2.86)

An application to allow Salford's public houses to stay open until 11.00pm on every weekday evening has been turned down for a second time by the city's licensing justices. (14.2.86)

It is hoped that work being carried out on the banks of the Irwell in Ordsall, part of a £1 million improvement scheme, may reveal the site of Woden's Den, thought to have been

destroyed in the last century. There is an authenticated description of the cave dating from 1780. If any traces of the Den are found, the Council will call in the archaeologists. (14.2.86)

In a meeting held at Pendlebury Miners' Club on Sunday, Salford's miners voted to stay with the National Union of Mineworkers and not to join the breakaway Union of Democratic Mineworkers. (14.2.86)

Salford's Bev Morris, World Karate Champion and four times European Champion, has decided to retire while she is at the top. (21.2.86)

On the occasion of her 103rd birthday Mrs Sarah Wigmore, a resident of Ivy Court, was visited by the Mayor and Mayoress of Salford, Councillor and Mrs Fred Brockbank. (28.2.86)

After being closed for more than a year for a £160,000 facelift, the Old Veteran pub on Eccles New Road reopened last night. (28.2.86)

March 1986

A fire in St John the Evangelist Church, Higher Broughton, on Friday night caused £25,000 worth of damage to the building, which was consecrated in 1839. (7.3.86)

Glass merchants Anders & Co of Liverpool Street have moved to Frederick Road to make way for the new Windsor Rail Link. (7.3.86)

Salford Rugby Club Chairman John Wilkinson has been on a fact-finding trip to West Germany to study artificial turf. (7.3.86)

The Salford & Manchester University Boat Race takes place on the Irwell tomorrow after an 11-year gap. The 3,000 metre course starts at Mark Addy's Bridge and finishes at the Mark Addy pub. (28.3.86)

The Broughton Hotel, Great Cheetham Street East

April 1986

The threatened closure of the upper reaches of the Manchester Ship Canal will not now take effect. The city's policy committee has been told that the canal will remain navigable as far as Salford, which will allow naval vessels and tall sailing ships to visit the city as tourist attractions as well as encouraging the development of leisure facilities in the Salford Quays project. (11.4.86)

The Grosvenor Hotel on Great Clowes Street, which had its name changed to the Hanky Park after a major refurbishment, has reopened again as the Grosvenor, after another major refurbishment to change it back. (18.4.86)

Miss Jean Pearson, headmistress of Pendleton High School for Girls from 1949-73 and principal when the school became Pendleton College until her retirement in 1979, has died at her home near Bristol. (18.4.86)

May 1986

After a gap of nearly forty years, the Salford Sunday Football League Lowther Shield has returned to the Willows. The final was played between Dukes and Moonraker, Dukes winning 2-1. (2.5.86)

Because of Rugby League's opposition to artificial turf, Salford Rugby Club's plan to build a £750,000 Super Stadium with an artificial pitch has been put on hold. (2.5.86)

After a major refit costing £120,000, the Royal ("Widow's Rest") on Eccles New Road is open again. (16.5.86)

A 76-foot long ocean-going ketch weighing 45 tonnes was launched at No.6 Dock on Monday morning. The vessel, the Greater Manchester Challenge, has been built by local unemployed teenagers under the supervision of naval architects. The boat will be officially named in June and handed over to the Ocean Youth Club, Britain's largest sail training organisation. (23.5.86)

Councillor Thomas Hobbs was invested as Mayor last week. (30.5.86)

A plan to build a £10 million shopping centre as big as Salford Precinct on the old Ward & Goldstone factory site at Orchard Street has been turned down by Salford Council. (30.5.86)

June 1986

Plans to build a "mini fishing village" at Salford Quays were unveiled on Tuesday. The scheme, named Merchant's Landing, will be built over the next two years and will consist of detached, semi-detached and terraced houses. It is the first residential project to be confirmed at the Quays. (6.6.86)

The Broughton pub on Great Cheetham Street, Higher Broughton, has just reopened after a complete refurbishment. (6.6.86)

The Swan public house on Eccles New Road has reopened after extensive refurbishment. (13.6.86)

Agecroft Rowing Club, celebrating its 125th anniversary this year, will launch the 100th Regatta tomorrow. (13.6.86)

Two Roman Catholic High Schools in Salford are to amalgamate. St Lawrence's on Weaste Lane and Cathedral High on Middlewood Street will join on the old St Lawrence School site and be renamed Our Lady of Mount Carmel. Cathedral High, which was formed from a merger of Adelphi House and Sacred Heart in 1977, is to close. (20.6.86)

An archaeological team is investigating a plot of land on Greengate, the site of the former Bulls Head Inn, which was pulled down in the 1930s. So far a few bottles, coins and pieces of pottery have been found. (20.6.86)

Salford's world-class Tug-of-War team collected a hat-trick of titles at the national championships on Saturday. The Kilroe team, based at the Unicorn Hotel, Lower Broughton, successfully defended their 720-kg and catchweight classes, won last year, and then went one better by adding the 680-kg crown. (27.6.86)

July 1986

Salford's most famous bride, Mrs Jane Brearley, is 102 years old. Her husband George is 91 and they were married in November 1983. (4.7.86)

There was a fire at the Salford Quays site on Monday in which the new £125,000 visitors' centre was burned down. (11.7.86)

Salford's 220 listed buildings are to

have their pictures taken. The Council will pay two students from Manchester University's School of Architecture to carry out a photographic survey and assess the condition of the buildings. (11.7.86)

The Lowry's ladies' darts team have had a bad season - they only won 35 trophies. Last year they won 43, in their first season in the Broughton 801 League. (18.7.86)

August 1986

Salford's annual Raft Race took place on the Irwell last Saturday. Twenty-eight crews took part, all in some form of fancy dress, hoping to raise £4,000 for charity. The race was won by the Titanic. (1.8.86)

Brothers David and Ronnie Mack are to close their tailoring business in Great Cheetham Street East, Broughton, and retire. Both men are in their seventies. The firm was started by their father Max in 1914. Ronnie, a master tailor, has worked there for 62 years and David, who looks after the book-keeping and buying side of the business, for 58 years. (15.8.86)

Angry parents are campaigning for the old Ordsall Board School to be pulled down. The school has been closed since Christmas and is becoming a dangerous playground for children. (29.8.86)

September 1986

The old Hyde Park Corner pub on Silk Street is to be demolished and a new one built in its place. (5.9.86)

The first season of the Salford & Eccles Quiz League has finished with Pendleton British Legion coming out on top, after losing only one of their fourteen contests. The League was set up, and is organised, by Mr Colin Roberts. (19.9.86)

The new Wellington pub on Regent Road opened yesterday. (26.9.86)

October 1986

A fire last Friday morning severely damaged the Spinners Arms on Oldfield Road. (3.10.86)

The new banqueting suite at the Carlton snooker and leisure centre on Cross Lane is now open. (17.10.86)

A public enquiry is to be held into plans to close the only working dock in Salford. The City Council wants to incorporate No.9 Dock into a water sports facility as part of the Salford Quays development. (17.10.86)

The biggest change to bus services for fifty years took place on Sunday. The service was deregulated, thus allowing private companies to compete with each other. This meant buses of all colours and sizes plying the normal routes. (31.10.86)

It was the end of an era on Saturday night when the last bus made its way into Salford's only remaining depot at Frederick Road, which is closing after 85 years of being home to trams and buses. The oldest Greater Manchester Transport bus on the last No.26 service of the day was driven into the depot at midnight by driver Terry Stevens, followed by a parade of seven vintage buses. (31.10.86)

A Salford man who ran for England in the 1924 Olympics and was a club captain of Salford Harriers died last week at the age of eighty-four. Mr Bill Nelson, formerly of Grange Street, Pendleton, was the oldest member of Salford Harriers and over the years won many medals for mile and half-mile distances. (31.10.86)

November 1986

Salford is to make a bid to house the Working Class Movement Library, which has more than 15,000 items. The Council wants to transfer the collection, put together by Eddie and Ruth Frow, to the former nurses' home on the Crescent. (7.11.86)

Broughton's new Olympic Wrestling Academy, off Great Clowes Street, was officially opened on Monday by Olympic runner Sebastian Coe. The purpose-built centre houses a sports hall measuring 45 metres by 18 metres, with seating for almost 1,000 spectators. (12.11.86)

The new eight-screen Cannon Multiplex Cinema on Salford Quays opened yesterday. The first films showing are "The Mission", "Labyrinth", "Cinderella", "Otello", "Howard", "War and Love", "Top Gun" and "Thérèse", with "Cinderella" and "Trans Formers" also showing at Nos. 4 and 6 at afternoon matinées. (19.11.86)

The last piece of Salford's Enterprise Zone land "went public" on Friday,

Mack Brothers' shop, photographed in the 1970s

with the launch of the Metroplex Business Park. (28.11.86)

1987

January 1987

A motorised push-bike capable of more than 20mph, and which can return 300 miles to the gallon, has been developed at Salford University. The bike was unveiled in September by University lecturers Dr Martin Tatnall and Dr David Myring, but so far there has been no interest from British companies because it is thought that British crash helmet legislation would deter potential customers. The bike has a 21cc motor which is fitted below the saddle, and can be converted from an ordinary cycle into a motor cycle at the flick of a switch. (2.1.87)

The Salford City Reporter, founded in 1879, will cease publication on 30 January. However, its name will live on. The Salford City Reporter and Advertiser will be launched on Thursday 5 February as a free newspaper. (9.1.87)

February 1987

Salford's licensing magistrates have announced an extra half hour's drinking time. From 2 March pubs in the city will be able to serve until 11.00pm every night except Sunday. (12.2.87)

Salford now has its own graffiti hit-squad. Ten of the city's long-term unemployed have joined the battle against the paint-spray gangs, in an attempt to clean up the streets. (19.2.87)

Mrs Sarah Wigmore of Ivy Court

Home for the Elderly, George Street, is 104 years old today. (26.2.87)

To meet local education cuts, either Langworthy Road Primary School or Halton Bank Primary is to be axed. Each school is campaigning to be the one left open. (26.2.87)

Parents in Pendlebury are clinging to a fragile hope that they can save their local high school from closure. They are contesting a ruling by the Education Secretary that Pendlebury High School should close instead of rival Wardley High School. (26.2.87)

Parents, teachers and governors of St John's Ellesmere Church of England School, Algernon Road, Walkden, are adamant that their school should not be closed in a bid to cut surplus pupil places. (26.2.87)

There are objections to the proposed name for the new hotel at Salford Quays. Councillor Joe Holt says that the name, "Copthorne Manchester" is a huge snub for Salford. (26.2.87)

March 1987

Irwell Valley High School and Broughton High School are to amalgamate, to become the new L S Lowry High School. (5.3.87)

The bridge which carries the Crescent over the south bank of the Irwell loop is cracking up and could cost £2 million to repair. It was built as part of the road-widening scheme in 1964. (5.3.87)

The Co-op store in Eccles is to close at the end of March, with a loss of 22 jobs. (5.3.87)

Fifteen-year-old Alison Howard, who is a member of the Salford Gymnastics Club, has been invited to compete in the Moscow News Tournament, where

she will rub shoulders with the world's greatest. She will also compete in a top match in Leningrad.

Alison has just clinched the British Schools' title, representing the North West. She took first place and also won a gold medal in the floor exercises. (5.3.87)

Salford actor Joe Gladwin, famed for the voice-over in the Hovis bread advertisements and for his part in "Last of the Summer Wine", has died. His funeral service was held at St Anne's Church, Crumpsall and afterwards at Wardley Cemetery. Joe was born in Salford and educated at Mount Carmel Roman Catholic School. His other notable screen appearances were in "Nearest and Dearest" as Stan the Pickler and in the film "Charlie Bubbles" with fellow Salfordian Albert Finney. (19.3.87)

The Carlton snooker centre on Cross Lane is to have live music from new and established local groups. The new venue, to be called "The Function" will open on Friday 3 April with band The Parade and singer C C Davies. (19.3.87)

Salford now has a branch of the Green Party. It was founded just after Christmas and has 21 members, who plan to spend the first year making their views widely known. (19.3.87)

St Paul's Church, Moor Lane, Kersal, which was ravaged by fire in January, needs £1 million to repair the damage. (26.3.87)

The recent exodus of Ladywell Estate tenants has meant that the Ladywell Community Centre is empty most nights of the week. Salford Social Services Department, who own and run the centre, are anxious that its facilities should be used. (26.3.87)

Next Tuesday marks the 40th anniversary of the running of Salford's last tram. The vehicle - Number 350 - gave forty-five years' service to the city. Its final journey took place on 31 March 1947 as the service No.70, leaving Ordsall Lane terminus at 10.38pm and arriving at the depot at 11.05pm. After this it was used to tow all the remaining Salford trams to the Hyde Road depot in Manchester, where they were scrapped. Tram No.350 was itself scrapped two months later. (26.3.87)

April 1987

An up-to-date security system has been installed in Thorn and Spruce Courts in Salford Precinct. It involves closed circuit television, a door lock and intercom system and a security guard. Tenants says that the new measures have meant less vandalism, cleaner lifts, stairs and passages, and even carpets and plants in the foyer. (2.4.87)

Following the announcement of plans by Salford Council to pull down a

The root of the problem: widening the Crescent in 1964

block of houses in Nadine Street, Seedley, residents are to get up a petition against the move. (9.4.87)

Millionaire Richard Branson will drop into Irlam at the beginning of May, wearing his "Clean Up Britain" campaign hat. He will be here to open the Irlam Linear Park - a major local project to brighten up and restore land around a derelict branch of the Manchester-Liverpool railway line. (16.4.87)

St George's Church, Charlestown, is to be knocked down. The church has been lying empty since October, and the effect of vandalism on the building has forced the decision to demolish it. (23.4.87)

Salford's win against Bradford on Tuesday night ensured that the Reds will stay in the First Division next season. Swinton, unbeaten at home this season, are already assured of their promotion to the First Division. (23.4.87)

Work is to start soon on the renovation of Kersal Cell. AUK Investments will begin development by the middle of May. (30.4 87)

The Nags Head in Irlam has reopened following a £50,000 refurbishment by Whitbread. (30.4.87)

May 1987

Lark Hill Place, the Victorian street at Salford's Art Gallery and Museum, has had a new sound system installed. Visitors will now be able to hear horse-drawn vehicles, clogs, factory hooters, church bells, a knocker-up, trams and many other sounds that recreate the atmosphere of a bygone age. (7.5.87)

A prehistoric settlement dating back to 1,000BC may lie hidden under a Salford farm. An aerial photograph of the field at Great Woolden Hall Farm in Cadishead shows areas where crop growth has been stunted because of buried features. As a result, the site has been excavated by the Greater Manchester Archaeological Unit's Salford Heritage project. (7.5.87)

The curate of St Paul's Church, Kersal Moor, has criticised talk of demolition and has pledged to save the building, which was consecrated in 1852, and see it restored to its former glory. (14.5.87)

Granada were filming in Salford this week to create a scene for a new thriller, "Game, Set and Match", which is about the exchange of spies from East to West. The film was shot mainly on location in Mexico and West Germany, but it proved impossible to film inside East Germany, so they turned a little corner of Salford - the car park at the side of Salford Station - into "Checkpoint Charlie" on the border. (14.5.87)

The new Salford Crescent rail station opened to the public this week. The line between Brindleheath junction and Agecroft junction closed last Saturday. Construction of the new station is still under way and is expected to be completed by October. (14.5.87)

A scheme to transform Salford's Art Gallery into a Lowry Heritage Centre got Government approval last week. This means that work on the first part of the project can go ahead in time for the Lowry Centenary Festival in October. The entire project will cost £480,000, of which 75 per cent will come from the Government. (14.5.87)

Salford's new Mayor is Councillor Charlie Schofield. (14.5.87)

The first phase of the Metroplex Business Park in Salford's Enterprise Zone was unveiled on Tuesday. It is expected to provide 300 jobs, rising to 1,500 when the scheme is complete. (21.5.87)

The bulldozers are ready to move in on the remaining Dales Flats area of Ordsall. The last business, the National Westminster Bank, moved to Chapel Street recently and now only the shells of the buildings stand awaiting demolition. (21.5.87)

The city's brand new Probation Centre on Redwood Street, Brindleheath, was officially opened last week. The centre takes over from the old Police Street building. (21.5.87)

Swinton Rugby Club rounded off a good season by winning the Second Division Premiership final at Old Trafford. Swinton are already runners up in the Second Division Championship. (21.5.87)

June 1987

Eleven blocks of flats on the Sutton Estate, Eccles Old Road, are likely to be demolished. The Sutton Trust plans to replace the flats with semi-detached or terraced houses. (4.6.87)

The new £14 million business park on Salford Quays, Waterfront 2000, was officially opened on Monday by radio and television presenter Brian Redhead. (4.6.87)

The new Novotel at Worsley will open next Sunday. (4.6.87)

Among the forty-four entries in the River Irwell annual Raft Race last Saturday were a World War Two fighter plane (the winner), a Viking longboat and Starship Enterprise. (11.6.87)

The Copthorne Hotel, Salford Quays, was officially opened this week by the Mayor of Salford, Councillor Charlie Schofield. The opening has created around 100 jobs. (25.6.87)

A collection of 5,000 books left to the city in 1949 has been discovered gathering dust in Pendlebury Public Hall. The Hall is to be demolished and the Council has now to decide what to do with the collection, which was acquired following the death of Dr Ghosh, an anaesthetist at Salford Royal Hospital between 1916 and 1948. (25.6.87)

Scott Camm of Worsley, who last month won the 68kg British Wrestling Championship, is competing for his country in the Grand Prix of Austria, which takes place in Linz tomorrow, 26 June. In August he will be representing Britain in the World Espoir Wrestling Championships in Canada. (25.6.87)

July 1987

Addisons, a new free house, has opened in renovated premises on Liverpool Road, Eccles. (2.7.87)

The spire of St George's Church rising above old housing in Charlestown

Bergin Court in Summerville Road, Irlams o'th'Height, was opened last week by Tom Bergin, former editor of the Salford Reporter, who lived in the area for most of his life. (16.7.87)

Salford College of Technology is to run a full-time BA degree course in Band Musicianship. It is thought to be the only such degree in the world. (23.7.87)

August 1987

Salford has won a top award in the Beautiful Britain in Bloom competition, the Commercial Effort Trophy. It was given for achievement in sprucing up the stretch of the city along the Crescent. (13.8.87)

The annual two-day Salford Show celebrates its 21st birthday this year and will be held as usual in Buile Hill High School grounds. (13.8.87)

Helen Brown, who has been a member of Salford's Green Party since it was launched in February, will stand as their first ever Council candidate in the forthcoming Pendleton by-election. (20.8.87)

September 1987

Salford's oldest resident, Mrs Sarah Wigmore, has died at the age of 104. She spent her last years at Ivy Court Home for the Elderly, George Street. (3.9.87)

The Salford Jets, who are getting together for a tenth anniversary concert at the Willows, will shortly re-release their most successful single, "Who You Looking At?" (3.9.87)

Valentine's Disco has opened in the Rialto Buildings, Great Cheetham Street West. (3.9.87)

In a joint venture between Wimpey Homes and Salford City Council, the 285 run-down flats at Ladywell are to be refurbished, to create 144 flats for sale and 141 for rent. The development will be called Canterbury Gardens. (3.9.87)

Whitbread are to close the former Threlfall-Chesters Brewery next May, with the loss of 132 jobs. (17.9.87)

Al Read, the Salford-born comedian, has died at the age of 78. He was born in Broughton, where his family had a sausage and cooked meats business. His biggest success on the radio was his "Such is Life" show, in which he was known for his catchphrase, "Right, monkey". (17.9.87)

Deputy Mayor, Councillor Joe Holt, is to take over as Mayor for six months, following the untimely death of Mayor Charlie Schofield while still in office. (24.9.87)

October 1987

Salford now has its own Labour History Library. The immense book collection of Ruth and Edmund Frow has been installed in Jubilee House, where it can be viewed by the public. The Frows, who live in a flat at the library, have been given the Frank Mullineux Award for their contribution to local history. (1.10.87)

The disused Park Manager's house in Buile Hill Park is to be converted into a £500,000 day care rehabilitation centre for drug addicts. The conversion should be complete by October and is being funded with a £407,000 grant from the European Community. (1.10.87)

The 5,000-book collection bequeathed to the city by the late Dr Jotindranath Ghosh is to be sold off. (1.10.87)

The derelict Irlam Shopping Centre is to be developed to create either private houses or a new shopping complex. (22.10.87)

The new Elmwood Church in Eccles Old Road has just been completed and members will move in next week. The £500,000 needed to build the church was raised by the 220 attenders in just five years. They have been in their present home, Eccles Evangelical Church on Half Edge Lane, for a quarter of a century; before that, the building belonged to Eccles Quakers, who moved out to take over their new Quakers' Meeting House at the Polygon, Wellington Road. (29.10.87)

DIAL, Salford's Disabled Advice Line, has moved house. It is now based in the Guild Hall, Guild Avenue, Walkden, in offices donated by the Council. (29.10.87)

November 1987

Last Tuesday, Princess Anne visited Pendlebury Children's Hospital. Then on Friday the Duchess of York came to Salford. During her visit she opened Carr-Gomm House in Gore Avenue and went on to open officially the L S Lowry Centenary Exhibition at the City Art Gallery. (5.11.87)

The old Langworthy Estate flats on Eccles New Road have been refurbished and are ready for people to move in. The development is now called St James' Park. (5.11.87)

The Church of the Nazarene, Great Clowes Street, Broughton, is to be demolished next month and a new church built to replace it. (19.11 87)

December 1987

Monday 21 December sees the opening of the Bell Tower Hotel, formerly the Angel Hotel, Chapel Street, after major refurbishment. (17.12.87)

1988

January 1988

The Lowry High School was officially opened last week by Salford artist Harold Riley, who presented his own painting of L S Lowry to the school. (14.1.88)

Wheelie bins are to be introduced to the city's refuse collection system as a cost-cutting measure. Fifty jobs will be lost as a result. (28.1.88)

February 1988

Work is going ahead on the widening of Regent Road Bridge over the Irwell, and the giant, pre-cast, arched beams that will support it are being made on the roundabout next to the Stowell spire. (4.2.88)

Coronation Street is to get a facelift - not the one on TV, but the real one, off Regent Road. The thirty-eight houses on the Barracks Estate street have been sold to the Pendleton Improved Housing Association, who will

The Duchess of York, in Salford for the Lowry Festival, 29 October 1987

renovate them for sale to first-time buyers. (4.2.88)

The eight-foot-high wall which shielded Salford Docks from the public gaze for so many years has been pulled down to reveal the new development at Salford Quays. (4.2.88)

The porter's lodge at Ladywell Hospital was knocked down last week. The site will be landscaped to create a smarter entrance to the hospital. (18.2.88)

Two of Salford's old red telephone boxes have been Grade II listed. One is outside the police station on the Crescent, the other in Worsley village, on the bridge over the Bridgewater Canal, and both are of the 1935 design by Sir Giles Gilbert Scott. (18.2.88)

A Salford couple who put down a reservation on a plot, expecting to buy a £55,000 house on Salford Quays were gazumped to the tune of more than £12,000. The house has been sold for an alleged £80,000. (18.2.88)

Cuts facing Salford's Health Service amount to some £727,000 and could mean the closure of Salford Royal Hospital. (18.2.88)

A new, speedy bus service, the M10, came into operation on 20 February, running every ten minutes between 7.00am and 7.00pm Monday to Saturday. The route is from the Brookhouse Estate to Manchester via Peel Green, Eccles, Pendleton and Lower Broughton. (25.2.88)

March 1988

The lych-gate at St Peter's Church, Swinton, a listed building, is being taken down, but will be re-erected a few feet back from its current position. The gate, built in 1920, commemorates those who lost their lives in the Great War and stands on soil brought back from Flanders. (10.3.88)

Last Friday, 4 March, the Mayor of Salford, Councillor Joe Holt, officially opened Canterbury Gardens, the new luxury homes created out of the old Ladywell Flats estate. (10.3.88)

Holy Angels Church of England, Moorfield Road, Irlams o'th'Height, which was only built in 1928, is facing the threat of demolition because £125,000 is needed for roof and brickwork repairs. (24.3.88)

The Keystone pub on Salford Shopping Precinct has reopened after being refurbished. (24.3.88)

Many of the blocks of flats in the Trinity area of Salford are in the process of demolition, as part of the £20 million improvement scheme in which flats and houses are being demolished, refurbished or converted. (24.3.88)

This weekend the newly-refurbished Sea Princess, a 42-foot, 55-seat passenger boat, starts operating its service between Salford Quays and the Mark Addy pub. This isn't the first time passenger boats have come up the Irwell: in the early years of the Ship Canal, passengers were carried from near Victoria Bridge to the Docks and there were pleasure trips on the river from the beginning of the nineteenth century. (31.3.88)

The Manchester & Salford University Boat Race near Albert Bridge

Some of the books bequeathed to the city by the late Dr Ghosh were sold in London last week, when 400 books from the city's museums raised £53,000 at auction. (31.3.88)

April 1988

Human remains have been unearthed during road works at Gore Street, just off Chapel Street. They are from the former burial ground of the Swedenborgian New Jerusalem Chapel, built in 1813, and it is believed that at least 2,000 bodies were buried there over fifty years. The site is being screened off while experts remove the remains for re-burial. (7.4.88)

The former Dawson Street Council depot in Swinton is to be converted into a workshop for the handicapped. (14.4.88)

The 550-ton, 80-year-old swing bridge which once took rail traffic over the Ship Canal was moved from its old position behind the cinema on Salford Quays and floated round on pontoons to be re-sited over No.9 Dock. It will eventually be opened as a pedestrian walkway. A film which was made of the event can be viewed at the Heritage Centre, Salford Quays. (14.4.88)

Last week three Salford lads just messing about on the river discovered a 6lb pike trapped in a shopping trolley. A sure sign that life is coming back to the Irwell! (28.4.88)

May 1988

Last Monday saw the annual Varsity Boat Race between Salford and Manchester, and for the first time in eighteen years Salford won the main race, the men's coxed eights. (5.5.88)

Salford Council has approved a plan to bring the new wheelie bins to the whole of the city. 66,000 bins will be bought on an operational lease system. (19.5.88)

Councillor Joe Holt, who took over as Mayor last October following the death of Mayor Charlie Schofield in September, was sworn in last week at the beginning of his true year of office. (26.5.88)

The Robin Hood pub at Clifton reopened last week following its conversion to a steakhouse. (26.5.88)

The Blue Bell at Monton Green has been converted to a Chef & Brewer Steakhouse. (26.5.88)

June 1988

Included in the City of Manchester's bid for the 1996 Olympic Games is a proposal to put the main stadium in Salford, on the site of the old Weaste sand quarry next to Ladywell Flats. The Olympic village accommodation would be in Worsley. (2.6.88)

A light aircraft crash-landed on the

M62 at Eccles, causing havoc on the motorway last Tuesday. (9.6.88)

In a Lancashire & Cheshire League cricket match between Swinton and Bollington last weekend, Swinton pace bowlers Simon Radcliffe and Jimmy McGuinness each scored a hat-trick. Radcliffe, who also plays football for Norwich City, took his with the last ball of one over and the first two balls of the next; his partner McGuinness completed his with three balls in the 17th over. (9.6.88)

Lollipop lady Hilda Dixon received the BEM in the Queen's Birthday Honours. She already has a gold medal awarded by Salford Council in recognition of her 23 years of duty, guiding children to safety in Liverpool Road, Irlam.

Two other Salford citizens received the MBE: Mrs Pauline Armitage of Worsley for services to adult and youth education, and Mr Gordon Trevett of Monton for his thirty-six years in the Greater Manchester Police vehicle workshops. (16.6.88)

It was the Great Salford Raft Race again last weekend. Fifty-six rafts took part in the eighth Irwell charity race. (23.6.88)

Salford's Lowry Centenary Festival was Britain's Arts success of 1987 and may result in a profit of as much as £18,000. (23.6.88)

Patients at Pendlebury Children's Hospital will be able to benefit from revolutionary ear surgery pioneered in Sweden. The technique for implanting a bone-anchored hearing aid was brought to Pendlebury by Mr Mike Rothera, the surgeon who will carry out the operations. (23.6.88)

Jane Brearley of Unwin Court, Fitzwarren Street, celebrated her 104th birthday this week. Jane married her third husband when she was 99, but sadly he died last year. (30.6.88)

Six old railway arches off Irwell Street have been transformed into business units. (30.6.88)

July 1988

The newly refurbished houses on Coronation Street, off Regent Road (not the one on TV) were officially opened last week by "Jack Duckworth" of "Coronation Street" (the one on TV), and already the thirty-eight houses have been snapped up at around £20,000 each. (7.7.88)

The new Salford University Business Park on Frederick Road was officially opened last week by the Mayor, Councillor Joe Holt. (7.7.88)

Salford Council is seeking permission to demolish the former chapel in Agecroft Cemetery; the building has stood unused for the past twenty years. (7.7.88)

Residents in Clifton, Pendlebury and Wardley say the new wheelie bin system is excellent. (14.7.88)

After twenty-six years the Metal Box Company's factory on Eccles New Road is to close, with the loss of 69 jobs. (21.7.88)

The Salford firm Insul-8 has won a £2.1 million contract to supply overhead conductors for the Channel Tunnel project. This will increase the company's turnover by half and create more jobs. (28.7.88)

One of Eccles' longest-serving hairdressers, Jack Pritchard, is to retire from his shop in Mather Road after fifty-three years in the business. (28.7.88)

The old Threlfall's brewery on Cook Street has been given Grade II listed building status. Brewing ceased there two months ago. (28.7.88)

August 1988

Furniture Store ELS shut down their Salford shop on Sunday. The store in Great Clowes Street was the company's oldest site. (11.8.88)

Salford Lads' Club on Oxford Street has been featured on the latest pop video of the group The Smiths, "The Queen is Dead". As a result, Smiths' fans have been turning up at the door, assuming that the group has some connection with the club. (11.8.88)

One of Britain's newest trade unions has opened its Regional Headquarters in Salford. Manufacturing, Science & Finance, formed when ASTMS and TASS merged this year, has its North West base in Acton Square. (18.8.88)

The human remains unearthed as a result of the Gore Street/Irwell Street road works were re-buried at Agecroft Cemetery this week. (25.8.88)

A new pub is being built on the site of the old Moorside farm at Swinton. When completed, it will take the name of the farm. (25.8.88)

Eccles-based paint company England, Hughes & Bell has closed down and axed 48 jobs. (25.8.88)

September 1988

The Druids pub on Silk Street is to be converted into a youth centre to replace the closed Peter Green Recreation Centre. The brewers, Banks's, have given up the site in exchange for a piece of land on Eccles New Road near the Stowell church spire, where they are to build a new pub. (1.9.88)

Salford lad Julian Ballantyne is fronting the new ITV Saturday morning show, "Motor Mouth". (8.9.88)

The old Custom House on Trafford Road is in the way of a road-widening scheme, but because the 85-year-old building is listed, it may have to be taken down and rebuilt, or even jacked up and moved up to twelve metres further back. (15.9.88)

The first of the ear implant operations by surgeon Mike Rothera will go ahead next month at Pendlebury Children's Hospital. The operation is possible ahead of schedule because of an amazing fund-raising effort by Mrs Kath Smith, who quickly raised £18,000 for the equipment. (22.9.88)

A proposal to bring French musical genius Jean Michel Jarre to Salford Quays for an outdoor extravaganza laser show has been turned down as it is thought that Salford could not handle the traffic and the Quays are not yet large enough to cope. (22.9.88)

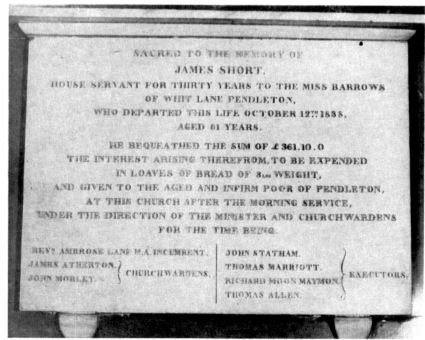

Memorial tablet to James Short at St Thomas's Church, Pendleton

Just 150 years ago a Mr James Short left a legacy of £361 to St Thomas's Church, Pendleton, to buy bread for the poor. The custom of giving out 3lb loaves after Sunday morning service stopped some years ago and now the church is using the rest of the money to stage an exhibition to celebrate two hundred years of its history and to raise more funds for charity. (29.9.88)

October 1988

L S Lowry's old house on Station Road, Pendlebury, is up for sale at £49,950. (6.10.88)

The new Adelphi Riverside pub overlooking the Irwell opened on Thursday 29 September. (6.10.88)

Workers at the Royal Ordnance Factory, Patricroft, were stunned on Friday 7 October, when it was announced that the entire plant will close by Spring 1990 and 1,200 jobs will go. (13.10.88)

Mr Edwin (Ted) Cole, clerk to the distributors of Booth's Charities, is to retire at the end of the month, after sixteen years in charge of the day-to-day running of 450 flats and the distribution of pensions to over 15,000 elderly Salford people every fortnight. The charity has been paying pensions to the elderly since 1630 and is one of the oldest surviving institutions of its kind in the North West. (13.10.88)

The Boundary Stone, a new pub on Bridgewater Road, Mosley Common, opened today. It stands almost on the boundary between the metropolitan districts of Salford and Wigan. (13.10.88)

Kersal Cell will reopen on 1 November as a pub and restaurant, following refurbishment and extensions. (27.10.88)

Salford met Wigan in the final of the Lancashire Cup last Saturday, but failed to bring home the trophy. They were beaten by 22 points to 17. (27.10.88)

November 1988

The old Skin Hospital on Quay Street, Manchester, has closed and a replacement unit has opened at Salford Royal Hospital, Chapel Street. (10.11.88)

Salem Church, Pendleton, is to be converted into an area office for the 4,000 council houses that surround it in the Precinct area. (10.11.88)

Residents at Linnyshaw, Walkden, are angry at Council plans to put a rifle range on the Linnyshaw nature reserve. The Salford Shooting Club's Eccles New Road range was closed down in June 1986 by the army because of poor safety standards. (17.11.88)

The new Moorside Farm pub, built on the site of the old farm at Moorside Road, Swinton, opens tomorrow, Friday 25 November. (24.11.88)

British Coal's plan to create the largest open-cast coal mine in Europe at the Lomax site on the borders of Little Hulton and Walkden have been turned down by Environment Minister Nicholas Ridley. Because of the presence of rare great-crested newts, British Coal will have to submit new plans that will protect the species. (24.11.88)

December 1988

Roe Green residents are fighting plans by a local antique dealer to demolish a 200-year-old cottage in Greenleach Lane and erect detached houses in its place. (1.12.88)

Pendleton College was closed down on Monday following a Legionnaire's disease scare. (8.12.88)

Local antique dealer Mr Michael Zammit has withdrawn his plans to demolish the 200-year-old cottage at Roe Green, following the protest by residents of the area. He now plans to restore it. (8.12.88)

Stowell Memorial School, Holland Street, Ordsall, will be closed for good on 31 December this year. (8.12.88)

Following the introduction of wheelie bins, Salford Council has sold its old-style bin lorries to Trafford Council for £3,500 each. (15.12.88)

After two years of traffic chaos, the widened Barton Bridge was finally reopened last week. (29.12.88)

1989

January 1989

There are plans to build a new road from Eccles into Trafford Park via a bridge over the Ship Canal. The scheme has been on and off the table for over fifty years, most recently in the 1960s when the plan was to provide a link to the East Lancs Road by way of Lancaster Road and Stott Lane. (12.1.89)

The former University chemistry block standing between the Peel Building and the City Museum and Art Gallery may be saved. Plans to demolish it were withdrawn following a suggestion that it could be converted into offices and let to local industries. (12.1.89)

Salford's entry has reached the top 20 in the "It's My City" competition, launched by Prince Charles at the end of last year. Now the judges will decide whether the city is to be placed in the top 12. (19.1.89)

The old Manchester and Salford Skin Hospital in Quay Street has been sold

The library, museum and art gallery overshadowed by the chemistry tower block of the university

for £3.2 million. The building will be developed as luxury offices. (19.1.89)

There are plans to restore the 193-year-old Clifton Aqueduct, which is Grade II listed, so that it will remain for future generations. (19.1.89)

Salford has added another Lowry to the city's collection. The painting "Industrial Heritage", was bought from the firm Kitchens Direct, who have had it in their boardroom since 1982. (19.1.89)

It has been decided that Halton Bank School will close by September 1990, although campaigners have vowed to fight the decision. (26.1.89)

Plans to transform the historic Worsley Old Hall into a gigantic leisure centre are being opposed by local residents. (26.1.89)

Ryan Wilson, son of Swinton Rugby player Danny Wilson, has been called up to train with the England Schoolboys' squad. Ryan, who attends Moorside High School in Swinton, is currently spearheading Salford's determined attempt on the National Schools' Trophy. He is already on the books of Manchester United. (26.1.89)

February 1989

Salford Show, which has been held for twenty-two years, has been axed this year owing to a shortage of organisers. (2.2.89)

There have been reports of ghostly activity at the Diamond XX pub in Patricroft. The weird happenings only started after the pub was given a facelift and a new inn sign was hung outside. The sign is supposed to depict Edward Diamond, the landlord

around 1880. One of the stories about the pub's name is that Edward was illiterate and instead of a signature, he used the mark "XX". (2.2.89)

The historic Packet House at Worsley is up for sale at £285,000, and a canalside cottage built in 1725 is to be converted into offices. (2.2.89)

Summervilles, the new private members' club on Bank Lane, Irlams o'th'Height, is opening on Wednesday 15 February, in premises which used to belong to Langworthy Rugby Club. (9.2.89)

March 1989

Salford Show, reported axed last month, will go ahead after all in August this year. It has been saved by city community group workers John Wallace and Marilyn Flitcroft. (2.3.89)

The former Pendleton Girls' High School is to close this year, but before it does, the school will stage an open day on Thursday 16 March. (2.3.89)

The latest recruits to Salford's Recreation Department are two shire horses, "William" and "Royal". They will be based at Clifton House Farm. (2.3.89)

Sarah, Duchess of York, came to Salford on Friday 10 March to open the new £1 million Skin Hospital. (16.3.89)

The Pier 6 café bar and grill at Salford Quays was officially opened on Wednesday, 8 March, by TV star Victoria Wood. (16.3.89)

Christ Church in Pendlebury Road, Swinton, is to sell its eight bells to St James's Church, Accrington. The money received will go towards the restoration work in progress on the

130-year-old church. The bells, originally installed in 1868, were renovated and rededicated in Christ Church in 1936. (23.3.89)

Most of the tenants have left Clement Attlee House flats in Aylesbury Close, Seedley, and the block could soon be bulldozed. (30.3.89)

Salford Methodist Community Church, Pendleton Way, which was only built twelve years ago, needs repairs to the roof and brickwork which may cost £150,000. (30.3.89)

Two pubs, the Punch Bowl, Chapel Street, Salford and the Queens Arms, Green Lane, Patricroft, have been made listed buildings, in the hope that this will prevent their character from being altered too much in the future.

There has been a pub on the Punch Bowl site at the Booth Street corner of Chapel Street since 1817, and it was once called the Waggon & Horses. The Queens Arms, Patricroft, was built in 1828, around the time that the Manchester/Liverpool Railway was being constructed, and is thought to be the first railway pub in the world. Originally called the Patricroft Tavern, the name was changed to Queens Arms in 1851, when Queen Victoria got off the train there on her way to Worsley. (30.3.89)

April 1989

Salford Council has made a cash award to help rescue Salford Playhouse, the only theatre in the city. The theatre went professional last year, but has failed to attract the interest it had hoped for. (6.4.89)

Barton Airport is up for sale, but it may be bought by the sitting tenants, Lancashire Aero Club. (6.4.89)

The old MFI warehouse on the East Lancashire Road, Worsley, is being converted into a thirty-six-lane bowling alley. The new GX Superbowl will be the largest in the country. (6.4.89)

About 800 Roman coins have recently come into the possession of Salford Council. They were unearthed by Mr Michael Donegan while digging on a Worsley housing site. (13.4.89)

One man was killed and five injured in a massive explosion at the Broughton firm, Featly Products, on Monday. (27.4.89)

A Victorian shop on the corner of Tatton Street, Barracks Estate, is to be saved by the Council, who will spend £60,000 on it rather than see it knocked down. The shop has fine examples of Victorian brickwork. (27.4.89)

May 1989

Salford's old red telephone boxes will be ripped out and replaced with new-style boxes over the next couple of years. The only two left will be those

The Punch Bowl, Chapel Street

which were given listed building status in February last year. (4.5.89)

The former Pendleton Girls' High School, Eccles Old Road, is to be sold for housing development and parts of it may be demolished. However, Summer Hill, the Grade II listed building on the site, will be retained as a feature within the development. Dating back to about 1825, it was once the home of the Agnew family, leading fine art dealers, who entertained many famous people there, including members of the Pre-Raphaelite movement, politicians like Gladstone, and Sir Charles Hallé. (4.5.89)

Swinton Rugby League Club made the finals of the Second Division Premiership at Old Trafford at the weekend, but lost 43-18 to Sheffield Eagles. (18.5.89)

The imposing chimney of Monton Mill, on the canal bank near Monton Green, was toppled in a cloud of dust on Sunday 14 May. Built in 1905, the mill was one of the last to be erected in the area and has dominated the Monton skyline ever since. Local conservationists had hoped to protect the building by getting it listed, but at the appeal stage the Department of the Environment ruled that demolition could go ahead. Soon the mill will follow the chimney to make way for a housing development. (18.5.89)

June 1989

It was announced this week that Eccles is to have a new fire station to replace the old one on Liverpool Road. It has not been decided when the new station will be built. (8.6.89)

Another piece of Salford's heritage is to go under the bulldozer - the Carlton Cinema. Built in 1937, it was the last to be opened in the city, until the new one at Salford Quays, and as well as films had staged a wide range of entertainments and variety shows: anything from the big bands of Teddy

Brown and Henry Hall to Phillip Roma, the world yo-yo champion. During the war the car park was used as an anti-aircraft station. In the 1950s films took pride of place once again, but rock'n'roll was taboo. The film "Rock Around the Clock" was banned and the management commented that if they wanted trouble they could get it any night of the week without looking. Later, the Carlton was used for bingo and then as a snooker hall. (8.6.89)

Thirty-seven rafts took part in the Irwell Raft Race at the weekend. Of the 35 finishers, "Fat Boy 2" was first past the post, with "Viking 89" the winner of the best dressed raft section. Both rafts were from Magnesium Elektron at Swinton. (22.6.89)

Salford's oldest resident, Jane Brearley of Unwin Court, Fitzwarren Street, was 105 years old on Sunday 25 June. (29.6.89)

Swinton Rugby Club is to open its new bar, restaurant, sauna and gymnasium on Wednesday 5 July. (29.6.89)

Salford and Swinton Rugby Clubs are to play for a new trophy in their pre-season matches. The old Hospital Cup has been replaced by the Agecroft Cup, which will be sponsored by British Coal. (29.6.89)

July 1989

Rukaya Bailey, born to mother Joanne on Monday 26 June at Hope Hospital, arrived after just 19 weeks. If she survives, she could be one of the smallest babies in Britain ever to do so. Rukaya is too small to be weighed, but is estimated at 8-10 oz. (6.7.89)

A compromise has been reached in naming the new roads on a housing estate in Swinton. Brackenlea Homes, the developers of the former Acme Mill site, wanted to call them after rock formations in Derbyshire and suggested Peaknaze Close, Bleaklow Close, and Castlenaze Drive, but

Councillor Derek Antrobus thinks that the names should reflect the local history of the area. Old Mill Close, Acme Drive and Peaknaze Close have been adopted. (6.7.89)

This year marks the centenary of the death of one of Salford's greatest sons, James Prescott Joule. The child of a wealthy brewer, he was born in New Bailey Street in 1818. A unit of energy is named after him and he is known to every student of science and engineering as the discoverer of energy conservation. (6.7.89)

The path across the locks at Mode Wheel, for many years used as a short cut by dock workers and others, has been railed off and locked by the Ship Canal Company. This means a long walk or cycle trip for those from the Salford side of the canal who work in Trafford Park. (13.7.89)

The Regent Road improvement scheme, which involved the widening of Regent Road Bridge over the Irwell, is now complete, and the official opening was on Friday 7 July. As a result, the Sportsman pub, formerly the Queens, is now accessible again after being marooned on an island surrounded by roadworks for many months. (13.7.89)

The Oldfield Road / Middlewood Street site of Cathedral High School will close on 23 July after more than twenty years. It opened as Sacred Heart Secondary School in 1965 and became Cathedral High 12 years later. (13.7.89)

After years of controversy and campaigns against the idea, brewers Joseph Holt have finally been given the go-ahead to build a pub on land at the corner of Liverpool Street and Ashley Street in Seedley. (20.7.89)

August 1989

Baby Rukaya Bailey, born prematurely five weeks ago, is making some improvement and has been taken off the critical list. (3.8.89)

A row of shops and maisonettes on Meadowgate Road, Weaste, has been sold by the Council to a developer, for conversion into private flats to be sold on the open market. (3.8.89)

It was the end of an era on Friday, when the last eight dockers employed on the Salford side of the Ship Canal left work for the last time. Bob Ward, Terence Harper and Robert Mould of Ordsall, David Mahon of Clifton, John Smith of Weaste, Newton Currie of Old Trafford, shop steward John Jones and another Salford man who refused to be identified all lost their jobs as a result of the abolition of the Dock Labour Scheme. The men were contracted out from the Manchester Ship Canal Company to Coopers Metals, but when the Scheme ended, Coopers employed their own men. (10.8.89)

Summer Hill, once the home of the Agnew family and later part of Pendleton High School for Girls

The last remaining tenant moved out of Adelphi Court, the derelict tower block of flats in Blackfriars, on Monday 14 August. (17.8.89)

In their pre-season Derby game, Salford were the first winners of the Agecroft Cup, beating Swinton 42-20. Mark Moran of Salford was the first winner of the Peter Smethurst Memorial Trophy for Man of the Match. (24.8.89)

September 1989

A chapter in Salford's sporting history was closed on 28 August, when Matt Marchant died in Ladywell Hospital at the age of 77. He was the youngest of the six Marchant brothers who were kingpins of boxing in Salford in the 1920s and 1930s. The others were Billy, Teddy, Jack, Mark and Albert. (7.9.89)

Newspaper publishers D C Thomson are closing their Chapel Street premises with the loss of 138 jobs. The work will be transferred to the company's more modern Scottish plant. (7.9.89)

The Kennedy Swinton Brass Band has just won the British Open, one of the top contests in their field. Nineteen bands took part in the competition at the Free Trade Hall last Saturday,

The former Co-operative Soap Works in Irlam

including the famous Black Dyke Mills Band. (14.9.89)

Less than a year after developers spent £1 million on converting the ancient Kersal Cell into a trendy pub and restaurant, it has shut. (21.9.89)

Salford Council is to look into the possibility of buying the jinxed Kersal Cell. (28.9.89)

October 1989

The TSB bank in Salford Shopping Centre has reopened after a complete refit. The bank has been operating from portable premises for the last fifteen months. (5.10.89)

The railway bridge between New Bailey Street and Irwell Street is to be given a £200,000 facelift. The Grade II listed bridge, built in 1844 and known as The Colonnade because of its ornate, Egyptian-style, cast iron columns, will be de-scaled, repaired and painted. (5.10.89)

The memorial to the Lancashire Fusiliers who served in the Boer War, which is sited at the corner of Oldfield Road and Chapel Street, is to be cleaned up and re-sited in a more prominent position a little further back. (5.10.89)

A 12ft by 8ft stained glass window which can usually be seen in Eccles Parish Church has been sent to Canterbury for specialist restoration work which will cost £20,000. The window is almost five hundred years old and depicts Jesus's entry into Jerusalem on the first Palm Sunday. It is one of only four pieces of pre-Reformation glass in the Greater Manchester area. (12.10.89)

Alvin Walkden Brass Band have just won the third section of the British National Championship, a victory which they last achieved 33 years ago. Two members, Bill Roscoe and Ken Mather, were in the band last time they won the title. (19.10.89)

Demolition of the Irlam Shopping Centre began on Monday 16 September, following years of campaigning to have it pulled down. When it is cleared, Mulberry Homes

Contractors working at Salford Quays

will build houses on the site. The last business to leave, the TSB, is still open among the rubble, waiting to move into new premises. (19.10.89)

November 1989

The former Co-operative Soap Works in Irlam, which was taken over by the Middleton-based soap company, Robert McBride, is to close in January with the loss of 150 jobs. (2.11.89)

The former Cathedral High School, Middlewood Street, has been bought by Swinton Insurance Company. They plan to demolish it and build a new luxury office block to serve as their headquarters. (16.11.89)

There was a fire at the former Pendleton Girls' High School on Sunday, bringing fears that the building may have to be bulldozed, rather than developed. (16.11.89)

Salford's run-down Clement Attlee flats are to be developed for private sale by the East Anglia company Lodgeday, who bought the block from Salford Council for just £625,000 in May. (16.11.89)

The London & North Western Hotel, Cross Lane, is lying derelict and will soon be knocked down. Built in 1884, it took over the licence from the nearby Railway two years later. (This was not the Railway across the bridge which was demolished in August 1979, but a much older public house of the same name.) The hotel was affectionately known to Salford people for many years as the Norwest, but its decline started when the brewers transformed it into a theme pub and called it that officially. It closed again for refurbishment once or twice, and was finally renamed "The End", which sadly it turned out to be. (23.11.89)

December 1989

Kersal Cell will reopen as a pub this weekend, under the new name "Byroms". (7.12.89)

Rosie O'Grady's American-style diner in Church Road, Eccles, opens this Saturday, 9 December. Work on converting the former Pearson's wine stores and the post office building next door to it has been going on since October, and the Pearson's part of the premises dates back to 1877. (7.12.89)

More than 12,000 fish weighing around 2,000lb have been put into the water at Salford Quays. The water, which is isolated from the main Ship Canal, is now clean enough to sustain fish such as roach, carp, rudd, perch, dace and chub. Fishing will not be allowed for two years. (14.12.89)

Rukaya Bailey, said to be the smallest baby in the world to survive, went home on Monday 18 December. Since she was born nearly six months ago, her weight has increased from an estimated 8-10oz to 7lb 5oz. (21.12.89)

Repair work on Crescent Bridge has finally begun, two years after it was closed. Temporary supports will be put in while workmen repair each of the 23 supports in turn. (28.12.89)

1990

January 1990

At King Street Youth Club, Irlams o'th'Height, prizes for the club's "superstars" competition were presented by Manchester United player and Welsh International Clayton Blackmore. (4.1.90)

Lowry High School and St Patrick's High School have been chosen to take part in a pilot safety scheme. Across the European Community 30,000 lives a year are lost as a result of domestic accidents and the aim is to educate pupils in a bid to cut this figure. The two Salford schools are the only UK representatives on the scheme. (4.1.90)

Salford's Chief Executive Roger Rees has been awarded the OBE in the New Year's Honours list. (4.1.90)

There is discontent in Boothstown over plans to convert the disused Grange Farm, Vicars Hall Lane, into a pub-cum-restaurant. (4.1.90)

Work is to start in February on restoring the lych-gate at St Peter's Church in Swinton. (4.1.90)

Local folk duo Tony Downes and Pete Martin are so fond of Salford that they have named themselves "Hanky Park" after one of the city's more famous areas, and have produced an album of songs called "Chimney Pot Skyline". (11.1.90)

A multi-million-pound scheme to transform the derelict Kersal estate may start this year. The original plans unveiled in October 1988 envisaged the demolition of six of the tower blocks and the estate's community centre and youth club. Now eight of the blocks of flats and two blocks of shops will go. Houses will be built in their place and the remaining blocks of flats will be refurbished. (11.1.90)

The Royal Ordnance Factory at Patricroft is to be closed, and there are now only around 25 workers left on a site which once employed 1,200. However, there is some hope for new jobs with the company Combined Power Systems which is moving to the premises. CPS builds environmentally friendly mini power stations. (11.1.90)

At Salford Quays this week a new Beefeater restaurant, "The Quayside", was opened at the side of one of the old docks, now named Ontario Basin. "Coronation Street" star Johnny Briggs performed the opening ceremony. (11.1.90)

Salford's self-proclaimed poet laureate, Adolf Chip-Pan is bringing his work to local pubs and clubs. Adolf, from Higher Broughton, likes to mix humour, social comment, nonsense and fun in his poems. (25.1.90)

A video rental shop in Langworthy Road has a sign on the door banning dogs and ferrets from the premises. The manageress said that lots of people had come in with ferrets and polecats, which left a bad smell, and that one customer had thrown a ferret at a member of staff after being refused an adult video. (25.1.90)

Oliver's nightclub in Station Road, Swinton, has closed, following complaints by police and residents. (25.1.90)

February 1990

According to a recently-published

Inside Salford House hostel in the 1960s

national report, Salford is the sickest city in Britain. Some 2.5 million prescriptions were issued to cover the city's population of about 250,000, an average of 9.7 per person over the year - the highest in the country. The national average was 7.18. However, at £5.716 the cost per prescription in Salford was lower than the national average of £6.023. (1.2.90)

Independent British Hospitals are to open a new cottage hospital, The Oaklands, in March. Sited immediately opposite Hope Hospital, it will accommodate twenty-eight patients and is said to have facilities on a par with a four-star hotel. (1.2.90)

Sharon Mills of Pendlebury has won a gold medal at the Commonwealth Games in Auckland. Sharon, who used to train at the Monton Judo Club on Carlisle Street in Swinton, beat Canadian Karen Hayde in the final of the middleweight judo competition. (8.2.90)

Two new industrial developments in Pendleton will create jobs for the area. The derelict Orient Mill in Lissadel Street is to be transformed into eleven light industrial units, and there are plans to build new factory and warehouse accommodation on a thirteen-acre site at the junction of Cromwell Road and Broughton Road. (8.2.90)

Figures published in the Times this week show that of all Britain's universities, Salford has produced the fourth highest number of first class honours graduates. Only Cambridge and Oxford, with Bath a close third, achieved more. (8.2.90)

Salford Council is to implement a £100

million plan designed to bring new life to the Chapel Street area. It is hoped that creating a new gateway to the city will increase tourism in this part of Salford, which includes the Lowry Heritage Centre, Salford Cathedral and St Philip's and Sacred Trinity Churches. (8.2.90)

The Social Services Committee has decided that the city's only hostel for elderly men is to close within the next two years. Salford House on Bloom Street was established in 1894. (8.2.90)

Following a review of the city's five Catholic high schools by the Diocesan Commission, two are threatened with closure: Our Lady of Mount Carmel in Weaste and St Ambrose Barlow in Swinton. (8.2.90)

Just a year after staging a come-back, Salford Show is in danger of being dropped again. The Show's organisers claim that Salford Council is not giving the necessary financial support. (15.2.90)

A fire completely destroyed the warehouse of DIB's Do-It-Yourself store in Bute Street on Wednesday 7 February. (15.2.90)

Army ambulances manned by troops and police are operating all over the city following strike action by the regular crews. (22.2.90)

The Sundorbon Restaurant (formerly Mothi Mahal) opens tonight, 22 February, at 40 Liverpool Road, Cadishead. (22.2.90)

Experts have said that unless £8 million is spent on major flood prevention work, it is only a matter of time before the River Irwell bursts its

banks. Up to 2,500 homes could be flooded. (22.2.90)

Another L S Lowry painting to add to the collection at Salford Museum and Art Gallery has been acquired with the help of a grant from the Victoria and Albert Museum. "Bargoed", painted in 1965, is one of only a dozen very large canvases by Lowry and depicts a scene in the South Wales valleys. (22.2.90)

Salford University has awarded a posthumous honorary degree to folk singer Ewan MacColl, who wrote over 300 songs, including "Dirty Old Town", which was inspired by his early life in Salford and "The First Time Ever I Saw Your Face", made famous by Roberta Flack. His many plays were widely acclaimed by the critics and in 1947 George Bernard Shaw remarked, "Apart from myself, MacColl is the only man of genius writing for the theatre in England today." The honour was received by Ewan MacColl's widow, Peggy Seeger. (22.2.90)

March 1990

Two valuable paintings in Salford Art Gallery, "Queen Victoria in Peel Park" by George Hayes and "The Five Wheeled Omnibus" by an unknown artist, were badly scratched by a vandal this week. It will take several months and cost £3,000 to repair them. (1.3.90)

Councillors on the city's Planning Committee have condemned plans to pump oxygen into the River Irwell in an attempt to improve the water quality. They say that there should be stronger curbs on industry putting pollutants into the river in the first place. (1.3.90)

Holy Angels Church, Acresfield Road, Irlams o'th'Height, has been made a listed building, thwarting plans to knock it down, sell the land and build a smaller church nearby. The church is badly in need of an estimated £400,000 worth of repairs. (1.3.90)

Salford City football team have booked their place in the final of the Manchester Premier Cup after a 2-1 win at Chadderton. The final will be played against Curzon at Old Trafford on Wednesday, 2 May. (1.3.90)

Planners have promised to work hand in hand with local residents when they develop the site of the former Pendleton Girls' High School for housing. (8.3.90)

If Canon Michael Arundel gets his way, St Mary's Parish Church, Eccles, will soon be registered as a museum as well. The church has around forty items of historical value, including a pre-Norman cross, two medals from the Battle of Waterloo and a tomb that dates back to Elizabethan times. (8.3.90)

Salford's Area Dean, the Rev Geoff Howard, is to have his book,

Dave Brierley and John Edwards fixing the mural at Broadwalk Library, 1990

"Wheelbarrow across the Sahara", published in June. The book relates his adventures while crossing the Sahara in 1975. He took a Chinese wheelbarrow - made up by an Oxford don from an ancient design - to carry his water and food. (15.3.90)

McDonald's have been given permission to open a new drive-in restaurant and a three-storey North West headquarters at Windsor Bridge, subject to a legally binding agreement that they will be responsible for clearing litter around the site. (15.3.90)

There's an unusual item on the menu at Barton Lane chippy in Eccles - frogs' legs. Owner Gordon Daniels says his time in the trade has taught him to supply whatever the customer wants. (22.3.90)

Salford Rugby League Club will play in the Second Division next season, following a 21-5 defeat by Hull at the Willows on Sunday 18 March. Coach Kevin Tamati, appointed in October, is hopeful that they will soon be able to bounce back to the top flight. (22.3.90)

Three years after the arson attack which caused nearly £1 million worth of damage to St Paul's Church, Kersal, the builders are starting the final phase of the restoration work. The congregation hopes to move back into the church by Easter next year. In the meantime they will continue to use the assembly hall of the nearby primary school for worship. (29.3.90)

The magnificent, 134-year-old gates which have adorned the Royal Ordnance Factory on Green Lane, Patricroft, since 1968, have been dismantled and returned to Woolwich Arsenal. (29.3.90)

April 1990

A new Sainsbury's supermarket opened on Wednesday 4 April at the bottom of Regent Road. It occupies the site of the former flats known locally as The Dales. (5.4.90)

Eccles' award-winning Co-operative Choral Society has disbanded after sixty-five years. In its heyday the society, which recently became known as the United Co-operative Singers, had 120 members and won competitions at music festivals throughout the North West. (5.4.90)

The Farmers Arms, Swinton, has been refurbished at a cost of £200,000 and the Vulcan in Walkden has had a £140,000 facelift. Both are owned by the Boddington Pub Company. (5.4.90)

Salford Council has closed the Brunswick Community Centre on Broad Street, Pendleton, claiming that it was under-used. The closure will save the Council £9,000 a year. (12.4.90)

The eight-storey Clement Attlee House, Salford's first high rise block of flats, has been given a complete refurbishment and renamed Kingsley Court. (26.4.90)

Following a protest by local residents, the city planners have refused an application for Cavendish House in Ellesmere Park to be turned into a Muslim religious centre. (26.4.90)

May 1990

The newly-formed Salford Federation of Anti-Poll Tax Groups want other poll tax protesters to join in their May Day march. The march will start by the old Carlton Cinema on Cross Lane and will end with a public burning of poll tax forms. (3.5.90)

Labour's traditional May Day march in Salford was called off at the last minute after infiltration by members of the Workers' Revolutionary Party. However, when the breakaway group rallied in Seedley Park several people burned their poll tax bills in a gesture of defiance. (10.5.90)

Salford City will have to replay the final of the Manchester Premier Cup after drawing 1-1 against Curzon Ashton at Old Trafford. The replay will be at Droylsden Football Club on the evening of Tuesday 15 May. (10.5.90)

British beef has been banned in schools throughout Salford in response to the "mad cow disease" scare. (24.5.90)

Local people are campaigning against the building of an indoor gun club on land off Summerville Road. Residents of the Duchy Road area are angry that they were only given twenty-four hours' notice of the planning meeting at which the proposal was discussed. (24.5.90)

Salford's new Mayor, Councillor John Smith of Cadishead, was officially sworn in this week. Mayor Sid Turner handed over the chain of office at a ceremony at the Civic Centre on Wednesday. (24.5.90)

Salford Council wants to turn Blackleach Reservoir and the surrounding land into a Country Park, creating a haven for wildlife. However, the Council may have to buy 21 acres of land from British Coal, who wish to build houses on the site at Walkden. Proposals to put up industrial units on land earmarked for a wild flower meadow have already been rejected by the planners. (24.5.90)

The Department of Performing Arts and Media Studies at Salford College of Technology has its own band, made up of three students and three music lecturers. Calling themselves the John Foster Black Dyke Mills Brass Band, they will be starting a tour of Japan next week as part of the Best of British Band Tour. (31.5.90)

Pupils from Windsor High School have taken part in a project to brighten up the area around Salford Precinct. Under the direction of local artist Walter Kershaw, they have completed a 30-foot mural along the outer wall of Broadwalk Library. The mural shows images of Salford. (31.5.90)

A walk along the River Irwell should be much more interesting from now on, following the erection of information

The Star, Greengate, once known as "Pawsey's", after a licensee who was there for many years until 1940. Closed and boarded in 1990, the pub was burnt out by June of that year.

boards at key points along the river bank. They give information about the city's history, telling of the legendary life-saving feats of local hero Mark Addy; of the sinking of the riverboat "Emma", which capsized at its launching with the loss of thirty-eight lives; and describing the prison which once stood on New Bailey Street near the river. (31.5.90)

Television cameras appeared alongside the Irwell on Bank Holiday Monday, and viewers were able to witness the sight of 15,000 plastic ducks plummeting from Agecroft Bridge for a "race" down the river. The event, part of ITV's Telethon 90 appeal, raised £8,000 for charity.

(31.5.90)

June 1990

Elim Pentecostal Church, Liverpool Street, celebrated its fortieth anniversary on the weekend of 9/10 June. The original mission was founded in Seedley Road in 1950 before moving to its present premises.

(14.6.90)

The last shift at Agecroft Colliery

Walter Greenwood Court, Pendleton, has reopened following a £1 million refurbishment. The high rise block, which was built in 1964, was closed in 1988 to be converted into special accommodation for the young, single homeless. (14.6.90)

Vatican ambassador Archbishop Luigi Barbarito came to Salford this week,

visiting Pope John Paul II High School, Britannia Street, and the Diocesan Offices in Gerald Road. (14.6.90)

Nurses dressed up in period costume this week as part of celebrations to mark the centenary of Ladywell Hospital. The foundation stone was laid on 22 May 1890 and the hospital opened on 15 June 1892. (14.6.90)

Miracle baby Rukaya Bailey, too tiny to be weighed when she was born, reached her first birthday this week. Now a healthy 12lb 5oz, she has been recognised as the most premature baby in the world to survive and is to be entered in the Guinness Book of Records. (28.6.90)

Also celebrating this week is Salford's oldest resident, Jane Brearley of Unwin Court, Fitzwarren Street. Jane was 106 years old on Monday 25 June. (28.6.90)

Two Catholic schools threatened with closure, Our Lady of Mount Carmel in Weaste and St Ambrose Barlow in Swinton, have been saved thanks to parent power. It was announced in February that the matter would be subject to public consultation and following talks with parents, governors and staff, the city's Diocesan Schools' Commission agreed on Wednesday 20 June to reverse their decision to close the schools. (28.6.90)

To mark the centenary of Salford Cathedral, the basement under the Cathedral bookshop is being transformed into a day centre. It is hoped that the centre will be in operation by the end of the year.

(28.6.90)

On Saturday 30 June Ruth Crofton will be ordained into the Christian Ministry at Weaste United Reformed Church and made pastor of Weaste and Patricroft churches. It is the first time that the two churches have had a woman minister and the first time they have shared a joint ministry. Mrs Crofton, a widow, was born in Gateshead. (28.6.90)

Civic chiefs have agreed a £50,000 scheme to brighten up the city boundary. A galvanised steel griffin

A photograph taken at Magnesium Elektron in the 1970s

four metres high and bearing the city's coat of arms is to be erected in the works of David Bentley, overlooking Trinity Way on the border between Salford and Manchester. The David Bentley company will contribute £10,000 towards the cost.   (28.6.90)

July 1990

British Coal plans to close down Agecroft Colliery because the pit has not reached production targets and has already lost £1.8 million this year. The 450-strong workforce has been told that there will be no compulsory redundancies. However, the union at Agecroft still has the right to appeal against the decision by asking for a review.   (5.7.90)

Potentially harmful methane gas from the old Lumns Lane tip in Clifton is to be harnessed to produce electricity. The company Landfill Gas Ltd has come up with a plan to extract the gas and convert it into fuel.   (5.7.90)

The Holy Ghost Fathers, a Roman Catholic religious community based in an ordinary house in Leicester Road, Broughton, plan to convert a garage into a chapel to help their work with young people.   (5.7.90)

The Duke of Edinburgh's reign as Chancellor of Salford University is due to end shortly. He has held the position for twenty-three years and has been the only Chancellor so far. The royal connection will continue because Prince Philip's daughter-in-law, Sarah, Duchess of York, will take over in August.   (5.7.90)

Pendleton featherweight boxer John White has made a big hit in the United States. The Americans asked John over after he beat one of Jake Lamotta's boxers in a contest in this country, and he was voted England's best performer in invitation tournaments which took place in New York and Boston. (5.7.90)

Swinton lad Chris Kendrick will be representing Great Britain in the World Free-Style Wrestling Championships which take place in Hungary this month.   (5.7.90)

The world's first degree in pop music was launched in Salford last week. The patron of the course is "the fifth Beatle" George Martin - the man who produced most of the Beatles' number one hits - and he was at Salford College of Technology for the official opening on Wednesday 4 July.
(12.7.90)

With the help of artist Walter Kershaw, pupils at Pope John Paul II High School have painted a 40-foot mural depicting William "Black" Douglas, after whom Douglas Green is named. Douglas gained notoriety locally because of his cruelty to the children who worked in his mill in the late eighteenth and early nineteenth centuries.   (12.7.90)

Agecroft miners have voted to accept the closure of their colliery. Production has ceased and redundancy notices will be received by the 450 workers on Friday, 13 July, although some will stay on to carry out salvage works at the pit. The men were producing between 9,000 and 10,000 tonnes of coal per week, but this fell short of the 13,500 tonnes required.   (12.7.90)

Part of the former No.9 Dock was used last week to unload a cargo of Portuguese timber. It is hoped that the pine timber, which is used for pallet making, will be the first of many loads which will bring new life to the Docks.
(12.7.90)

Salford City Football Club has a new team manager, former Rossendale boss Steve Connaghan. Last season, under manager Dave Russell, the team reached the final of the Manchester Premier Cup, which they lost after a replay.   (12.7.90)

Irlam Town Football Club player Paul Winter has been selected for the under-14 England Squad which will travel to Finland to play in an international tournament at Helsinki. Paul lives in Cadishead and attends Irlam High School.   (12.7.90)

Salford-born actor Robert Powell received an honorary Master of Arts degree from Salford University last week. The award is made to mark his contribution to the world of film, theatre and television. Former Eccles MP Lewis Carter-Jones and Sir Robert Reid, Chairman of British Rail, were among others honoured at the same time.   (19.7.90)

St George's Church in Whit Lane was pulled down two years ago, following

problems with dry rot and vandalism. But now, if the Rev David Knight and his parishioners can raise the cash to refurbish and adapt Charlestown Park Lodge, a new church may be created just thirty yards away from the old site.
(19.7.90)

Salford will lose one of its longest-serving traditional craftsmen next month, when cobbler Bill Heslop shuts his shop in Liverpool Street, Seedley, for the last time. Bill has worked there for thirty-two years, thirty of them as owner of the business. He refused to make concessions to the modern age and entering his shop, with its collection of old sewing machines and hand-crafting tools dotted about, has always been like stepping back in time.
(19.7.90)

An archaeological dig in the grounds of Ordsall Hall is expected to continue for several months. When it is completed, the grounds will be landscaped and restored to look as they did in the seventeenth century.

(19.7.90)

Last week Sainsbury's supermarket on Regent Road had to get in extra supplies to cope with demand from the Rolling Stones. The group was playing at Maine Road football stadium over the weekend and a roadie came to stock up with food, mainly pies and onion bhajis. When he reached the checkout, the bill came to £600.   (26.7.90)

A fire which burned down a third of the main stand at Salford's rugby ground, the Willows, this week is thought to have been caused by children.   (26.7.90)

Halton Bank School, Pendleton, closes its doors for the last time today. The

The Top House, Eccles

school, which stands in a prominent position on Bolton Road, was considered one of the best in Salford, but the site has been earmarked for other uses, including commercial development and housing. Most of the pupils will move to Langworthy Road School. (26.7.90)

The Mayor of Salford, Councillor Jack Smith, has opened a new £15 million chemical plant at Magnesium Elektron Ltd. The company, based in Lumns Lane, Clifton, will now be the world's leading supplier of zirconium, which is a chemical alternative to lead used in paint and a variety of other products. (26.7.90)

August 1990

Salford's Hope Hospital is to be used as the setting for a new Granada Television drama series called "Medics", to be screened later this year. (2.8.90)

The management of National Power have declared that they have no plans to close down Agecroft Power Station, despite the fact that 5,000 jobs are to go throughout the country. Agecroft has already suffered a major blow this year with the loss of more than 400 jobs when British Coal's pit opposite the power station closed. (9.8.90)

Work has begun on a new mini-port at Irlam flanking the site of the former Irlam Steel Works. The Manchester Ship Canal Company is to spend £500,000 on a new quay at the former ore wharf off Liverpool Road. It will be designed to take ships of up to 10,000 tonnes. (9.8.90)

Brewery bosses have promised to restore the façade of the Top House

Hall's Building, one of the oldest in Eccles

pub in Eccles to its former Victorian glory. The original façade was taken down earlier this year, without planning permission. (9.8.90)

A 400-year-old stained glass window showing Christ's entry into Jerusalem was returned to Eccles Parish Church last week, after being away for two years for restoration. The work, which was carried out in Canterbury, is likely to cost £23,000. The window originally came to England from France after the Napoleonic Wars and was formerly in St John's Church, off Deansgate in Manchester. (16.8.90)

Pendleton barber John Wallwork today celebrates fifty years of being a

barber in the same shop on Langworthy Road. John started as an apprentice in the shop at the age of fourteen in 1940 and eventually took over the business in 1972. (16.8.90)

Salford's first poll tax protesters are due to appear in court on Tuesday and Wednesday 4 and 5 September. Meanwhile, Salford Anti Poll Tax Federations are calling on protesters to turn out in force for demonstrations at the courts. (23.8.90)

Plans have been announced for an £8 million scheme to revitalise Eccles town centre. The plan includes the pedestrianisation of Church Street (to be completed by 1993), a new market

A view across the Ship Canal towards the old Irlam Steel Works

and bus station and a new Light Rapid Transport terminal. (23.8.90)

Following a major investigation into housing demands in the city, the Council is to sell or demolish ten of its high rise blocks of flats in the areas of Salford Precinct, Ordsall and Trinity. It is hoped that a buyer will refurbish some as private accommodation, and some of them will be sold to house students. (23.8.90)

If Environment Secretary Chris Patten approves the proposals, a boundary change could see 700 Bolton residents moved into Salford later this year. The plan is to realign the boundary along the natural line of Unity Brook. The present line cuts in half a housing estate at Clifton and it is felt that the residents' needs could be better met if they were all under one council. (23.8.90)

September 1990

More than 150 poll tax demonstrators turned out at Salford Magistrates' Court on Tuesday 4 September to cheer on the 200 people due to appear for not paying their bills. However, only 24 defendants turned up and many cases were heard in the absence of those charged. (6.9.90)

Salford Council plans to demolish

A rare photograph of the Royal Ordnance Factory, Patricroft

Windsor House on the Islington estate for a new service road behind Chapel Street. There are only eight residents left and most of the block is boarded up and vandalised. (13.9.90)

The former Druids Home on Silk Street, which closed as a pub some time ago, has been refurbished and transformed into the new Peter Green Centre, a youth club for youngsters in the Trinity area. This replaces the old Centre, which had to be demolished to make way for road developments. (13.9.90)

Work is to start in January on a multi-million-pound revamp of the Pendleton Shopping Precinct. It will involve the covering over of the malls with glazed panels, attractive porticos and internal canopies and a complete re-tiling of the floor areas. (27.9.90)

A former Salford Grammar School pupil has been promoted to Superintendent in London's Metropolitan Police. Superintendent Paul Cunliffe is the elder son of Detective Superintendent Wilf Cunliffe, who was with Salford City CID. Paul has already spent three years with the Royalty Protection Branch at Buckingham Palace with the rank of Inspector. (27.9.90)

Kersal Festival was held last weekend, when thousands of spectators turned out to see an impressive parade of carnival floats, live entertainment and a guest appearance by racehorse Red Rum. It is hoped that this will be the first of many such festivals. (27.9.90)

The Bowling Green pub on Bolton Road, Pendlebury, has reopened after a complete refurbishment. The pub was opened in 1853 and the original cellar steps still remain. (27.9.90)

October 1990

Salford planning bosses have authorised a £3,500 feasibility study to look into the future of the seventeenth century Hall's Building, a timber-

The lych gate at St Peter's, Swinton, before it was moved back from the traffic which caused its structural problems

framed, black-and-white house behind the shops on Church Street, Eccles. The study is to make sure that renovation is feasible and to suggest possible uses for the building, which is believed to be the second oldest in Eccles. (4.10.90)

Business will soon be booming on the new Northbank Industrial Estate on the former Irlam Steel Works site. As well as the mini-port for the Manchester Ship Canal, there are plans for more than twenty light and medium manufacturing companies to move into the estate, creating jobs for the Irlam area. (4.10.90)

Salford Rugby Club nearly gave world champions Widnes a shock in the Lancashire Cup Final at Wigan on Saturday 29 September. In a closely fought game Salford were in front 18-12 and looked as if they were about to lift the trophy. However, they allowed Widnes to draw level and in the dying minutes Martin Offiah clinched the victory for Widnes with a try which was converted, making the final score 24-18. (4.10.90)

Salford's Arts & Leisure Department has plans to put commemorative plaques on nine of the city's oldest and most important buildings. Among them are two public houses: the Braziers on Hodson Street, Blackfriars, an example of a house-pub dating from 1824 and the Three Crowns (now Buskers) in King Street, where a meeting took place to plan the first Trades Union Congress in 1868. The Salvation Army building in Oldfield Road and the Caxton Hall on Chapel

Street have also been selected and famous Salfordians will be remembered in plaques affixed to their former homes: L S Lowry (Station Road, Pendlebury), Harold Brighouse (Ellesmere Avenue, Eccles), John Byrom (Kersal Cell) and comedian Al Read (Kipling Street). (11.10.90)

Thousands of people watched on Sunday 14 October, as eight of the twelve multi-storey blocks of flats in Kersal were demolished in a spectacular controlled operation. The buildings had been rigged by demolition experts with 6,000 explosive charges, set to detonate just split seconds apart, with the initial blast due to go off at 11.00am. The whole procedure took just a few seconds, as everything went according to plan.

It is thought to have been a world record explosion and the Guinness Book of Records has been approached with a view to having an entry in their book, although no category exists at the moment. The blocks demolished were Burns, Shakespeare, Jonson, Browning and Milton Houses and Keats, Chaucer and John Bacon Courts. (18.10.90)

Beatles producer George Martin was at Salford College of Technology this week to mark the 50th anniversary of John Lennon's birth with presentations of the new John Lennon awards, which are backed by the Performing Rights Society, to outstanding students from the college's popular music and recording courses. The three winning

students were Andrew Greenwood, Paul Spencer and Rory Meredith. (18.10.90)

A competition to name the new pub on the corner of Ashley Street and Liverpool Street, Seedley, first announced in April and organised by brewers Joseph Holt and the Salford Reporter, has been won by local resident Alfred Wharton. The hope was that someone would come up with a name which reflected the local history of the area or recalled a famous local resident, and Mr Wharton has been able to do that. He claims that before the houses were built, a brook ran through the area. It is now culverted under the motorway and can no longer be seen, but the pub has been named the Ashley Brook. (18.10.90)

Residents of Irlams o'th'Height have launched a fight to save two former weavers' cottages which were part of the old Height village. The owners, Agecroft Investments, want to bulldoze the 200-year-old cottages to make way for new developments, but local people are hoping to get a preservation order. (18.10.90)

Salford councillors have criticised the local bus companies for failing to provide transport at Christmas. Under the newly-announced package, buses will operate a skeleton Sunday service on Boxing Day, December 30th and New Year's Day, but there will be no buses at all on Christmas Day. (25.10.90)

A report by Salford Council's new accident investigation and prevention unit says that road accidents in Salford cost the community £27 million last year, and also lists the city's top ten accident blackspots. The number of accidents which were fatal or caused serious injury has dropped, but the overall number of accidents on the city's streets continues to rise, with 1,224 last year. (25.10.90)

Popular Salford publican Walter Wheeler - landlord of the Worsley Hotel in the 1960s and then the Flat Iron (formerly the Royal Hotel) until 1971 - has reason to be proud. His son Peter has just been appointed Assistant Regional Organiser for the Labour Party in the North West. Peter will be based in Warrington. (25.10.90)

November 1990

Mario's Fish Bar in the Eccles Shopping Precinct has been included in a new book, "The Gourmet's Guide to Fish and Chips", which lists the best 500 chippies in the country. The shop is owned by Mario Paphitis, who opened the takeaway back in 1969. It was included not just because of the excellence of the fish and chips, but because of the impressive premises, which have wood-panelled walls and chandeliers hanging from the ceiling. (1.11.90)

One of many Salford pubs demolished in the 1960s and 1970s: the Coomassie Hotel, Hanky Park, photographed in 1968

When officials of Swinton Cricket Club visited the Deansway Road club house on 25 October, they discovered that vandals had broken in, wrecking furniture and stealing what they could find. However, the club house had been closed since the end of the season in September, so there was not much to steal and the club, which is a hundred years old this year, will be able to continue its centenary celebrations as planned. (1.11.90)

The new Green Lane Technology Park on the site of the former Royal Ordnance Factory, Patricroft, was formally opened on Wednesday 31 October. To date, 214 new jobs have been created. (1.11.90)

Pupils from Buile Hill High School were the guests of the respected scientific body The Royal Institution in London last week. The pupils were giving a performance of their play, "James Joule", which has been highly praised for the way it brings together drama and science. The play reflects the life and works of Joule, who was born in Salford and gave his name to the unit of energy. (8.11.90)

Salford Council has won its fight to turn Blackleach Reservoir into a Country Park. Agreement has been reached with British Coal, who wanted to develop the site themselves, but will now sell it to Salford for £300,000. (8.11.90)

Two former Salfordians will be contributing to the success of the rock musical "Grease", which opens at Manchester's Palace Theatre this month. Graham Gill, who lived in Laburnum Street, Seedley, as a youngster and attended De La Salle College, still has family in the area.

Now an actor based in London, Graham will be returning north to play the rôle of Doody, while the show's choreographer will be Salford's own Arlene Philips. (8.11.90)

An invention by Higher Broughton optician Sol Taylor may mean that drivers no longer need to worry about "blind spots". Mr Taylor has just patented the "Mirror Mate", which is clipped on to an existing car wing mirror to give the driver 100% visibility along the side of the vehicle. (15.11.90)

"Beyond the Stethoscope", a report drawn up by Salford's Director of Public Health, Dr Ian Greatorex, reveals that where you live in the city is an indication of whether you will be healthy or not. Statistics collected between 1984 and 1988 covering heart disease, lung cancer, mortality rates and children's birth weights show that Swinton, Worsley and Boothstown are much healthier areas than Little Hulton and inner city areas such as Blackfriars. (15.11.90)

The Phoenix Theatre, off Liverpool Street, reopens with the launch of a new play, "The Hardman", on Tuesday 20 November. The theatre will be run by a group of professional actors on a permanent basis. The last attempt to make a go of the Phoenix failed in February 1988, when a production of "The Tempest" had to fold because the audiences were too small to support it. (15.11.90)

Planners have given the go-ahead to an ambitious scheme for a new marine aquarium in Wilburn Street, Salford. The first of its kind in the UK, the proposed development would be on three levels and would include a

crocodile pit and an aquarium in which members of the public can walk through an acrylic tunnel and see sharks swimming above and around them. Shops, restaurants, exhibition areas and offices are included, and it is hoped that the complex will attract visitors from the successful Granada Studios Tour nearby. (15.11.90)

Work on restoring the lych-gate at St Peter's Church, Swinton, was completed in time for Remembrance Sunday. When the gate was built, two caskets containing earth from World War One battlefields were placed in it and during a special rededication service on Saturday 10 November, these were reburied inside the renovated gate. (15.11.90)

Regulars at the Jollies on Oldfield Road (formerly the St Philip's Hotel) scored 422,427 during a twenty-four-hour darts marathon last weekend and raised £450 for good causes in the process. The pub already holds the Champion of Champions trophy awarded by the Royal National Institute for the Blind to the pub that raises the most money for the charity. (15.11.90)

The 200-foot-high chimney at Courtauld's Textiles, Manchester Road, Walkden, was blown up last week. The site is to be sold for redevelopment and a large weaving shed and several smaller buildings were also demolished. The honour of pushing the plunger to set off the explosion went to the winner of a raffle held in aid of St Ann's Hospice, Little Hulton, but the holder of the winning ticket, Mr John Taylor of Swinton, passed on the privilege to his wife Linda. (22.11.90)

Meadowbrook, the new £3.5 million mental health department at Hope Hospital, opens this weekend. The 88-bed facility is part of the region's move towards more community-based units in preference to the traditional, large institutions. (29.11.90)

December 1990

The Ashley Brook, the new Joseph Holt pub on Liverpool Street, opened on Tuesday 4 December. (6.12.90)

Halton Bank School, which closed in July, has been saved from demolition. The Portico Housing Association has bought the building with the intention of turning it into luxury flats and building twenty new houses in the playground area. Work should start next year. (20.12.90)

The Oddfellows pub on Liverpool Road, Patricroft, popularly known as "Wangies", has just reopened after a complete refurbishment. There have been many theories as to how the pub got its nickname; the latest is that it was the after-work meeting place of the ladies from a nearby mill known as Wangers. (20.12.90)

Working on Phase II of the transformation of Salford Art Gallery & Museum in 1990

Index

Italics refer to illustrations and captions.

This old photograph of Broad Street clearly shows some of the large houses with gardens in front stretching up to Brunswick Methodist Church on the corner of Upper Gloucester Street. Brunswick Sunday School is on the extreme left of the picture and the Congregational Church on the right

Redevelopment in the Ellor Street area, with John Street School in the background

Seedley Baths

*Demolishing the Big Derby in Ordsall. The pub closed on 22
July 1978*

Salford Fire Brigade in action at Ward & Goldstone's in November 1979